Self-Help and Popular Religion in Early American Culture

Recent Titles in
American Popular Culture

Self-Help and Popular Religion in Early American Culture

An Interpretive Guide

ROY M. ANKER

AMERICAN POPULAR CULTURE
M. Thomas Inge, *Series Editor*

GREENWOOD PRESS
Westport, Connecticut • London

Library of Congress Cataloging-in-Publication Data

Anker, Roy M.
   Self-help and popular religion in early American culture : an
interpretive guide / Roy M. Anker.
     p. cm.—(American popular culture, ISSN 0193–6859)
   Includes bibliographical references and index.
   ISBN 0–313–31136–6 (alk. paper)
   1. United States—Religion. 2. Self-help techniques—United
States—History. I. Title. II. Series.
BL2525.A567   1999
 277.3'07—dc21   99–21280

British Library Cataloguing in Publication Data is available.

Library of Congress Catalog Card Number: 99–21280
ISBN: 0–313–31136–6
ISSN: 0193–6859

First published in 1999

Greenwood Press, 88 Post Road West, Westport, CT 06881
An imprint of Greenwood Publishing Group, Inc.
www.greenwood.com

Printed in the United States of America

The paper used in this book complies with the
Permanent Paper Standard issued by the National
Information Standards Organization (Z39.48–1984).

10 9 8 7 6 5 4 3 2 1

To Ellen,
in gratitude for support, good humor,
and much much else

Contents

Acknowledgments

This book owes a great deal to many people and organizations. It took shape in a National Endowment for the Humanities Summer Seminar led by Professor R. Laurence Moore of Cornell University in 1981. It developed during a fruitful sabbatical leave from Northwestern College in Orange City, Iowa, spent at the Institute for Ecumenical and Cultural Research at St. John's University in Collegeville, Minnesota. The project was further supported with a summer research grant from Northwestern College and a Calvin Research Fellowship from Calvin College, Grand Rapids, Michigan.

Throughout this long project I owe much to the wonderful hospitality of away-from-home hosts, to the warm support of colleagues in Iowa and Michigan, and to my splendid family—my dear wife and our three wonderful children—whose patience has been very great and for whom I have measureless gratitude and appreciation.

Chapter 1

Introduction

This is the first of two books that examine the relationship between popular religion and the self-help tradition in American culture, specifically, the way in which the former has given rise to the latter. The relationship between these two has long been regarded, often with very good reason, as a mainstay of American historical understanding. A traditional supposition has been that at times in American history, popular religious ferment has, in response to conditions in the larger culture, fostered distinct and very important configurations of attitudes, values, and meaning on which historians have subsequently bestowed the label of "self-help." For many historians, there has been a sufficient number of these unique and prominent expressions, although individually different in kind, to compose a readily identifiable "tradition." Further, this distinct tradition of self-help has contributed greatly, it has often been argued, to the formation of an individualism that lies near the center of a generalized American character, although many historians now question the accuracy and usefulness of this sort of sweeping generalization about America, Americans, or a unique national character. Presently, though, quite apart from what academic historians deem important or true, a plethora of social commentators, best-selling psychotherapists, and media pundits regularly invoke segments of the self-help tradition, like the Protestant Ethic, as all-purpose explanations and prescriptions for what is both right and wrong about contemporary America. Indeed, to a degree that is hard to overestimate, the concept of self-help as part of a distinctive American character of individualism remains firmly imbedded in the nation's civil discourse, and within that discourse, the notion of self-help has become a pervasive and provocative emblem of deeply felt, albeit usually unarticulated, ideological allegiances. When we encounter many of the myriad aspects of individualism or self-help, we tap into a host of strongly held conceptions and, unfortunately, misconceptions of the American past.

Potent historical constructions of this sort pose difficulties for understanding American culture. Perhaps the largest of these has to do with the lack of terminological precision in each of the key terms deployed here, "self-help" and "popular religion." Individually, each points to an indisputably central, large, and energetic current in past and present American cultural history. In common usage the term "popular religion" can refer to everything from America's founding Puritans and Quakers to contemporary fundamentalist snake-handlers, Christian televangelists, and New Age gurus of natural medicine and spontaneous healing. As we shall see, the word "popular" in popular religion has numerous descriptive uses and, on top of that, numerous strong connotative attachments. Nor is exactness much greater for the term "self-help." There again the range of reference is so broad that it is almost without semantic value. Indeed, on one hand, the term recalls the sober, ascetic discipline of what is called the Protestant Ethic and, on the other, what some see as its opposite, the attitudinal "feel-good" conditioning of mid-twentieth-century positive-thinking strategies. As descriptive labels, then, neither term carries a useful measure of terminological precision. What semantic heft they do still retain is put to use as brickbats in public policy and ideological warfare. In this role, the terms serve as broad-brush catchwords that, in a verbal thumbnail, seek to praise or condemn what makes large segments of American culture tick. In short, they both lack historical precision and connotative neutrality. While the disappearance of either of these terms is unlikely, we would hope for some greater accuracy in their use, and it is hoped that this book might help a bit in bringing that about.

Beyond the great generality in nomenclature, a second substantive difficulty with the terminology arises with the plain accuracy of the historical interpretations that have, over the years, accrued to the terms or components of them and have since undergone significant historical revision. What we used to think of as unequivocally true, we are not so sure about anymore. That is perhaps nowhere more true than in the case of the idea of a Protestant Ethic, first set forth speculatively by sociologist Max Weber in 1904–1905 and then published in book form as *The Protestant Ethic and the Spirit of Capitalism* (1922). Weber suggested that the Protestant Reformation gave rise to a new spiritual ethos that greatly advanced the rise of capitalism. Weber's primary purpose in the book was to suggest that religious ideas do have social and cultural consequence, and the emergence of capitalism proved the point. Here religious ideas gave rise to economic change, which was a proposition exactly the opposite of what later Marxist historians were to contend, namely, that human activity, including religion, was economically driven. In any case, ever after in Europe and North America historians of all kinds—religious, social, and economic, for the most part—have debated, sometimes furiously, the accuracy of Weber's speculation, particularly as it applies to that hotly disputed relationship between Puritanism and the rise of capitalism. In the case of American historical writing, Weber was adapted by American Progressive historians like Vernon Parrington and, taking their cue from Weber and Parrington, by popular journalists like H. L. Mencken and countless successors who have promoted and flailed the image of the Puritans as calculating misers who used their religion as a cloak for religious and financial self-aggrandizement (some contended the Puritans' goals were also religious but only so because they supposedly sought economic success to prove that God liked them and that they were saved). Political conservatives were also perfectly happy with only a slightly softened version of this image, for it supported the idea of economic self-reliance as originally and normatively American. The difficulty is that this notion of Puritan as relentless entrepreneur has prevailed and grown into a handy stereotype—despite the ardent scholarly controversy that initially greeted and has ever after surrounded Weber's hypothesis. So entrenched is this caricature that the impressive revisionist work of recent social historians of New England has yet in the least to temper the historical lore carried about by pundits and the like.

Similar kinds of interpretive constriction have also played a role in the study of popular religion, depending on how the word "popular" is interpreted. For a complex array of reasons, "popular" has often been taken to mean simple or unsophisticated and consequently unworthy of study. Religious history has received a great deal of study, but until very recently that enterprise has almost exclusively focused on ecclesiastical and theological history. While institutional and intellectual histories of faiths and churches surely deserve close attention, for long these topics were virtually the only subject matter in the study of religion. The history of religion was "church history," scrupulous records of institutional and doctrinal change within particular denominations or theological traditions, such as Reformed, Methodist, or Roman Catholic. In part, this resulted from the fact that the writers of these histories were themselves highly trained academics who found most interesting and worthy the history of people much like themselves, members of an intellectual elite, in this case, religious leaders, thinkers, and scholars. As a consequence, the religious significance and experience of the ordinary has been routinely overlooked. What ordinary people themselves have believed, experienced, felt, or thought has received scant attention.

In the context of academic or secular historical writing, the kind done for the most part outside church-supported colleges, seminaries, and historical societies, the study of popular religion has, to some extent, suffered the same fate, largely because it has often smacked of the deviant or eccentric, a mode of behavior or thought that departs from clear standards of "normalcy" and rationality. Those religious people who have strayed from the well-traveled paths of "normal" in religious interest or expression have been supposed to lack sense, rationality, and even intelligence, candidates for membership in fringe groups or cults. Neither church historians nor secular academic historians of religion have been disposed to study those who depart so markedly from the scholars' own canons of logic and plausibility in matters of belief. As historian Laurence Moore has pointed out, academic historians of religion have been no more inclined to understand the experience of ordinary people than church historians have been interested in writing the histories of the ordinary person in the pew or at the camp meeting (*Outsiders* viii). A rarely stated assumption is that "popular," especially when it comes to religion, necessarily entailed inordinate credulousness, superstition, and a host of attitudes that intellectual elites have deemed of little historical interest, implicitly unworthy of study, or plainly unhealthy insofar as they oppose the predominantly rationalist values of secular elites.

In looking at popular religion and the self-help tradition in America, this book focuses on those junctures between popular religion and the self-help impulse that historians have deemed of critical importance in the development of American culture. To be sure, not all popular religion gives rise to self-help impulses; nor do all self-help strategies and creeds emerge from popular religion. We are, then, interested in those occasions on which historians have understood the two to intersect. In this pursuit, individual chapter discussions employ those approaches that provide the most efficient and thorough path through the pertinent history and the historical judgments that have deemed this or that religious figure or movement to be of importance in the history of self-help. In some instances, particularly with well-established movements and figures that have, over the years, received enormous amounts of scholarly attention, as with Puritanism and Benjamin Franklin, historiographic issues are clear, and the discussion focuses primarily on those issues, utilizing only the directly pertinent historical information and interpretive approaches. In the case of Benjamin Franklin, for example, the chapter focuses on Franklin as a popular writer and ventures into those portions of his philosophy that help to explain the message he communicated to his vast audiences. We necessarily exclude other dimensions of his thought or his academic status as a philosopher, scientist, diplomat, or bon vivant, which are portions of his legacy that were without great consequence in shaping the economic and ethical messages he communicated to his vast audiences. In the case of lesser known figures and movements, such as Phineas Parkhurst Quimby and the rise of New Thought, discussion attends, first, to the historical backdrop and contours that gave rise to the mixing of popular religion and self-help, the birth and rise of different specific expressions of the mix of self-help and religion, and, last, to the numerous interpretive debates that have surrounded these events. In all cases, in surveying the historical and scholarly materials that depict the history of popular religion and self-help, the narratives and commentary emphasize the historiographical debates—sometimes enormously significant ones—that shape interpretation of the ideas and figures within these prime junctures in the development of the religious self-help tradition in the United States.

All writers of history, even historians of history-writers, have their historical limits, shaped and prescribed as they are by their own time, temperament, and ideological perspectives. This examination tries to transcend those limits, to be sure, but point of view nonetheless surfaces in selection, representation, and judgment. One of the main purposes of this work is to point to the particular intellectual, political, or religious perspectives that sometimes inform and shape historical treatments. History is far more than "just the facts" but, also crucially, the effort to suggest what the facts mean about people, societies, cultures, and history itself. Very often facts themselves are in dispute, and even more in dispute are the interpretations that derive from a given set of facts. It is terribly important to note a common-sense notion, one that is often overlooked: historians do not have omniscience. The best of them know that and approach their work with a gracious cognitive humility and an exploratory openness, hoping always that scrupulous study of the historical record will tell them more about "how it was" and provide new insight into the cultures of humanity. Indeed, most historians try to do the best they can at telling it "like it was," given the limits of historical retrieval—how much we can really come to know about the past with certainty—and the inescapable limits of any era's models of historical understanding. The best research data suggest more perceptive views of history and historical understanding. Besides simply recounting the historical backdrop and factual record of assorted popular religious expressions of self-help, the discussion emphasizes what is called historiography, the points of view from which historians write history, by compactly discussing the perspectives that are evident in individual approaches to the subject matter. With this in mind, the book regularly points out, perhaps tiresomely, that the telling of history is often shaped by a prior opinion or ideological commitment that then supplies the goggles through which the history is told and understood. The history of American historical writing well shows that sometimes scholars and popular critics gerrymander historical realities in order to make this or that religious or political point. More than a tendency, for many historians it has been a habit, putting history to the service of a particular ideology.

This book, then, seeks to be a reliable introductory, interpretive guide to major self-help figures and movements that have had their origins in popular religious movements. In order to keep this examination efficient and helpful, this book undertakes a narrow reckoning of exactly where in American history popular religion and self-help have reputedly and actually intersected. Often, renditions of American history by scholars and popularizers alike ascribe causes to particular phenomena that are tenuous at best, and that is perhaps no more true than with the history of the Puritans and the self-help movement in general. Some commentators suggest, for example, that Puritan influence was and remains so potent that it accounts—all-purpose scapegoat that it is—for most of the maladies in contemporary American cultural life, everything from greed, to workaholism, to sexual repression. So this book avoids sweeping cultural generalizations and tows a strict line in tracking only conspicuous critical intersections of popular religion and self-help, intently disregarding ancillary or derivative figures or ideas, no matter how intriguing or timely they might prove. Still, while it means to be thorough, it cannot be exhaustive, particularly on such broad and pervasive topics as popular religion and self-help. That is particularly true in specific topic areas such as American Puritanism and its relation to the Protestant Ethic, a topic on which enormous quantities have been written and to which just about everything in early American history is, if only for its value as contrast, in some way relevant. In its broadest construction, then, some topics seem almost inexhaustibly interrelated to all there is in American culture. Given this prospect, there necessarily are authorial focus, judgment of significance, and, as a result, exclusion of some areas and figures, topics that others might think vital to adequate understanding.

Putting together popular religion and self-help still makes for one very big topic—expansive, virtually all-inclusive, and frequently unwieldy—for just about everything in American culture seems sooner or later in some way or another to connect to a supposedly distinctive American individualism that seems to have at least some of its roots in the persistent symbiosis between popular religion and self-help. This book does not attempt a sweeping or exhaustive enumeration of every pertinent idea, book, figure, or movement. The temptations to compile such a lengthy list of figures and ideas are great, for such catalogs are invaluable aids in charting the contours and parameters of America's many different meldings of popular religiousness and self-care. There are, however, several problems with this approach. First, in the case of the United States, the list would be almost limitless, for the seemingly perennial fusion of self-help and religion has in recent decades gone from strength to strength. In short, the admixtures of religion and self-help seem to be more and bigger than ever. For example, the New Thought movement, absorbing many different currents of unconventional religion and spirituality, has generated multitudinous groups, and the compression of all these and their antecedents into one even very lengthy volume would test the patience of readers. Second, a great deal else in American culture is, at the very least, tangentially related to either individualism or religion, thereby expanding to unmanageable lengths. The volume would become no more than long lists of interconnections between this and that group and would not, in the end, prove very helpful for the curious reader. Third, the venture would be redundant, for this invaluable enumeration has to a large extent already been accomplished. Happily, many "histories" of American self-help and numerous reference guides to popular religion, produced by a handful of tireless scholars, have, in large part, already surveyed this territory. Many prominent figures and movements identified and briefly described in these surveys now deserve extensive primary research, but that task cannot be accomplished within the limited scope of one or even two volumes.

Because of the existence of a large body of helpful, although often conflicting, histories and interpretations, the intention here is to construct a historical narrative that highlights these critical junctures in order to make them more understandable and to relate them to prominent historiographic debates in the study of American culture. This book, then, in addition to providing reliable historical narrative, is very much about who has said what about what and whom. Within that venture, this book is meant to occupy a middle place between the specialized scholarly enterprise and the sketchiness that necessarily characterizes reference guides oriented to "first-step" research. In order to make the scholarship of others as accessible as possible to both students and scholars, this book does as much direct quotation as permitted by cost and copyright rules. Students read the language that scholars use in describing their subjects and in talking to each other, and scholars hear the nuances and texture of argument and perspective that shape the telling of history. While this tactic might, at times, strike the reader as cumbersome, it has the additional benefit of letting scholars speak for themselves on hotly debated interpretive matters, of which there are an abundant number in this survey. Additionally, ample citation lessens the possibility of authorial bias rearing its own unseemly head.

Chapter 2 recounts in some detail the perspectives and conclusions of previous histories of American self-help, which compose an important resource from which students might learn much about self-help and about the perspectives from which previous histories have been written. Taken together, they paint a broad canvas that includes just about every figure and movement that might possibly occupy a niche in the history of the self-help tradition. The review begins with the first book-length survey of self-help in America and proceeds to the present to include several books from related areas that have pertinence for the understanding of the history of popular religion and self-help. While the approaches of almost all of these studies are direct and transparent and can be fairly and efficiently summarized, a few tax the reader's patience, and in those instances some care and space are taken to interpret the historical interpreter. The chapter also includes analyses of several important related works that affect the usual understandings of self-help and suggest avenues for future research. Last, the final section of the chapter enumerates the often excellent reference resources available to both first-time students and scholars of either popular religion or the self-help tradition. Happily, a growing handful of historians have labored to supply an increasing number of reference books and bibliographies that expedite both research and understanding. The books recounted in this introductory survey of prior work in the area of popular religion and self-help do much to recover and recount the lives of ordinary people, a collective enterprise that has gone a long way to dismantle the preemptive judgments of traditional church historians and academic scholars of religion about the significance and meaning of ordinary lives.

The remainder of the book treats the pertinent junctures chronologically, looking first at the lastingly controversial idea of a distinctive Protestant Ethic, as first formulated in the early twentieth century by German sociologist Max Weber in *The Protestant Ethic and the Spirit of Capitalism*. As suggested earlier, Weber's thesis has largely been accepted as a truism: Puritanism in Europe and America, but especially in New England, was a major catalyst for the rise of economic individualism, the rationalization of business and the marketplace, and, following upon those two, the rise of capitalism. After explaining in some detail Weber's thesis—and Weber meant it to be no more than a thesis—and the controversy surrounding it, Chapter 3 examines at length the social thought and history of New England with the specific intent of assessing how well literary evidence and the recorded history of the place and time support Weber's contentions. The gist of the new field of social history, which has pursued a new focus and means in doing history, has in the last several decades called into serious question the main contours of Weber's thesis and traditional understandings of the Puritan social vision and the texture of socioeconomic relations within that society. Similarly, Chapter 4 again turns to the legacy of Weber in examining the influence of American legend Benjamin Franklin, whose *Poor Richard's Almanac* and *Autobiography* exerted enormous influence in the shaping of early America. Weber contended that Franklin's life and thought made him the premier example of the fruition of the Protestant Ethic, even though in his youth and ever after Franklin discarded all Puritan religious commitments. Once again, recent scholarship divides on the question of the "Puritanism" of Franklin and how well his celebrated work ethic takes its inspiration from his Puritan forebears. As with the social history of New England, the verdict on Franklin greatly affects the plausibility of Weber's thesis and, simultaneously, how American historians should talk about the origins of the self-help tradition in American cultural life.

From Colonial and Revolutionary America, the history of popular religion and self-help shifts to a markedly different cultural setting, a wholly different wellspring, and an entirely different configuration of meaning. Beginning about 1800, America went through a series of seismic tremors that would permanently alter the ethos of America culture and provide the origins of what is now the dominant posture within the self-help tradition in modern America. Amid the dislocations of westward expansion and early industrialization came two movements that constituted radical departures from Puritanism and most other forms of American religious life: first, the very large evangelical Christian revival of the Second Great Awakening and, second, its more intellectually sophisticated and less religiously orthodox cousin,

Transcendentalism, a peculiarly American expression of the larger intellectual movement known as Romanticism. From this markedly different "mood" in the young United States emerged the mental healing movement generically known as "mind-cure," a little-known, but profoundly important, reimagining of the human person and the nature of reality. Chapter 5 provides a historical survey of early nineteenth century, focusing on those central cultural changes that prepared the soil, first, for the emergence and, then, for the relatively eager reception of mind-cure. The specific character of the Second Great Awakening receives considerable attention for its markedly different patterns of religious experience, particularly its embrace of experiential religion and epistemological subjectivity. If revivalism prepared the soil religiously, then American Romanticism provided a notably fresh, idealist, philosophical rationale for the possibility of mental healing. Finally, the chapter follows the arrival in America of the physiological theory known as mesmerism, which offered important clues to early mental healers, especially Maine clockmaker Phineas Parkhurst Quimby, about the effects of thought and attitude upon physical health. From among the approximately 12,000 patients Quimby treated come the many founders and later impressive proselytizers of what is now called the New Thought movement.

A second volume, *Religion and Self-Help in Modern American Culture*, continues this historical survey with a chapter on the most famous patient of Quimby, Mary Baker Eddy, the founder of Christian Science (denominationally known as the Church of Christ, Scientist), the most prominent, successful, controversial, and distinctive of all the groups whose inspiration scholars trace to the healing and intellectual influence of Quimby. Eddy visited Quimby in 1860 after years of ill health and was healed, at least temporarily, and it was to Quimby that Eddy turned when she sustained injury from a fall upon the ice in Lynn, Massachusetts, in February 1866, an accident that Eddy later claimed led to her discovery of what she eventually called Christian Science. After examining the unique cultural conditions that shaped Eddy and made late nineteenth-century America receptive to Eddy's message and church, the chapter traces the history of Eddy's highly controversial life, career, and church, all of which contain notable ambiguities that are still hotly debated, since few students of Eddy or the Church of Christ, Scientist, seem to muster detachment from their subject. The survey concludes with a review of scholarly analysis of Eddy's theology and the reasons for her very considerable appeal and the rapid growth of her movement.

Chapter 3 in the second volume examines the primary conduit for the entrance of the mental healing tradition into the mainstream of American culture in the mid-twentieth century: the career and enormous celebrity of preacher Norman Vincent Peale, the author of the perennially best-selling *The Power of Positive Thinking* (1952) and for decades the famous preacher of Manhattan's famous Marble Collegiate Church. The son of an Ohio

Methodist minister, Peale's own journey from moderate evangelical Protestantism to his embrace of his positive-thinking version of New Thought
in many ways forecast the path that many of his followers would take, people
from the gray-flannel mainstream who felt a gnawing discontent with the
perspectives and promises of traditional Protestantism. Peale played a key
role in the widespread religious revival of the 1950s, and his stupendous
positive-thinking best-seller ignited enormous controversy, eliciting vigorous
denunciations from the likes of eminent theologian Reinhold Niebuhr. So
great was the storm of criticism that Peale for a while considered resigning
his pastorate. The chapter traces Peale's life and career and the controversies
that followed upon his success. Peale's message and the criticism it has
drawn receive special emphasis. Chapter 4 looks at the life and career of
Peale's successor, possibility-thinking television preacher and author Robert
Schuller of Garden Grove, California's Crystal Cathedral. Like Peale, Schuller's message and strategies have often elicited furious controversy, although
Schuller has, for the most part, wisely avoided the political entanglements
that hounded Peale. It is important to note that Peale and Schuller constitute, except for evangelist Billy Graham, the public face of mainstream
American Protestantism in the second half of the twentieth century in the
United States. Other Protestant preachers have had their day, but it is ar-
guable that none have reached so many Americans as Peale and Schuller,
the cheerful descendants of New Thought, although the pair have usually
diminished the measure of their indebtedness to what they themselves would
deem a heterodox fringe group within American religious life.

Chapter 2

Academic Histories of Self-Help

For all the supposed prominence and influence of self-help and individualism in American culture, very few books have dealt specifically with self-help ideologies or American individualism. Nor has any scholar undertaken an adequate, comprehensive history of self-help in relation to American popular religion. This situation is particularly unfortunate. In the last several decades, academic historians have come to modify traditional interpretations, ones still deeply entrenched in popular media and public myth, toward more complex renditions of the American past. While historians have often changed their minds about the origins, shape, and texture of American individualism, in which self-help plays a major contributing part, electronic media commentators, newspaper pundits, and countless academics, including many historians, still unblinkingly accept and even venerate ideas about the American past that have become, at the very least, historically ambiguous. Some of the most important realignments pertain directly to those widespread public understandings of self-help and popular religion in which many of the central themes of older historical accounts have undergone rather severe questioning. A prime example, recounted through two chapters of this guide, involves what has become known as the Protestant Ethic, an idea first set forth by sociologist Max Weber in the early part of the twentieth century. Weber set forth his idea as a speculative model that meant to explore the extent to which religious belief can influence social change. So attractive was Weber's idea to many historians, especially the liberal Progressive historians, that it was readily embraced as fact and has since largely been accepted as a well-established historical certainty in the popular media, amounting now to cliché and shibboleth. Subsequent historical work, largely by social historians of Puritan New England, suggest that there are large holes in Weber's own construction of seventeenth-century New England and its religious and social ethos. Nonetheless, Weber's assumptions persist in the culture as a whole and among many historians.

In some instances, fundamental reappraisal of the historical record is already under way due to new historical information, as is partly the case with the new social history, or because of what historiographer Gene Wise called "paradigm shifts" (*Explanations* passim). With the latter, for example, the new cultural models set forth by the "annales" group in France and by anthropologists such as Clifford Geertz in America have inspired significant reinterpretation and research. One marked effect, especially for a study like this one, has been to alter the old disposition among historians to regard elites as the whole or only notable subject matter for historical writing; in recent decades, more and more historians and literary critics have examined the lives and worth of ordinary or "common" people, whether they belong to a minority or inhabit the anonymous "faceless mass." Similarly, useful again for this study, the usual reductive social and psychological approaches to religion—ones that view religious engagement as deviant or abnormal—are receiving a second look. In the eyes of Geertz and others, religion generally plays an indispensable cultural role of positive value in providing shared structures of meaning that allow for the cohesion necessary to the survival of individual societies. Within the historical profession itself, the work of a distinguished group of American historians has suggested the invaluable role of American religious life in the creation of American culture's most significant moral, social, and political accomplishments. Together these trends bode well for the exploration of the way ordinary people think and feel and believe.

The soundness and sensitivity of future historical writing always depend on knowledge of the past and what others have written about it. While no comprehensive study of religion and self-help has appeared, in recent decades a host of interpretive articles and books on historical and ideological segments of American popular religion and self-help has appeared. Their value is immense. First, these books have, by and large, traced the currents and parameters of the self-help impulse in American religion as well as in the culture as a whole; they provide a helpful sense of the size and terrain of the territory before we set out to explore. Second, they collectively provide some fullness of perspective as they individually utilize different interpretive frameworks for understanding their subject matter. Some are markedly political in orientation, trying to assess what salutary or destructive effects different self-help proponents and movements have had in American history. Others attempt to understand self-help as a shaping myth or artifact in American culture. Still others work to clarify literary strategies as they strive to convey meaning and invite popularity. Last, still others look at best-selling self-help authors as mirrors to gauge the sundry dysfunctions of American culture.

I

Given the persistence of self-help literature, the study of this theme as a reflector or index to American culture is a recent development, as are most studies of American popular culture. The first book-length study to appear was Irvin G. Wyllie's *The Self-Made Man in America: The Myth of Rags to Riches* (1954). Confining himself largely to the late nineteenth century, Wyllie was general and modest in approach, more or less charting the territory that later scholars would examine in more depth and detail. By and large, Wyllie sets forth the critical perspective that many popular writers on religion and self-help have since readily accepted, although it is difficult to tell if Wyllie merely reflected the prevailing attitudes of his time or, in fact, contributed in some measure to long-reigning historiographical conventions. His study was the first of its kind and has periodically reappeared in paperback editions. For the most part, Wyllie ties the notion of self-making closely to economic success, asserting that Americans have historically given only lip service to other sorts of success than wealth-getting. All the while their hearts were really after money and riches. His attempt, then, is to delineate "the saga of an idea that had power among the people" and explain its "origin, nature, and content," including "something of its relation to religion, education, and general movements of thought, something of its propagation, and its social uses; and something of the men who loved and despised the idea" (6). As such, Wyllie's book remains a useful place to start, especially for novices, although much of its research has since been greatly enlarged upon and its points of view questioned by subsequent scholars. For example, his introductory survey of America prior to the Gilded Age indicts Puritanism for fostering the wealth-getting ideal. Consequently, following Weber and Griswold, Cotton Mather and Benjamin Franklin are lumped together as Puritans, and Franklin is seen as the chief promulgator of an ideal whose time had finally and fully come with the Industrial Revolution. By the Civil War the publicists of self-made wealth had taken over, and out of the war "came rich new opportunities for acquisition . . . and a well-ordered gospel of business success" (20).

The book is thereafter organized by chapters on particular values and motifs of self-help literature. While useful, this approach scants chronological development and the distinctions between one writer and another. For Wyllie, the success strain in American culture is cultic, univocal, and unchanging. Within its mythic configuration of values, character became the key to success, not economic good luck or opportunity, and poverty fast became "the equivalent of sin in Calvinist theology, an evil to be struggled against and overcome" (22). Nonetheless, says Wyllie, poverty was glorified as ample incentive to rise. Rural life and inspiring feminine influence, whether in mothers or wives, properly equipped the aspiring young man (girls were wholly excluded from the dream). Energetic pursuit and perseverance, what was called "industry," made up for lack of genius or aptitude. Frugality, sobriety, punctuality, reliability, and initiative followed close behind.

Wyllie is not entirely clear in spelling out the role of Protestant Christianity in the Gilded Age, specifically in clarifying the depth of the church's ambivalence toward wealth. On one hand, he emphasizes that the "get-ahead values of the business community" were, for the most part, sanctioned and celebrated by a large section of Protestant Christianity; many of those conduct standards did, after all, replicate or at least echo age-old Christian standards for a good and full life (56). Insofar as this was true, "the way to wealth passed through the church" (66). Along that path to riches, however, as Wyllie notes, lay many perils, and the churches raised significant objections to greed, selfishness, and ill-gotten wealth. For countless preachers, the means to wealth posed more of a problem than the goal itself, which was to have riches in order to contribute "to the social welfare" (71). The ideal of stewardship was the capstone of the churches' vision in its advocacy of money-making. Profits were not (repeating here the sumptuary laws of early Puritan society) to be spent in extravagant or riotous living; wealth was for the betterment of the whole community. Wyllie leaves the reader to wonder which views predominated when and where. Indeed, Wyllie seems to spend a good deal of time questioning his own assertion of the churches' comfortable complicity in hallowing the quest for wealth—that Beecher, Abbot, and Conwell proselytized for the success gospel while complaining just enough to restrain excesses and protect it "against the charge of godlessness and materialism" (60).

This ambiguity carries into other topics as well. For example, Wyllie devotes a lengthy chapter to the heroic ideal for self-making, whose hallmarks were fairness and philanthropy. These standards varied to some extent depending on who evoked them, but those two keystones obtained throughout the self-help mythos. Robber barons were excluded from the pantheon in favor of men like Andrew Carnegie, George Peabody, Peter Cooper, and Ezra Cornell, all of whom became major philanthropists. Even Carnegie, whose Darwinist leanings forbade him from aiding the poor directly, resolved to die poor by giving his money to socially useful causes. Aside from Carnegie, few of the rich or their apologists took much guidance from a Darwinist model that could potentially advocate ruthlessness or unscrupulousness in the marketplace or in employee relations. For most, wealth and its getting were to be socially useful, a goal that discouraged speculation and exploitation. If proponents of the gospel of success failed their public, Wyllie suggests, it was in their naïveté about the tenacity and deviousness of evil. Their free-enterprise faith trusted the innate moral equilibrium of the marketplace to punish, largely through financial failure, offenders against a high moral creed. Somehow or another, the cruel and greedy would be found out and expelled for their excesses.

Wyllie subsequently devotes chapters to education, whose utilitarian value was only grudgingly and gradually admitted; to the dissemination of the gospel of success through biographies, manuals, textbooks, and sermons; and to conservative and liberal protest about the success dream, whose possibilities were limited by environment, materialism, corruption, and quickly shrinking opportunity. In a concluding chapter on the role and value of the rags-to-riches myth, Wyllie suggests that prior to the Civil War the dream reflected and, in part, inspired the larger democratic ethos of opportunity that was very much in the fabric of Jacksonian America. After the war, the dream was more and more used by "the business class . . . to maintain its superiority and consolidate its control" (154). Notions of universal opportunity were slowly supplanted by reminders that only the strong of character succeed and that not everyone could be rich. Mounting radicalism in the last decades of the century fomented still stronger conservative defenses of the social utility and model individualism of millionaires. An epilogue carries the book's story into the twentieth century, where the self-help ideology of character and opportunity was revived in the halcyon days before the Great Depression. In addition, Wyllie mentions that newer self-help manuals began to define success in terms of managerial status as opposed to the older definition of success as ownership. Correspondingly, the guides increasingly emphasized personality and psychological poise alongside old-style character traits. Wyllie seems to expect the imminent demise of the cruel joke that was the self-help credo. His hopes were foiled by the publication of the pastoral encouragements of Norman Vincent Peale and a host of others.

II

Insofar as it carefully chronicles the origins, distinctions, and changes in America's understanding of success, John Cawelti's *Apostles of the Self-Made Man* (1965) is a far better book. In addition, Cawelti is far more cautious and reflective about his analytic methods, shifting from one critical approach to another in order to yield a full and complex portrait of the tradition. As such, the book is, in large part, traditional intellectual history, devoting individual chapters to Jefferson and Franklin, Emerson, Horatio Alger, and John Dewey. Beyond this traditional approach, two chapters examine the general social context in which the dream of success at different times flourished, and two others look at popular culture to examine the dream's purveyors in best-selling fiction and self-help guides. Thematically, Cawelti argues for the existence of the "three main strands of thought and feeling" within the tradition: a "conservative tradition of the middle-class Protestant ethic" that emphasized calling and found success in "a respectable competence in this world and salvation in the next"; second, often at odds with the first, an aggressive financial quest that encouraged social change and industrial growth; and lastly, a stress upon "individual fulfillment and social progress," an old tradition revivified by recent social and psychological thought and positive thinking (4, 5).

The third strand begins with Franklin and Jefferson, which is where Cawelti begins and ends, for if there are heroes in Cawelti's vision of America, they are these two early American political philosophers. The more important of the pair for the tradition of self-made success is Franklin, who "exemplified in his own person and articulated in his writings a new hero, different in character from traditional military, religious, and aristocratic conceptions of human excellence and virtue" (9). Franklin's beguiling and "assiduously cultivated" public image of commoner-made-good embodied that ideal of the heroic, just as his writings sought to encourage it (11). Behind this was, in Cawelti's judgment, "a broad, humane and responsible idea of human development" (13). According to the Franklin of the *Memoirs*, the paths to human happiness and social good coincided with the path to wealth. In *Poor Richard* and other places, Franklin used the prospect of wealth as a carrot to lure common folks toward goodness and "virtue," of which self-discipline was the chief element: how "better stimulate men to the practice of [industry and prudence] than by showing that wealth and comfort could be achieved by this means?" (15). Unfortunately for Franklin's historical and literary influence and reputation, only Franklin's counsel of self-discipline for wealth-getting has remained prominent, and this has overshadowed his emphasis on self-discipline as the path to wisdom. It is important to note here that this view has retained substantive interest by later historians, as narrated in the chapter on Benjamin Franklin. Cawelti's view constitutes an extended apology for Franklin's thought and argues for a considerable discrepancy between his authorial intentions and popular interpretation—Franklin intended to foster virtue and wisdom as well as economic prosperity. Those unsympathetic to Franklin would accuse Cawelti of gliding over Franklin's glib embrace and advocacy of utilitarian and prudential personal and social ethics.

Cawelti's other early American hero, Thomas Jefferson, hoped for "the growth of strong, relatively self-sufficient and autonomous local communities" wherein capable and meritorious persons might rise to leadership roles founded on the rise of industrialism and centralism (26). In looking at both Franklin and Jefferson and their influence, the reader must wonder about Cawelti's treatment of Franklin and even the inclusion of Jefferson. The part of Franklin on which Cawelti focuses has seemingly had little influence on American culture. Similarly, as noble as it might be, Jefferson's democratic localism never really had much chance or attracted much enthusiasm. The idealism of either never really became popular at all. In mid-nineteenth-century America, which was the heyday of the self-made man, popular culture embraced the lesser part of Franklin's counsel, the dream of "social and economic advancement," and largely neglected Jefferson's ideal of meritorious leadership and social usefulness. Later writers, such as Emerson and

Dewey, showed traces of Jeffersonian ideas, but they played an incidental role at best.

Amid the industrial and population expansion of the Gilded Age, what Wyllie referred to as the character ethic predominated. As Cawelti aptly summarizes, "the majority of Americans sincerely believed what they publicly professed: that individual economic advancement and productivity was the best way of assuring both the individual and the general welfare" (45–46). Realized opportunity created more opportunity, and thus the society as a whole flourished. In spite of this heartening faith, brandished everywhere by success publicists and preachers, the public showed increased apprehension about many dimensions of the success dream, specifically about how easily the virtuous might be diverted into greed, vanity, or corruption, either personal or commercial. Thus arose, in Cawelti's mind, a central paradox of the self-help tradition, one that had earlier afflicted Puritans: all were to work hard within their own calling, working for the sake of work and morality but not lusting for riches or status. This same ambivalence characterized the era's popular sentimental fiction by authors such as Sylvester Judd and T. S. Arthur. To be sure, these best-selling authors' self-made heroes, once they had it made, "attack the moral laxity, extravagance, and corrupt business practices of the new industrial cities," and ultimately in the stories, the heroes' merit derives from religious and moral achievement and not social status (60). In most midcentury novels of this kind, personal accomplishment in business through hard labor and virtue does not prove to be the causative factor in the hero's rise. In fact, proclaims Cawelti, there is "hardly a single instance where industriousness, frugality, and piety are operative factors in the hero's rise" (62). Instead, luck or coincidence appears to solve the hero's problems with "a kind of magic rather than by a clearly envisioned process of cause and effect"; as a group, the novelists "resort to supernatural intervention to insure the worldly success of the morally meritorious" (62, 63). The implausibility of the fictional models and the conspicuous amorality of actual business practice prompted ample satire.

The very appearance of popular self-help occasioned some protest. Novelist and patrician James Fenimore Cooper and historian Francis Parkman both inveighed against the erosion of cultural standards and the social privilege that they thought sustained civilization. Opponents of this position, such as William Ellery Channing and Ralph Waldo Emerson, advocated individualism but saw economic achievement as simultaneous with spiritual development. In their minds, self-making meant self-culture, the full maturation of all human capabilities, especially the spiritual. After all, Transcendentalism believed in "the tremendous creative potential" that lay deep within the soul of every individual and advocated lyceums and lectures for workingmen (85). As much as Emerson and other Romantics liked to see individual mind and spirit romp free and advance, they, too, were troubled by the specter of figures like Napoleon whose unbridled narcissism and deceit crushed their optimism. Emerson's major contribution to the self-help movement was philosophical in providing a theology for the later New Thought and positive-thinking movements; that is, his "belief that the truly self-reliant individual could be transformed by uniting himself with powerful universal forces" (97).

Cawelti's discussion of the most famous of all self-help promoters, novelist Horatio Alger, clears away a number of notable misconceptions about Alger's message. The first is that Alger was not the first to feature unfortunate, poverty-stricken boys who rise to success. A host of others prepared the way for Alger's popular rendition of the myth. Second, Alger's heroes never rose to great fortune but only to modest means and the prospect of future solid income. Alger gave them something still more important, which was middle-class morality and respectability, "a happy state only partially defined by economic repute" and roughly equivalent to "spiritual grace" (110). Always the rise of Alger's boys came much less from the celebrated virtues of self-discipline and labor and far more from good luck, a fact that the boys always readily acknowledged. These implausible denouements were only slightly less strained because of the nonetheless deserving nature of the fortunate. Alger's novels abounded in "sympathy for the underprivileged" and "humanitarianism in their emphasis on practical good works and frequent insistence that Americans extend opportunities for worldly success to the juvenile proletariat of the cities" (117). Alger partakes of "the middle-class ethical tradition of industry, frugality, and integrity, and the sentimental Christian version of a benevolent Providence" and, as such, is not "an exponent of free enterprise" as it was to be understood in the twentieth century (120, 121).

Cawelti devotes another chapter to Alger's contemporaries and their affirmations of the traditional self-help ethos. Unfortunately, the best-selling Gilded Age novels of Mrs. E.D.E.N. Southworth and minister E. P. Roe are too briefly treated to justify Cawelti's conclusions about the novelists' views of a changing American society. Southworth is faulted for simplicity and nostalgia, which she surely displays, and Roe is criticized for nativist reaction to immigrant "forces which are identified as hostile to the prestige and traditional ideals of the native middle-class," a charge that is not confirmed by the rest of Roe's considerable canon (134). Mark Twain, William Dean Howells, and Henry James are examined for their "attempt to understand the deeper cultural implications of the new industrial society, a more critical view of the traditional ideal of self-improvement, and a questioning of the middle class's claim to be the sole repository of virtue in America" (139). The three largely concur about the corruption, injustice, and barrenness of America's practice and vision of easy wealth. However, these minority voices of protest were drowned out by a revised turn-of-the-century image of success that better reflected and justified economic realities of the new corporate order. The new apologists of success fully dispensed with lingering notions about the moral and religious usefulness and meaning of work. With a thin Darwinist intellectual rationale, competition and wealth were embraced as the means and end of individual effort. The old Christian defense found new apologists in "success specialists" Russell Conwell, Orison Swett Marden, Elbert Hubbard, and George Horace Lorimer (175). Since most Americans labored tirelessly hard in mines, stockyards, and factories but advanced not at all, a new formula for success had to be improvised, and that new decisive "something" in the self was celebrated as nerve, confidence, willpower, and initiative. The prize now went to those who dared, those who risked. The decisive balance had shifted away from "traditional moral virtues" to the "qualities of personality" necessary to acquire riches (184). Here the New Thought movement with its emphasis on power supplied inspiration and rationale, eventually giving birth to the power of positive thinking. Business itself was sanctified and exalted in advertising man Bruce Barton's *The Man Nobody Knows* (1925). In Barton's view Jesus was the perfect account executive who had discovered service as the key to success.

For Cawelti, the ideologies of positive-thinking success literature of the twentieth century reveal a fundamental ambivalence about the worth of the success dream—whether success was indeed a dream come true or a rat race. Through industrial expansion and trade unionism, many more people had achieved the hallowed dream; however, the fruit of attainment did not seem an unmixed blessing, for the getting and keeping of more and more wealth seemed to result in less repose and peace of mind. People seemed confused about the relation between inner tranquillity and material wealth and about which is the means to the other. The writings of Norman Vincent Peale, Napoleon Hill, and Dale Carnegie all urged attitudinal transformation as the key to repose and success. One could neither reach nor enjoy the latter without the former. The repose was necessary to release, in Romantic style, the reservoir of personal power and magnetism that could activate will and shape and bend circumstance. Thus, for Cawelti a contradiction arises: the positive thinkers "ultimately . . . seem more concerned with inner certitude and serenity than with the conquest of the external world, more with personal joy than with upward mobility," but they are "unable to envision peace of mind without the sanction of material success" (213). Similarly, they seem not to be able to decide whether their message is, at heart, science or mysticism. The positive thinkers' unspoken ambivalence about the worth of success by itself is repeated overtly in the novels of William Faulkner, Robert Penn Warren, and F. Scott Fitzgerald, all of whom yearned for a return to older and more holistic virtues of success. For these modern novelists, "the tragedy of success is more a spiritual than a social failure . . . a collective failure of the moral imagination which has resulted in an over-emphasis on the need for individual economic accomplishment at the expense of the rich diversity and complexity of human capacities and motives" (235). A way out of the modern success predicament is suggested in Cawelti's closing discussion of philosopher John Dewey, whose work harks back to the localism first suggested by Jefferson.

By and large, Cawelti offers an excellent survey, rich in methodological diversity and insight. Different readers might wonder about the inclusion of certain authors within the book or particular interpretations, but *Apostles of the Self-Made Man*, at once sympathetic and critical, remains the single fullest, fairest, and most sensible account of the tradition. In only a couple of instances does Cawelti's interpretive penchant get the better of him. The penchant itself might be made clearer, but cloaking such interpretive biases, often naive or wholly unconscious, is not unusual among historians and critics. On occasion, Cawelti suspects a kind of oligarchic conspiratorial intent behind popular or intellectual movements, just as he does with the conservative insistence that lower classes remain contented in their callings: "the ethic of self-improvement had reflected the anxious attempts of an established elite to control the development of a materialistic society" (170). At other times, even though he eschews the practice in his Foreword, the otherwise cautious and astute Cawelti assumes an omniscient stance in suggesting the exact role popular fiction played for ordinary readers (ix–x). Southworth's fiction, for example, provided "a vicarious fulfillment of dreams which had little chance of realization" (128). Similarly, he ascribes to Protestants of the early nineteenth century secret delight "in the amoral enterprise of fictional Sam Slicks and real-life Commodore Vanderbilts; overtly, they gave their approval to the idealized version of success embodied in self-improvement handbooks and didactic novels" (74–75).

III

The single most exhaustive and simultaneously the most helpful and the most bothersome survey of self-help is *The American Idea of Success* (1971) by Richard Huber. Huber tries to situate his book somewhere in a middle ground between popular exposé and serious historical study. Part of the bother comes from Huber's journalistic style, half humorous and half muckraking in tone. On the other hand, these authorial choices capture some of the energy and spirit of the figures and movements he describes. There is also in Huber's choice of style the demand for the pithy epigram, a formulation for which Huber has considerable skill. Huber, despite his limitations, does convey a large body of information, considerably more than any other work on self-help. The largest difficulty with Huber's survey is his often simplistic rendition of success ideology, which he aligns along rather stark poles. While he is good at describing those poles, repetition often takes the place of clarifying historical origins or the consequences of a particular idea. Huber seems to change his mind midway through *The American Idea of Success.* His introductory chapter fails to mention that America had ever entertained ambivalence, if not outright denial, on the value of wealth or status. In spite of this introductory omission, that ambivalence toward wealth and success becomes a major theme in later stages of the book. Attitudinal shifts also seem to occur with his esteem for the character ethic, which rises as he compares it to late nineteenth-century New Thought alternatives to traditional success ideology. At times, Huber's work comes off as a lampoon or diatribe against a benighted American economic and social conscience, especially as it is wooed by positive-thinking proponents; at other times, there is a grudging admiration for the struggle to humanize the inherent self-seeking of the American economic system. Only a third of the way into his survey does Huber concede that there has been more to the American venture than the rank pursuit, in the words of Huber's title to his introduction, of money, status, and fame.

Huber's gift for pithy summary works least well in his treatment of the Puritans, as he regularly reduces historical complexity to convenient catch-phrases. Under the influence of Weber, he concludes that the Puritans succeeded in inverting traditional Christian values: "what had been considered a vice in the Middle Ages . . . had to the Colonists' economic system become a virtue" (11)—that is, specifically, the coequal pursuit of salvation and fortune, a view that has since been seriously questioned by some intellectual and social historians. Cotton Mather's advocacy of two callings gave warrant to worldly pursuit, which, according to Huber, for Puritans became as important as or exceeded religious devotion. While numerous historians, such as John Cawelti, defend Franklin's social vision, Huber focuses solely on Franklin's exaltation of wealth-getting as a means to leisure and whatever one wished to define as virtue. For Huber, from a perspective of historical progressivism, the explanatory pivot for American history is economic, as well indicated by assertions that the "colonists were eager to get ahead in a nation on the make" and that such impetus occasioned the American Revolution (16). Franklin differs from the Puritans only insofar as he secularizes "the Puritan belief that God was a means to success," which puts an unprecedented level of economic utility in Puritan religion (19).

Religious and individualistic justifications for work continued into the nineteenth century. However much both espoused the identical means to wealth, the motivational impetus for each differed markedly. The schoolbook readers of William Holmes McGuffey exerted their sway and then were succeeded by the mixture of advocacy and caution in advice-giving preachers like Henry Ward Beecher in *Lectures to Young Men* (1844). In midcentury the advice guides and novels of Timothy Arthur Shay encouraged personal enrichment as long as the public was also effectually served. Eclipsing the prominence of any other profession, in an era bursting with opportunity and optimism, the businessman soon "moved front and center on the stage of American life" (35). The prophets of the businessman were popular success writers like Horatio Alger, William Makepeace Thayer, and Russell Conwell. With Alger, Huber repeats the comments of Wyllie and Cawelti, adding the biographical detail of pedophilic homosexuality that lost Unitarian minister Alger his first and only parish. Thayer's specialty was the biography of the self-made man, tales in which Providence played key roles and public service was a chief end. Finally, Baptist minister Conwell, "America's greatest salesman of opportunity," became a national icon with his pamphlet "Acres of Diamonds," which he gave in lecture form some 6,000 times (55). Conwell glorified wealth for the good it could do and from that premise argued that it was therefore the duty of every Christian to become as rich as possible. Like Carnegie and other rich people (for Conwell became rich on his sermon but gave away a good part of his proceeds), Conwell refrained from giving charity to the poor because in a land of opportunity like America the only reason for poverty was sloth.

Like Irvin Wyllie, Huber devotes a chapter to examining the content and influence of Social Darwinism, a movement to which historians have usually given substantial attention. While a couple of self-made men, most notably, Andrew Carnegie, did find within it some personal justification for their great personal wealth, Social Darwinism's prime exponents were paid "spokesmen for specific business interests, such as lawyers and ghost writers, and 'impartial' savants, for instance professors and assorted intellectuals" who "used Social Darwinism to defend a laissez-faire economy, business consolidation, and the elimination of inefficient competitors" (73–74). The businessmen themselves ignored it because they were themselves deeply imbued, "heart and mind," with the "Christian and humanitarian" success ideal that in significant ways ran counter to the amoral world posited by Social Darwinism.

Amid a wave of late-century criticism of business, a defense of enterprise came from an unexpected source, Elbert Hubbard's 1,500-word tract "A Message to Garcia" (1899), which became an overnight sensation and "the most effective and widely distributed tract in the history of success literature" (80). A self-made soap magnate, Hubbard in midlife took up a literary career as writer and publisher. Hubbard himself constituted an odd mixture of bohemian self-publicizer and entrepreneur. The message of "A Message" was its ringing praise for individual responsibility and especially for the burdens carried by owners and managers who must do their best with a lazy and unruly workforce. Less sympathetic but still hopeful of conciliation between business and labor was liberal preacher Lyman Abbott, who became the "religious spokesman for reform-minded, middle-of-the-road Progressivism in the forty years following Appomattox" (87). Protestant preachers as a whole, Huber finds, "offered sensible answers to the problem of reconciling God and Getting On" by reasserting "the obligations of successful men" and placing "checks on the sin of runaway greed" but also by lambasting illegality and business self-interest. While they "poured blessings by the bucketful on the virtuous duty of accumulating wealth," they also added "strict words of caution about the perils of drowning in materialism" (91). Whatever was ignoble in the "character ethic" was redeemed, at least in part, by its long struggle with demands for stewardship and public service.

Huber argues that the entire drift of American thinking about work and wealth underwent a major shift with the emergence of New Thought, a movement "which has largely been ignored in histories of American thought" (125). Huber sees the movement arising from America's pragmatic thrust, melding together ancient traditions of mental healing with religious idealism and modern psychology. Such comments suggest that Huber would undertake a serious examination of the content and context of New Thought. Unfortunately, he makes little of these philosophic and cultural roots and currents. Instead, he rather fully dismisses its stance and insights as fantastic strategies of infantile wish fulfillment. His language borders on the intemperate: New Thought "was a woman's kind of religion" that offered "a downy way to achieve your heart's desire" (131, 132). To illustrate the history and character of New Thought and to substantiate his disdain, Huber follows the careers of two of New Thought's least admirable proponents, Prentice Mulford and Orison Swett Marden, who together stretched mental healing into money-getting. In their writings, the traits of the character ethic were replaced with the power and potential of thought and wish; thinking and hoping now became the only effort necessary to achieve what one wanted, a formula of which Huber is more than a little skeptical. Moreover, New Thought served to shore up the conservative business establishment because it argued that opportunity was simply a matter of attitude and had little to do with actual socioeconomic conditions. In spite of its supposed emphasis on spirit, its preoccupation and ends were materialistic.

In a latter chapter, Huber does try to understand some of the cultural changes that made New Thought "a theological panacea" for so many Americans' "troubled, unhappy lives" (165). The much-studied dislocations in Gilded Age thinking and living created psychic needs that "the character ethic left unsatisfied" and to which New Thought responded, largely by bridging the widening rift between science and religion and by promising just about everything. Prominent amid its promises of "health, wealth, harmony, energy, [and] abundant life" was "economic redemption in this world," a kind of "self-seeking magic" that "arrogantly sought to coerce God into granting . . . desires" (170, 171). During the same years, the hopefulness and strategies of New Thought found secular expression in new psychological, attitude-altering autosuggestion techniques introduced by Frenchman Emile Coue.

The biggest purveyor of modern self-help ideology was eminently successful and multitalented advertising executive, politician, and writer Bruce Barton, whose *The Man Nobody Knows* (1925) viewed Jesus as the prototype of the modern businessman. As a writer and publicist for the rightness of American business and its methods, Barton set out to inspire ambition, justify money-making, provide techniques, and finally, in his most momentous phase, "justify the role of business by surrounding the successful businessman with the glory of Christ" (202). To make his point, Huber compares *The Man Nobody Knows* to a previous religious best-seller, Charles Sheldon's Social Gospel novel *In His Steps*. Sheldon's concern had been to summon readers to the hard task of emulating Jesus' ethics; Barton's purpose, in contrast, seems to sanctify the businessmen by indicating how much they were already like Jesus. Barton's major emphasis was the extent to which service was the common purpose of both Jesus and business culture. So insistent was his point that it began to look utilitarian—serving others, paradoxically, became a way of making oneself rich. In any case, Barton's emphasis on service as the heart of business was shared by other innumerable success writers, so much so that it became the rallying cry in the commercial world of the early twentieth century and displaced the old character ethic's stewardship credo. At one and the same time, the banner of service staved off attacks on business, fueled a production economy, vindicated individual self-interest, and reassured the religious conscience. Following the tradition of Barton, Huber devotes a series of vignettes to other less illustrious stars in the early twentieth-century constellation of publicists of success and service. The founder of a financial magazine that still bears his name, B. C. Forbes "represents the counterpart of Bruce Barton in the secular interpretation of the character ethic" (212). For Forbes and countless others, service became an all-purpose notion, parrying attacks on business, justifying personal business success, fueling economic expansion, and sanctifying self-interest.

The biggest success molder of them all was Dale Carnegie and his 1936 best-seller, *How to Win Friends and Influence People*, a book that would forever change the face of the success ethic. In Carnegie's book, old-fashioned good manners and etiquette became utilitarian. While success literature had always had a utilitarian undercurrent dating back to Franklin, never had it been so bald-faced, thanks to a mixture of New Thought and applied psychology. With anecdote and rules, Carnegie urged readers to find success through the manipulation of others, placating and flattering their desires and opinions. Carnegie's enormous success begat numerous books and success prophets that together constituted a personality ethic as opposed to the old character ethic. More and more success would depend not on internal resources that, through hard work, could make an imprint on the business but on how one got along with others and how pleasing a personality one could present. Unfortunately, according to Huber, what "the personality ethic lacked was the nineteenth century's passionate defense of honesty as a moral absolute ingrained in our character" (259). Not only work but now interpersonal relations rested on a cash nexus. Sincerity and transparency went by the boards. Again, the failure to succeed "was the fault of the individual, not social and economic conditions" (264). A changing ethos in the business world focused increasingly on pleasantness and niceness as necessary qualities for success, a shift that is amply indicated in the expense-account business lunch. If the "character ethic served the needs of an economy of small proprietors," the personality ethic of manipulation and "getting along" seemed better fitted to survival in the large corporation. Out of this came "a creeping conformity which was subtly tyrannous in its pressure to play the game according to the most effective rules, even though the rules might violate a person's ethical principles" (290).

The loss of identity and individual purpose in the new corporate state led to other psychic crises and the "search for power" through such books as Claude Bristol's *The Magic of Believing* (1948), a "wide-ranging summary of the secular mind power school of success literature" (296). This and other secular books pointed to the subconscious as a reservoir of energy that could be tapped through techniques of autosuggestion, visualization, attraction, and thought transference. Huber suggests that the New Thought tradition supplied energy and inspiration for the demands and toll of the personality ethic: "The New Thought believer wanted power because he felt insufficient to meet the demands of life," offering "the timid . . . a source of personal magnetism as dazzling as bolts of electricity. The fearful and isolated, the alienated and helpless could connect with a celestial power plant mighty and magnificent enough to conquer all those forces which seemed so overwhelming in modern life" (310). For its diffusion through American culture, Huber points to the Unity School of Christian Living, Napoleon Hill's *Think and Grow Rich*, and finally, the foremost proponent of this school, Protestant preacher Norman Vincent Peale and one of America's all-time best-sellers, *The Power of Positive Thinking* (1952). With Peale, the reader gets "the straight New Thought message" dressed "in a particularly attractive package" (323, 321). Peale utilizes the full repertoire of New Thought control strategies—affirmation, visualization, and the like—all of which seek to tap into the Divine Supply.

For Huber, Peale is a prime exemplar of the fate of modern American culture, partaking especially of the "religion-in-general" return to piety of the 1950s. Positive thinking was essentially socially and politically conservative, faulting the individual, rather than social or economic structures, for failure. It differed from the character ethic insofar as it presented a means to money-making rather than a justification, as did the stewardship notions of the older character ethic. Further, paradoxically, the New Thought tradition used "philosophical idealism" to achieve a "worldly materialism" (333). And lastly, Peale and others pragmatically perverted traditional interpretations of Christianity. Results became the test of truth, an approach that values God primarily for personal use and turns traditional theology into "hash" (334).

For the remaining twenty percent of his book, Huber seems to lose focus, partly due to the fact that his historical narrative ends with Peale. He does chronicle a number of other faddish approaches to success, ranging from memory improvement to vocabulary. A late chapter is entitled "The Failure of Success," but Huber fails to make clear in what way success has been a failure in America. He does cite the lasting conflict "between capitalism as an economic system of organized selfishness and Christianity as a value system of unselfish love," a tension that New Thought effactually obscured (361). This dilemma is traced over again, making for some repetitiousness, through chapters on politics and art, often using literature to provide evidence and insight into American ambivalence toward wealth and getting ahead. The broad contours of dissent are indicated, ranging from Thoreau to Reinhold Niebuhr. Through the last two-thirds of the book, it is clear where Huber's sympathies lie, which is with the old character ethic that, despite its limitations, at least grappled with the realities of American economic life and the hard demands of orthodox Christianity. New Thought is viewed as a major culprit, among many, for eroding the tough perceptual and moral realism of Protestant Christianity.

IV

This judgment is shared by Donald Meyer and provides the informing viewpoint for his book on *The Positive Thinkers: Religion as Pop Psychology from Mary Baker Eddy to Oral Roberts* (1980), which is an expanded version of an earlier survey that followed "the American Quest for Health, Wealth and Personal Power" from Mary Baker Eddy through Norman Vincent Peale (1965). Put simply, as he does in his Preface, Meyer blames the New Thought tradition for diverting American Christianity, particularly Protestantism, from significant, widespread engagement with social problems. Commitment and energy have been "wasted in religion as therapy, as cult of reassurance, as psychology, as peace and positive thinking" (xii). Meyer makes clear his belief that "schisms in the cultural heart" of America have produced a "pervasive disturbance in the capacity of established ideas and institutions to satisfy" the deeper longings of the self (21, xv). From this situation have come many popular religions and psychologies. Even with this situation in mind, Meyer is clearly dismissive of the usefulness, truth, or integrity of the New Thought tradition. While Meyer does see the world more complexly than Huber, he sees it no more sympathetically. Throughout, his interest lies more with judgment than understanding, an approach that at times breeds disdain if not ridicule. More seriously still, Meyer's historical, analytic method does not pay close heed to original texts or documentation. The historical method and the writing style are rather more impressionistic than scrupulously supported or reasoned. At times his commentary borders on glib, ascribing to his authorial point of view superior sensibility that spontaneously intuits past cultural reality.

Meyer's narrative fastens on the historical junctures most important for his topic. His account begins with Dr. George Beard's attention to the malady of American "nervousness" brought on by the incompatibility between the "human neural apparatus and modern society" (26). Within this changing cultural context, Meyer locates unconventional religion from Swedenborg to Phineas Quimby, who inflated "practical healing into a psychology and then into philosophy and religion" (34). The need for such an approach to life was particularly evident in the anomie felt by newly leisured and feminized middle-class women who searched "for something to do" (49). So began the modern female penchant for "conspicuous consumption" and shopping (50). Without significant work or purpose women were made to become delicate, sentimental, and superfluous, themselves in danger of becoming possessions or ornaments, thus having "to will themselves to be creatures without will" (53). Thus cornered emotionally, behaviorally, and vocationally, an inviting recourse for self-assertion was to "get sick." Meyer's speculative judgment is harsh:

To be sick was a route for the pure but weak, neither the masterful, aggressive reform of reality by the strong nor the anarchic selfish rebellion of the weak and impure. To make oneself sick was an escape, for it invited a project which at the same time did not require one to wrestle with the world [and the] project of getting well could be pursued entirely within oneself. (59)

This sad condition for women was not helped by doctors and clergy. The new medicine attacked only the physical, and the Protestant tradition carried a rigid and unfeeling spirituality. The old Calvinism "tried to live in the naked glare of the Father alone" to the exclusion of the Son (64). Sickness then seemed a psychically cogent option:

The sick got taken care of. To those who were ill, attention was paid. . . . Sickness might be, not ego-alien, but a project of the ego: for people who were underemployed, a form of occupation, for the lonely, a demand for intimacy. Sickness might constitute a means for bringing lives otherwise diffuse to a focus. (70–71)

Into the circumstance, ideally suited, bursting with opportunity and hope, came New Thought, thoroughly American in its origin and flavor. To the needy it gave "the closure of absolute assurance" by replacing divine sovereignty with divine supply, a godhead that "was the immediate projection of uninspected wish" (76, 81). Departing from traditional theology, Christ became a principle, and the Father became Mother. At the same time, modern psychology discovered the unconscious, a speculative notion that seemed to gel with New Thought assertions about the nature of the human spirit.

By the early twentieth century, psychosomatic illness attracted the serious attention of doctors and just everybody else, again emphasizing the role of attitude of faith in matters of health. How one felt came to be seen as the product of how one believed, and to feel well, Meyer thinks, Americans would believe just about anything. Many believed "what . . . was helpful and healthy and pleasant to believe" in order to shelter them "from the blighting refutations of the reality-principle." New Thought religion had "become purely the projection of wish, neither humbling the ego nor requiring action to reform the world" (101).

In the fifty years surrounding the turn of the century, the New Thought movement continued to stress a selfish individual security as seen in its followers' charitable constraint and financial accumulation. Politically, the movement had little consequence on either end of the spectrum, tending always to fade into visions of transcendent harmony. Instead, Meyer struggles to catch the effects of the New Thought ethos on what we might call "personality style," but at best his language remains frustratingly abstract. From there, Meyer goes on to discuss in general terms the disintegration of the old character ethic as became evident in the mounting personal, social, and economic tension. Stewardship notions did not quite suffice, and labor unions came to care only for narrow bread-and-butter issues. Instead of substantive confrontation with the social disturbances in American culture, those afflicted could escape in adjustment-oriented, therapeutic psychology and religion. The last gasp of the work ethic came in Frank Haddock's *Power of Will* (1907), part of the "Power Book Library," in which Haddock discarded the notion "that will followed what mind grasped of the intentions of God." Haddock defined mind as purposeless, and that conclusion finally severed "the cord of piety" that had ennobled the dying work ethic (165). Haddock believed that willpower could make anyone into anything, an automaton, and appease anyone, thus first raising "the problem of sincerity" in the emerging personality ethic (166). Willpower for success soon gave way to the mind power of "magical psycho-science" or "psycho-metaphysics" (understandably, Meyer cannot decide on the best verbal formula for the curious amalgams of New Thought; 168, 169). The "eccentric and mostly magical notions" of Napoleon Hill and Claude Bristol find an audience among those "on the fringe, men with some, but only precarious and hazy, schooling, men without special skills, men of the underworld of earnestly struggling underpaid unimportance, clerks, stockroom assistants." (170). These "weak" and failed men, "sleepwalkers in the routines of modern organizational society," suffered from "an almost total incapacity to generate or identify with any kind of coherent social myth or philosophy, or politics." Adrift and aimless, "they undertook their own transmutative self-hypnosis" so as to "vibrate with the mystic ether of money" (171). Those for whom individualism and the corporate state were too much took a lesser route through psychic pablum and escape.

Meyer looks at the standard success figures of Bruce Barton and Dale Carnegie. He ascribes to Barton "a liberal version of Jesus" that focused Jesus' "blithe spirit" on "individual creative energy and self-transformation," messages of New Thought, and the new business ethos (177, 78). Insofar as Barton correlated "Jesus' personal magnetism" with "the purported qualities of business leadership," Barton gave business its "supreme sanction" (179). Carnegie supplied "the means for achieving a self-automated caricature of Barton's personal-magnetism ideal" (180). Meyer notes the moral burden of artificiality and the advocacy of "the impersonality of personality" that talked much about liking but little about friendship (187). The new theme of interpersonal harmony in industrial and corporate settings "simply added another layer of imposed socialization upon consciousness already severely burdened" (193).

The character ethic at the center of the "nineteenth-century social imagination" was supplanted by the "vision of a system," and the incarnation of the vision was Henry Ford (195). Abundance replaced scarcity in a new "lyric of plenty," as Meyer calls it (199). In all of this, under the counsel of New Thinkers and economists, the consumer "was weaned from saving and hoarding so that he might spend, weaned from piling up possessions in order to expedite planned obsolescence, weaned from ascetic discipline that he might respond to every innovation, weaned from work identities that he might have the time for consumption" (205).

V

In *The American Myth of Success: From Horatio Alger to Norman Vincent Peale* (1969), Richard Weiss looks closely at changing varieties of American success ideology as displayed in the literature that served as their chief purveyor. The survey largely falls into two parts, the first half dealing with what is generally called the "character ethic" and the second treating the substance of New Thought literature. As a study in the history of ideas, the book seems balanced, fair-minded, and revisionist in import, especially in its analysis of the character ethic. Weiss repeatedly insists that well into the late nineteenth century the "message" of success was subdued, if not chaste, and not at all what historians have generally deemed it to be. Popular lore about Weber's Protestant Ethic and Horatio Alger's "Ragged Dick" has generally misunderstood the substance of these benchmarks in American cultural history. Contrary to intellectual prejudice, Puritan America was much concerned to temper the desire for wealth and the corrosive social effects of its attainment. Religion was not a warrant for unfettered greed: "In the Puritan conception, economic activity was subject to both moral and social considerations. . . . they believed that government could and should supervise individual economic activity and make it conform to the commonweal. Economic liberalism advanced only with the decline of the influence of the clergy" (23). The Puritan ambivalence toward wealth-getting, while commending the virtues likely to achieve financial increase, would ever after affect American success literature.

Benjamin Franklin offered the first real departure from the Protestant ethic insofar as he secularized it and encouraged social and economic mobility, a possibility that ran contrary to the medieval social vision of Puritan culture. For Franklin, "proper behavior . . . brought rewards," and Franklin himself not only popularized the ideal of social mobility but became its first symbolic representative" (28, 29). On the other hand, the famous readers of William H. McGuffey expressed a Puritanical distrust of wealth and were far from the agents of social control and exploitation that they are often made out to be by historians. Again, as a corrective of the truisms of the historical profession, Weiss argues that McGuffey's readers "contained more idealism than ambition" and were deeply apprehensive about the encroaching capitalist order of individual economic pursuit (34). Even though they might celebrate accomplishment and the virtues necessary to achieve it, the guidebooks of early America "uniformly gave virtue precedence over wealth" (40). Moreover, as America became increasingly urban and rampantly commercial, guidebooks became increasingly nostalgic for a past social and economic order of rural communalism (43).

The ambivalence toward wealth and wealth-getting that Weiss finds in the Puritans, McGuffey, and other early success writers, he finds, again contrary to historical clichés, in the work of Horatio Alger, Jr. Rather than a symbol of Gilded Age greed, in Alger's work there is "a critique of the post–Civil War period—of industrialism, urbanization, mammoth fortunes, and the general decline of morals" (59). Alger resented the new economic order and the urban world that was its arena, especially as these imposed a heavy toll upon children. Weiss also examines the attitudes of five best-selling Christian novelists—Augusta Jane Evans, E. P. Roe, Charles Sheldon, Gene Stratton Porter, and Harold Bell Wright—who saw their work as offering practical spiritual and moral counsel to their many readers. While advising discipline, thrift, and integrity, all denigrated the values of economic self-interest promulgated by the new merchant class. Their heroes and heroines never became magnates but achieved a modest prosperity through hard work and good luck. Success for them had little to do with money or status but depended on quality of one's moral life, especially as their actions affected those about them. As a group they were far more likely to indict than to celebrate the accumulation of wealth. While always emphasizing the importance of character, novelist-minister Charles Sheldon became, with his *In His Steps*, a major voice of the Social Gospel. By and large, success literature "contained much advice on the general conduct of life, very little on the art of accumulating fortunes" (97).

In the second half of his book, Weiss turns his attention to the emergence of a new message in American success literature that was better suited to the impersonality of life within an emerging corporate structure. While Weiss concurs with Donald Meyer's thesis about the ego-corroding effects of the mind-cure movement, at the same time he argues that mind-cure addressed Gilded Age religious confusion with historical insight and social sensitivity. Weiss views mind-cure as a pragmatic modification of the philosophical idealism that informed Transcendentalism. The effect of his treatment is to pull the mind-cure tradition in from the fringes of American religion and thought. In its motives and its popular ideas, mind-cure articulates an ideological disposition—a creative and sustaining myth—that lies closer to the elusive American center than is generally recognized. As such, observers need not wonder too much at the ease with which the "ideas of Quimby and New Thought have penetrated the mainstream of American Christianity and beyond" (229).

Weiss differs considerably from Christian Science apologists in identifying a specific forebear for Christian Science and mind-cure in the philosophical idealism of Transcendentalism. For Weiss, this "renascence" of idealistic thought in the New Thought movement was, most of all, a reaction against the increasing materialism and depersonalization afoot in the Gilded Age (134). Mind-cure emerges as a reaction to the religious and social crises of the late nineteenth century. The new science clearly tended toward materialism, and the rationale and practice of the new industrialism "fostered a naturalistic world-view which contradicted theological notions of a purposive and moral universe" (129). The latter found its concrete embodiment in the danger that the machine might "dwarf the individual" (128). The joint assaults of scientific realism and impersonal technology effectively "shattered the psychic prism" through which the average person understood self and society. That confusion wrought by the new mundane and intellectual conditions spelled the demise of "the belief that Christian virtue led to worldly well-being"—the end, in other words, of the older Protestant Ethic of character (129).

The strategy of mind-curists, as with the Transcendentalists before them, was to assert the claims of the spirit in determining responses to questions, in William James's terms, of "God, free will, and immortality" (139). In the Gilded Age's new social and intellectual settings, the ontological preeminence of "mind" became the chief vehicle for preserving "belief in the power of self-direction" (140). In the older Protestant character ethic of the self-help tradition, the "classic virtues of prudence and frugality" were means to personal and social fulfillment and satisfaction; in the postbellum successor, "states of mind rather than traits of character were the keys to success or failure" (133). This orientation on the part of mind-cure writers illustrates, first, their continuity with Transcendentalism and, second, in its pragmatic applications, "the interrelatedness" between apparently disparate elements of culture, namely, "the common ground between what is probably America's most distinctive contribution to Western thought and what is generally regarded as one of the crudest expressions of popular philosophy" (138). The innovative, utilitarian stroke of New Thought theology pushed toward the "melding" of a strong American minority tradition in Transcendentalism and the emerging appeal of philosophical pragmatism (139).

With New Thought's distinguished roots in the idealistic and pragmatist traditions, Weiss finds little to fault in its impulses and basic ideas. Their problem, it seems, was in their habitual "overstatement that brought them to the edge of absurdity." Working toward a revised estimate of New Thought's social legacy, Weiss locates its chief contribution in maintaining the possibility of hope in personal and social realms, specifically with regard to politics. As with leaders in spiritualism, many of the early mind-cure advocates were also social reformers who saw the "preservation of an optimistic world-view as a social necessity" (156). The intellectual and religious themes of the movement contained implicit reformist emphases: democratic individualism, unlimited personal potentiality, openness to science, confidence in an immanent "orderly and harmonious universe," and physical and psychological health in a social world (164). Far from an exclusive stress on a selfish instrumental application of New Thought principles, early New Thought popularizers regularly inveighed against abuses of power by social and economic elites. The impulse for personal development could not be entirely separate from the necessity of providing ample opportunity for its expression in economic spheres. In summary, then, mind-cure, or at least a sizable portion of it, was entirely democratic, denied the existence of natural elites of any kind, and exalted

all people equally as the chosen creatures of God. Condemning human suffering as wrong and unnecessary, it does not offer the rewards of an after-life as a *douceur* for present miseries . . . it holds that all men can and should experience fulfillment, happiness, and success here on earth. In short, it is a humanistic doctrine. (233)

Not until the ascendancy of the most famous New Thought writer of them all, Norman Vincent Peale, did mind-cure assume a markedly conservative character. While Peale's message was "little more than a restatement of what mentalistic self-helpers had been saying for more than a half-century," he imbued it with conservative implications by giving "exclusive emphasis to the importance of subjective psychic factors in the cause and cure of human problems. . . . By promoting the illusion of limitless individual power, the ideology of success [in the Peale version] obscures certain social realities, and thereby serves a stabilizing function for the established social order" (233).

While differing with Donald Meyer on the political substance of some mind-cure, Weiss shares some ground with him in viewing the New Thought tradition as a response to the reduction of the individual within the modern industrial state. As men increasingly became mere "cogs" in the corporate machine, their concern for "individual power" mounted, and New Thought provided something of a recourse wherein they might retain some sense of "unique value and importance" (234). In the end, Weiss does leave open the question of the actual social role the mind-cure success tradition has played, whether reformist or conservative, and simply acknowledges that both elements were present. If it finally worked to accommodate people to oppressive social realities, as Meyer contends, this judgment lies outside Weiss's scope since his is not an empirical study of mind-cure effects. Seemingly, he is content to suggest that the mentalist success tradition, as with the character ethic before it, was not as nearly "monolithic" in its pursuit of selfish accumulation as intellectual historians have usually insisted (7).

Much to the contrary, Weiss regards New Thought as a genuine spiritual protest with "symbolic significance" (231). "Whatever its premise of material rewards, success ideology is rooted in the idealistic tradition" that views the human person as "free and prepotent" (229, 230). By identifying mind-cure in impulse and doctrine as a "revival of transcendentalist dogma," Weiss effectively places mind-cure nearer the intellectual mainstream, shearing it off from its marginal and fringe status within the American past. This push is furthered by its later association with some of the impulses and strategies of pragmatism. Here Weiss employs a strategy similar to Stephen Gottschalk's in order to normalize a variety of thought that has most often been relegated to a disrespectable fringe. In its spiritual reaction and its creative use of significant "high-culture" American philosophic traditions, New Thought or mentalistic self-help becomes nondeviant, even though its rhetoric was much given to histrionics and exaggerations in behalf of "an illusion of independence" (13). Like Meyer, Weiss cannot finally repeat Gottschalk's embrace of a full-blown idealism as a way of contravening the bothersome press of adverse reality. Weiss wished to move the tradition more toward the center of the continuum, but he cannot entirely regularize it as a sensible approach to life. In its extremes, with Coue and Peale, much of the good sense within New Thought ends up as instrumental triviality.

VI

A model of its kind, Daniel Rodgers's prizewinning 1978 study of *The Work Ethic in Industrial America 1850–1920* carefully surveys the major challenges to the work ethic during America's development into a modern industrial state. Rodgers insists that for mid-nineteenth century, middle-class northerners, work had been "the core of the moral life," a "distinctive credo," and "ideology" (xi). In the seventy years following, through mechanization and routinization, the nature of "work itself was radically remade" in such a way as to render its traditional rationales inapplicable. Ironically, "the industrial revolution in the end left in tatters the network of economics and values that had given it birth" (xii). Rodgers contends that even after the historical context that had given rise to the work ethic had disappeared, "the equation of work and virtue continued to pervade the nation's thinking." Beset by confusion and contention, "the record of the work ethic, at any rate, was at once one of failure and persistence" (xiii). Defenders and moralists of the old vision of work would seemingly ever after struggle "to haul work and values back into accord" but to no avail (240).

In the opening chapter, Rodgers sets forth the ideological roots of the work ethic, first briefly spelling out the historic visionary tension in Western culture between leisure and work and then concluding that nineteenth-century America wholly embraced the latter: "the elevation of work over leisure involved not an isolated choice but an ethos that permeated life and manners" of the middle class (7). The Puritan heritage, moderately construed here by Rodgers, emphasized the benefits of work in individual social usefulness, character formation, and moral discipline. Quite apart from the lure of success and material reward, "the sanitizing effects of constant labor offered at once a social panacea and a personal refuge" (12). Expanding economic opportunity in the middle part of the nineteenth century fueled standard rationales for work into frantic, success-impelled busyness. As industrial expansion ran apace, it smothered older forms of domestic and craft shop manufacture. In the new factories, "size, discipline, and displacement of skill" enormously increased productivity. "Between 1860 and 1920, the nation's population a little more than tripled, but the volume of manufactured goods produced increased somewhere between twelve- and fourteen fold." By 1910 the United States more than doubled the industrial output of its nearest rival (27). Yet out of this expansion and its requisite "transformation of labor" came a "maze of paradoxes" that devoured ideals and assumptions about "the moral preeminence of work" (28). Massive and penurious factories undercut the old hope that labor begot economic betterment. Moreover, in the new factories, work proved uncreative and artless, fully capable of performance by machines and drones. The very material success of industry undercut Protestant asceticism with "a noisy gospel of play" (29).

Among many disjunctures, one major battleground arose between the promises of the old work ethic and the effects of the new factory system. The old creed held forth the model of a "society of economically independent workers" wherein anyone who labored hard might advance and prosper (31). In contrast, in the faceless and regimented world of the new factory, the average worker more resembled a permanent slave or hireling; modest prosperity or rise became an insubstantial dream. Success literature downplayed the efficacy of work and dedication in favor of personality or attitudinal attributes, such as those featured by New Thought. Labor and industrial theorists proposed a number of strategies to counter the trend of shrinking opportunity. Profit-sharing schemes and piecework wage scales revealed, on the part of all, "an intense longing for industrial harmony" (46). Through all of this, Rodgers contends, the crucial question focused on the worker's freedom, on "self-direction," on whether the worker was "owned and mastered for all practical purposes by his employer, chained to his task without hope or profit or escape." Such a circumstance simply violated everyone's convictions of "what work should be" (63, 57).

The circumstance directly affected questions of worker autonomy and creativity in the workplace. Long hours of monotony—of "specialized, repetitious, machine-paced, and, often, deadeningly simple" work—had its effects in "spiritless, discontented labor" (67). Creativity and dignity largely disappeared. Uneasy middle-class moralists, such as industrial expert Carroll D. Wright, justified these deadening processes by arguing that they instilled order, discipline, and intelligence in workers' personal lives, most of which were, in Wright's estimate, notably inferior to their employers. Dissenting from the elitist and optimistic rationale were late-century muckrakers, who took inspiration from such British aesthetic reactionaries like John Ruskin and William Morris. On a practical level, the protest against industrial tyranny took shape in Elbert Hubbard's handicraft movement. Chicago social worker Jane Addams hoped to enrich the worker's life by teaching the "connection of one's work with the social whole" and the historic value of work within community and tradition (83). The most common remedy for too much bad work was to do less of it, a prospect that predictably frightened many conservative moralists. More leisure, especially if allowing for escapist and sensational outlets, could foster waste and dissipation.

The nature and necessity of "Play, Repose, and Plenty," Rodgers's fourth chapter, became a preoccupation of the moralists and labor leaders. The views of Henry Ward Beecher, the era's most famous preacher, fluctuate between a youthful, rigoristic view of work and morality and a more mature appreciation of leisure, indicating uncertainty about the true route to personal wholeness and contentment. As Rodgers comments, what was at stake in the public debates were "at once a moral code and a set of interrelated psychological, religious, and economic premises" (99). Almost everyone was torn between the moral and spiritual effects of work, as the old work ethic contended, and the recuperative and energizing benefits of leisure and relaxation, modes of being that invited a mystical contemplation of life. "From the 1850s on . . . in pace with the accelerating economic changes, one can trace a steadily mounting attack on the excesses of work and a growing praise of play and recreation as antidotes to the violent, all-consuming busyness" (102). At least some of the counsel to relax came from the phenomenon of neurasthenic exhaustion, for which many doctors advised total rest. Theologians like Horace Bushnell and popular writer Hannah Whitall Smith, author of *The Christian's Secret to the Happy Life* (1883), advised passivity and receptivity; New Thought writers Trine and Towne echoed the same as a means to tapping into the divine plenitude and flow in the universe.

Nowhere were the subtle, but sure, changes in the work ethic more conspicuous than in the fiction for adolescent boys, the imaginative domains inhabited by Ragged Dicks and Henry Wares, which was a flourishing publishing enterprise in the nineteenth century. While we cannot be sure what elements, whether adventures or morality or both, might have enticed readers, these novels do, nonetheless, offer access to author's intentions and messages, especially to the changes therein. In the fiction of the early nineteenth century, "incident and moral fused together in a common didactic purpose" to emphasize "that systematic, self-disciplined work" resulted "in happiness, in contribution to the common good, and in tangible reward" (132). Amid changing values in the workplace, the influence of Romanticism, and the rise of the sensationalistic dime novel, this traditional counsel "grew increasingly split and uncertain" (136). The immensely popular novels of William T. Adams, under the pen name of Oliver Optic, initially promulgated the work ethic but then moved decisively toward entertainment, their "fundamental code" shifting "from restraint to impulse, from work to deeds of nerve and daring" (139). Rodgers summarizes the frequent criticism that Horatio Alger, enamored of bestowing large quantities of luck on his heroes, "was all but incapable of actually showing the steady, sober advance he talked about so much" (140). In the last quarter of the century, novels increasingly emphasized solidarity over individuality, "chivalrous, heroic virtues" over discipline and steadfastness, and "the romance of victory" over "the reward of effort" (144). After the turn of the century, tales of "wish fulfillment" in athletic prowess continued a trend where winning received more attention than the hard drudgery of training. Joseph Altsheler's frontier stories of young Henry Ware featured evasion of civilized responsibility through escape into the wilderness. All in all, novels for adolescent boys more and more dramatized simple escape or luck, all the while continuing lip service to traditional work ethic models. Abstraction and fantasy settings supplanted older attempts to place young men in "real-world," practical situations. The gradual change suggests, at the very least, writers' ambivalence toward the continued truth and cogency of the old models.

Obviously, boys were not the only young to have specific models and visions set before them. Rodgers spends a chapter describing the fate of women's roles within an industrializing society that profoundly affected the work world of women, both domestic and commercial. The feminist issues of the late century went beyond suffrage to raise questions of work, productivity, and idleness. The works of famed novelist Harriet Beecher Stowe contained many of the ambivalences of the age's women. On one hand, Stowe "poured out a pent-up sense of the hardness of woman's lot" but complained simultaneously that women of her time "had fallen to the cult of fashion and lost the will to labor" (184). The Victorian cult of sentimental femininity posed the greatest threat to women; the idle woman—sunk in selfishness, antidomesticity, and "aimless deadening vacuity"—had a higher calling of usefulness, whether within or without marriage, a consideration that placed Stowe in the company of some feminists. Charlotte Perkins Gilman, the most widely read of turn-of-the-century polemicists, responded to women's plight by arguing that all women should work outside the home, thereby highlighting economic realities and opportunity for women. Most often writers and reformers necessarily walked a middle way between assertion of a "desexing" masculinity and idle and sentimental womanhood. Those women who did enter the industrial or commercial workplace were severely disillusioned with the romantic popularizations of feminine labor promoted in countless magazines and books. The work of the factory and office proved hard, demeaning, and unfulfilling. While "the hunger ran deeply for something more demanding and useful than ornamental daughterhood, something far broader and less constrained than unmitigated tending of home and children and something more independent than submissive wifehood," actually finding satisfying work outside marriage and home was not easy (189). Those feminists who did look closely at the world of female factory work were rather taken aback at what they found in the work and those who did the work, for work did not finally seem to have the liberating, ennobling, or satisfying capacities for which they were looking. Nor was it easy to live within the poles of idleness and work.

The agendas of the new labor federations or unions included the length of work, payment formulas, the dignity of work, absenteeism and turnover, scientific management, and a host of other issues, but most of these had at their root changing conceptions of work and idleness, all of which were highly charged politically. Social radicals of various sorts, from populists to Marxists, accused company owners and managers of idleness, of not working for the proceeds for which the "workingman" labored physically. Conversely, owners condemned idleness and suggested that those who protested current conditions were guilty of a kind of incipient laziness, of wanting more return for their labor than it deserved. Always the debate seemed to swirl around questions of genuine labor, its value, and who actually did it. For Rodgers this unceasing dispute was inevitable given "a society conspicuously dedicated to the value of work" (215). Utopian dreams of leisure did not enter into political discussion, for all parties in the debate, no matter how radically opposed to one anther, believed in the practical and moral necessity of labor. Neither side abided the poor and shiftless. Conservatives were the most extreme in their censure, not merely seeing the poor as "sufferers from their own incapacities" but believing also that they "were at once a moral contagion and a severe economic burden" (223). Gilded Age charity organizations feared helping the poor would bring them to a condition of permanent dependency. Only later would sociology come to fault specific social problems for pauperizing so many people. The notion of individual responsibility, especially the obligation to work, carried enormous rhetorical and emotional power well into the twentieth century. In a society where "work has served so long as a moral imperative, it is not surprising that the charge of laziness should have touched so vital a nerve." It pervaded politics because it "turned question of policy into the more vital language of myth and moral drama" (231). The debate carried into the twentieth century, preoccupying such cultural luminaries as Harvard University president Charles William Eliot, who tirelessly sought to sustain the ideal of dignified work, a dream that the realities of the industrial workplace were making ever more unrealizable.

VII

Elizabeth Long's *The American Dream and the Popular Novel* is a cautious and astute argument about exactly what can be fairly derived about national or cultural attitudes or moods by reading popular fiction—in this case the shape and status of the tradition of the American Dream. Long finds in the popular novel an intriguing and trustworthy mirror to the shifting aspirations and struggles of middle- and upper-class Americans in the three decades following World War II. Moreover, the evidence from hardback best-sellers notably modifies the often simplistic, idiosyncratic, and gloomy analyses of the national climate by recent sociologists.

Long devotes a full chapter to a discussion of methodology, in which she argues that the "sociology of literature must examine the interrelationship between authors, channels of distribution, and the wide range of reading publics, in order to understand the cultural significance of books" (19). She concludes that there are continuity and commonality in composition and experience between the book industry and the taste and concerns of the middle- and upper-class reading public. Further, she contends that, by its very popularity, popular literature is a "social phenomenon" that provides and clarifies the "central markers of the categories through which we perceive the world" (51, 19), because reading "is an expressive behavior," and "reading patterns embody each individual's life-print" or response to crucial central issues in the reader's personal and social life (51). Insofar as these are shared by innumerable other readers, novels become best-sellers, in part, because they articulate, reflect, or "resonate" with their readers' values, "the wishes and fears, their hopes, uncertainties, desires, and dreams" (26, 45). Recurrent thematic content in best-sellers and changes in the treatment of that content allow interpreters to "infer general shifts in the cultural ethos" (21). The study of popular literature can yield some fix on "cultural meaning" (53). In general, the thematic content and its complexion are transparent and unambiguous but allow for only a narrow range of sensible cultural interpretation (57–58).

With this analytic frame in mind, Long's study reveals a significant shift in the broad-scale public definition of the nature and potential of the American Dream. About forty percent of the best-sellers in the decade after World War II "celebrate a vision of entrepreneurial success" that strongly links "the individual's saga of independent self-improvement to the triumphant advance of world progress" (63). As heroes fulfill their own goals of individual business success, they simultaneously contribute to the larger community, thereby transcending narrow self-interest. In an automatic and optimistic fashion, private success results in social good. The prevalent postwar notion of an ever-expanding commercial world allows for the melding of self-aggrandizement with the noble goal of forging a better world. The single-minded businessman is heralded particularly in religious novels, such as Lloyd C. Douglas's *The Big Fisherman* (1948), where the apostle Peter is depicted as the village fishing magnate (70). Such novels identify Christianity with secular pursuits and sanctify an American capitalistic vision. Heroes in the best-sellers of this period are enthusiastic and untormented by conflicting motives or dubious judgments or actions. The drive for success is a natural and pure sphere for human activity in which the individual can unblinkingly expend the soul. Women, by and large, are relinquished to subordinate roles from which they venture with peril.

By the mid-1950s, this model, hitherto ideally rendered, begins to fray. Conflict between the demands of work and family begins to emerge, and dependence on the corporation overshadows individualistic commercial freedom. In this " 'corporate-suburban' model," the hero's saga is

less one of conquest than one of integration of a set of disparate tasks and roles. Work is described as a fragmented and abstract process rather than as the creation of a product, and the hero's search for a sphere of mastery draws him increasingly into the private world of domestic and affective ties.

The personal and social satisfactions of commercial success, while not wholly discarded, are edged aside in favor of success as " 'the good life,' a balanced whole in which work is valued only insofar as it permits material comfort and familial happiness" (82). Sloan Wilson's novel *The Man in the Gray Flannel Suit* and William Whyte's sociological study *The Organization Man* betoken the beginnings of this significant shift. For Wilson, the world is no longer "a simple backdrop for heroic initiative" but "problematic, fragmented, and full of conflicting memories, responsibilities, and demands" (84–85). Realism and tragedy come to the world of business and domesticity. Heroes begin to wonder if the costs of actually attaining the dream offer a poor bargain.

Second thoughts about the worth and attainability of the traditional entrepreneurial dream result, in part, from profound structural changes in American life, a process of change that will continue apace for decades to come. Success is no longer personally or socially self-justifying; nor is it an end in itself. Instead, success in modern America becomes a means to something else, self-fulfillment, a sphere of activity and meaning that is private and emotional. The broad dispersion of affluence, the coming of a consumerist heaven, displaces the ideal of "entrepreneurial independence, thrift and self-discipline" (1). Novels in Long's second period, 1955–68, become "fictional explorations of the landscape on the far side of affluence" (91). Normal everyday Americans now have "access to the objects and experiences that had symbolized success to earlier generations," and thus organizing and shaping "metaphorical power of success as a moral imperative" wanes (92). The goal of success loses "its power to suffuse the individual's life with a sense of moral purpose, its ability to meld self and world into a progressive and meaningful totality" (94). The world of work breeds conflict and alienation, and the corporate monolith dwarfs and smothers individual effort. In its place the family is idealized and becomes the justification for work. Or, in the case of the more sensational novels of the time, glamour and luxury offer ample cause for labor and money-making. As might be expected, given the new ambivalence toward success, the number of best-selling novels dealing centrally or peripherally with success shrinks by roughly half during this thirteen-year period. With these novels, "a central cultural message has shifted" from the nobility of work as a moral venture to the utility of work for self-satisfaction. In the larger culture, there are "a new heterogeneity and relativism, organizational complexity, bureaucratic concentration, and social unrest" (101). Bureaucracy, technology, and impersonality encircle and shrink human aspiration and space for achievement. In such a world, the human need for meaning, warmth, and intimacy results in the apotheosis of sex in a vision of "fleshly intimacy engendering spiritual communion" (110). Religious and elite novelists proffer otherworldly solutions in which personal satisfaction—here rendered as peace or tranquillity—emerges from either inner or transcendent sources.

A last period of best-selling fiction, 1969–1975, Long labels "the failure of success," for novel after novel exhibits "a world-view in crisis." Not only has "economic or vocational success lost congruence with personal happiness or moral worth . . . but other definitions of personal fulfillment are also perceived as deeply problematic." Amid "the disappearance of moral sanctions and ideals," the search for satisfaction becomes more desperate, often culminating in extreme and brutal sexual practice whose sensate experientialism offers some sort of anodyne to inner vacuity (118). Further, the "naive sense of good and evil, heroes and villains, that characterized popular novels after World War II have evolved beyond openness and relativism to an arbitrary and destructive moral leveling." A new tone of "exhaustion, cynicism, and despair" accompanies a veneer of tolerance and sophistication. The most the reader can now expect from the widespread lowered expectations from work, hope, and life in the American system is seen in main characters of disaffection, alienation, and tenuous psychic survival. The happy ending disappears before "an increasingly difficult and unpalatable reality" (119). In the work world, style replaces morality, taste replaces merit. During this period, proportionally more novels deal with dropping out of careers, are outlandishly escapist sensation, or have settings in non-modern or fantasy locations. In other words, discontent is high, and any equilibrium is sensed as fragile. Even religious novels, bastions of hope and happy endings, "manifest a continued attenuation of the confident 'progressive' religiosity that in the earlier periods was the spiritual prop of entrepreneurial individualism" (141–42). One religious response comes in the novels of the demonic, Levin's *Rosemary's Baby* and Blatty's *The Exorcist*, and another in decidedly populist and antimaterialistic tales, such as Holmes's *Two from Galilee*. "Clearly, the earlier comfortable faith in God, which was coextensive with an equally comfortable assurance about progress, success, and the American way, has been significantly eroded" (143). In sum, the novels of this period call "into question the most private sources of character and aspiration, and almost every institution—familial, occupational, educational, religious—that constitutes the wider social realm" (146). In the midst of this cultural crisis of confusion and lostness is "at the very least a sense that traditional verities are too simple to handle the complexities of modern times" (147).

Long concludes from her survey of three decades of fiction that while the entrepreneurial ideal is not dead, "it has lost its certain connection to broader moral and social progress" and retains little plausibility as an ideal (192). The loss has been gradual but real, and it is clear from the "diversity of novelistic responses . . . that no new cultural ethos has emerged . . . to replace the entrepreneurial dream of success" (196). The slow demise of

the entrepreneurial ethos has shattered our cultural conventions for both knowing and feeling—engendering a predicament that is not only intellectual, but also emotional or spiritual, since both the ideational and moral maps that have guided our pathways through the social world are out of kilter with the experiential landscape. (198)

VIII

Another survey of American fiction and notions of success and self-help is Ruth Miller Elson's *Myths and Mores in American Best Sellers, 1865–1965* (1985). The survey is useful for noting the range of types of best-sellers, both fiction and nonfiction, their obvious content, and into what broad streams of American thought and feeling they fit. Given the scope of Elson's overview, the level of precise analysis that characterizes Elizabeth Long's book on *The American Dream and the Popular Novel* is not here possible. Nonetheless, the survey ties together diverse books that appeared decades apart to establish significant thematic configurations or channels that, over time, have transmitted and promulgated ideas. This listing, alignment, and analysis constitute the primary value of Elson's book. A major deficiency is Elson's simplistic approach to myth, one of her central organizing categories, insofar as she credits it with more effective power for individual readers than it has probably ever exerted. For example, in commenting on traditional, formulaic, good-vanquishes-evil fiction, she asserts that the "reader, soothed by the confirmation of his/her prejudices, was freed from the necessity of coping realistically with life as it was" by venturing into a realm of "wish fulfillment" (8). Similarly, she concludes her study with the unequivocal assertion that the myths contained in the best-sellers brought "order into a confusing world and a pattern of mores that allowed a comfortable and unquestioning adjustment to those myths" (309). Realistic fiction, social and psychological, invariably receives higher aesthetic and cultural marks. Such a view shows a marked preference for high culture and a truncated view of the role of myth within culture. Her interest in best-sellers lies more in presenting than in understanding, as she says, "a history of American cliches" (14).

Elson's chapter on religious best-sellers is a helpful overview of the kinds of religious literature that attracted and shaped the American public over a century. In language choice, secularization is clearly evident (177). Narratively and thematically, conversion or redemption plays a major role in early Gilded Age fiction, especially in the fiction of Augusta Evans Wilson and E. P. Roe. Elson notes the concern for the afterlife in Elizabeth Stuart Phelps *The Gates Ajar* (1868) but dismisses its subject matter as escapist rather than noting its social context and marked postwar cultural significance. Novelistic responses to the Gilded Age crises of faith are duly listed and described. Along the way, Elson rightly notes most religious novelists' regular support for conservative social and economic attitudes. Such endorsements appear in characterizations of Jesus in different religious classics. Russell Conwell's popular lecture and pamphlet *Acres of Diamonds* (1887) identifies wealth-getting with true Christian faith and ethics. Conwell, Douglas, and Peale all see poverty as a moral failing, which is a dubious reading of all three. Birth into poverty is unavoidable and can build character, but no more than that can be said for its moral status. Bruce Barton's life of Jesus in *The Man Nobody Knows* (1924) "reveals Jesus as an extraordinarily successful executive who forged an organization that 'conquered the world' by the use of modern business methods" (186). This strain culminates with Billy Graham's *Peace with God*, an extended tract that endorses middle-class attitudes and mores with its "simplistic and heartily conservative social philosophy" (206). On the opposite side, a sizable number of writers—H. G. Wells, Harold Bell Wright, and Charles Sheldon—regularly depict a Jesus who is on the side of the poor and likely to subvert a comfortable stratified social order.

A third major area of religious response, which Elson delineates well, is the emerging movement of New Thought, pointing specifically to Ralph Waldo Trine's *In Tune with the Infinite* (1897) and Frank Haddock's *The Power of the Will* (1907) as preparing the way for Napoleon Hill and Norman Vincent Peale. The New Thought movement marked a significant departure from Protestant evangelicalism as represented by Roe, Phelps, and Wilson. The techniques offered in best-sellers for tapping God's power became "techniques for getting ahead in the world," for "achieving power on earth rather than salvation in heaven" (206). Trine's *In Tune with the Infinite* features this emphasis. So successful is New Thought that by 1927 it is a subject for satire by Sinclair Lewis in *Elmer Gantry*. The ideas of New Thought received support, though without overt connection, from popular novelist Lloyd C. Douglas in *The Magnificent Obsession* (1929). Douglas's physician-hero fuses pseudoscientific and biblical notions of divine power and supply as a means to forge and prosper his career. Napoleon Hill published his best-selling *Think and Grow Rich* in 1937. The crowning articulation and success of this orientation come in Norman Vincent Peale's *The Power of Positive Thinking* (1952), which sees religious faith as an "exact science" that "is not something piously stuffy" but offers a "procedure for successful living" (209). Again, Elson emphasizes the degree of Peale's departure from evangelical Protestantism: in method, the endless tales of success in this world and its untrammelled optimism make the book a compendium of the American Dream. Religion is designed not to sweeten one's character but to enhance one's personality and popularity so that one can get ahead. God is a means to an end, an earthly, a material end. One becomes a success not by using the old virtues of thrift, hard work, persistence to produce something, but by becoming a more attractive personality. Instead of self-denial, devotion to one's fellow human beings and to God, one is to be absorbed in self-development; one is to exalt oneself by positive thinking. One praises oneself rather than God, and guilt and therefore redemption are left by the wayside (209). Thus, the "aim of Peale's transcendence is mainly a material one" (210).

In some of the book's strongest and lengthiest précis, Elson well summarizes the marked change in the spiritual ethos and moral end of twentieth-century Christianity. While she occasionally overstates her case and thinks modern readers are wholly uncritical, Elson forcefully describes the difference between nineteenth- and twentieth-century Christianity: the divinity of the nineteenth-century books is "omniscient, omnipotent, august, a Creator whose existence is accepted quite apart from human beings," and within this scheme humanity's duty is to serve God. "By mid-twentieth century, however, God seems to exist mainly to serve man: to assure him peace of mind, a stable society and prosperity." Not only does God begin to look a lot like humankind, but he is "almost wholly secularized." Putting the matter another way, Elson ventures that while in the previous century people called on God "to give the strength to conquer pride, selfishness, laziness, sinfulness," in the present one, God is called upon "not to strengthen one in the virtues espoused by Christ and Christianity, but to enlarge one's ego, to develop the pride and self-centeredness of Positive Thinking, to become a pleasing personality" (213–14). The God of the Protestant Ethic fired a public to produce; the God of the twentieth century functions within an economy of distribution and consumption.

Chapter 3

The Protestant Ethic
and Puritan New England

In seeking to locate the origins of the self-help tradition in American culture, historians have usually pointed to the first decades of European settlement in New England, that part of the New World settled, for the most part, by English Puritans in the early seventeenth century. Popular lore depicts these people as rugged individualists who were primed by their special kind of Protestant religious zeal to tame the wilderness for liberty and God—and to get rich in the process. As we will soon discuss, the accuracy of that portrait has formed the center of much debate not only about American history but also about the rise of capitalism in the Western world. The question has, in fact, occasioned, in the words of one scholar, "one of the most significant and well-publicized disputes of twentieth-century scholarship" (MacKinnon 211). What we are talking about here, of course, is the idea that a distinctively "Protestant Ethic" fostered the rise of capitalism, a notion first set forth by German sociologist Max Weber just after the turn of the century (1904–1905). Not only has the controversy over the "Weber thesis," as it is called, run the whole length of the twentieth century, but it has very recently, as scholars have gathered new information and reexamined the sufficiency of old arguments, heated up all over again (Zaret 245). One scholar has recently likened the whole, long-running dispute to a Hollywood movie monster, "the thing that would not die," akin to a creature whose character and visage cannot finally be either accepted or defeated by the people whose lives are shaped by its presence (Oakes 285). Just how important the topic is appears in the very persistence and range of the discussion it has inspired, for its depiction of American beginnings continues to influence many crucial contemporary political and cultural debates about national heritage and future purposes. This chapter briefly recounts the substance of the dispute over the Weber thesis, reviews traditional popular cultural images of America's Puritan past, and finally assesses at some length the extent to which aspects of the early history of New England support Weber's contention. Making use of both social history and literary-theological evidence, this last portion examines the culture of Puritanism and its historical record.

THE WEBER THESIS AND THE LEGACY OF PURITANISM

Just over ninety years ago, German sociologist Max Weber published two essays that suggested that the psychological effects of two prominent Calvinist theological doctrines, specifically, calling and predestination, hastened in Europe and then in New England the development of the economic system known as capitalism. Whether intended or not, the effect of Weber's thesis for many historians and especially in the popular lore of American history has been to cast the Puritan as the founder of American economic individualism. In the legacy of Weber, the Puritan became the prime catalyst in the emergence of modern capitalism and thus the prototype for the sometimes rapacious capitalism of later American history. Regardless of Weber's real intent or method of inquiry, both of which are also matters of lengthy debate, *The Protestant Ethic and the Spirit of Capitalism* gave rise to the image of the Puritan as one who was impelled, willy-nilly, to money-making in order to find earthly tangible proof of personal eternal salvation, which for the Puritan was God's ultimate blessing. Weber rested his argument upon the emergence of two ideas in the Calvinist or Reformed wing of the Protestant Reformation. The theology of French theologian John Calvin prominently emphasized a new understanding of calling, vocation, and work. Calvin rejected the idea that the only "holy" calling for the believer was work in some clerical capacity in ascetic retreat from worldly activity; rather, Calvin and his followers proposed that all work was holy when the worker labored to transform all domains of human experience into the kingdom of God. Calvin's idea thrust believers into worldly work in behalf of God and his world.

With this new conception of work, Weber mixed the old and peripheral Christian doctrine of predestination, a largely Calvinist notion that argued that God had before creation and human history arbitrarily and inscrutably chosen those who would be saved, those known in Calvinist circles as the elect. Unfortunately for the believer, since this God and life were essentially mysterious, usually concealing divine intentions and judgments from human knowledge, believers could not be sure of their soul's destiny in a cosmic scheme that closely resembled a divine lottery. Thus, with heaven and hell heavily on their minds and spirits and suspecting the deep human potential for self-deception in assessing one's spiritual estate, Puritans supposedly searched for some outward empirical sign, a tangible proof, of divine hope and favor that would confirm their hope of salvation. That came, so goes the argument, in work and wealth—by getting rich in the emerging marketplace of capitalism. Freed now from ascetic retirement to work in the world and fueled by dread of damnation, work and works became viable means of validating one's eternal selection. Taken together, these ideas of vocation and predestination threw the Puritan into a frenzy of worldly activity and prepared the way for the Puritan embrace of work and success. Economic success came to suggest God's providential favor and signaled that the successful had already been chosen for eternal salvation. Cultural historian Catherine Albanese explains the subtle process by which works came to supplant faith as a marker of salvation: as Puritans

became anxious about the question of their salvation, they looked to their behavior to seek assurance. One of the signs of saving faith was, after all, a righteous and reformed pattern of living. Gradually though, the saints in practice began to attach more weight to this pattern than to their faith, to put the cart of good deeds before the horse of grace, so to speak. It was not too much of a shift to begin to see external righteousness, good works, as a guarantee of salvation—and a guarantee which could be strengthened by more and more good action. Thus, ironically, an ethic of works and work came to flourish at the center of the religion which had taught justification by faith. (*America* 89)

So great was the psychic burden imposed by predestination that the Puritan initiated a new rigor in labor, discipline, and rational improvisation (called rationalization by sociologists) for the getting of wealth. Here began, then, so the story goes, new and heavy emphases on punctuality, frugality, dependability, hard work, and, the farthest extreme, entrepreneurship. As one Weber commentator summarizes,

the performance of "good works" in worldly activity became accepted as the medium whereby . . . surety [of salvation] could be demonstrated. Hence success . . . eventually came to be regarded as a "sign"—never a means—of being one of the elect. The accumulation of wealth was morally sanctioned in so far as it was combined with a sober, industrious career; wealth was condemned only if employed to support a life of idle luxury or self-indulgence. (Giddens 5)

Predestination, then, an "awesome" doctrine, as historian Sydney Ahlstrom has dubbed it, placed the Puritan on a psychospiritual rack, and the consequent anxiety served as an engine that propelled the Puritan into relentless economic activity with such resolution that capitalism reached its full modern state (*History* 118). Puritans thus became culprits, for they initiated the inexorable process that brought forth the modern economic state, and the chief hallmark of that state features the rigid industrial workplace that turns its workers into joyless, mechanized drones.

Unfortunately, Weber's largely speculative notion, which was how he himself thought of it, has become very much a shibboleth, a standard and unquestioned supposition, useful fodder in the academic marketplace of ideological contention, whether from the Left or Right. The "Weber thesis," as it has become commonly known, has undergone relentless and voluminous scrutiny and controversy, a debate that continues to this day. Critics have attacked Weber's work on virtually every possible ground, from methodology to historical accuracy; defenders, in turn, point to the critics' sloppy reading, to the practice of "decontexting" it from Weber's larger work, and to the thesis's essential correctness when one ignores particular mechanisms to appreciate its broad contours. Whether true, wrong, or some admixture of both, there is no question about *The Protestant Ethic*'s deep and lasting influence on intellectual and popular understandings of Puritanism and its role in shaping modern culture.

Calvinists mustered remarkable and, according to Weber, desperate spiritual and intellectual energy that worked to rationalize and regularize the methods of business, which fast became the means to getting wealth. With this vision of the interrelation of Calvinist ideas and economic history, Weber sought to counter reductionistic, materialist views of history, such as those set by Marx and others. In any case, Weber's suppositions quickly disseminated through the international intellectual community, but they did not receive wide dispersion in North America until the publication in 1930 of *The Protestant Ethic and the Spirit of Capitalism*, a translation of Weber's book-length version of his early essays on the topic. Ever since, a long train of many kinds of sociologists and historians have hotly, lengthily, and perpetually disputed the validity of just about every aspect of Weber's postulations.

By and large, the less ideological academic historians have exercised ample caution about the truth of Weber's thesis, usually proving unready to affirm its truth without sufficient historical evidence to resolve the many points of controversy within Weber's work. That hesitancy has not, unfortunately, characterized the posture of what we might call American popular intellectualism. For assorted reasons, this distinct "class" of opinion makers long ago accepted the Protestant Ethic as an important hallmark in the formation of American culture. Here Weber's ideas have been used to support two opposing ideological purposes. On one side of the cultural spectrum, political and religious conservatives have esteemed the Puritans for their supposed rigor in personal morality and for a courageous individualism that in the struggle to survive in the New World dutifully embraced self-reliance and hard work. In conservative discourse, images of Plymouth Rock and Thanksgiving are meant to evoke a lost "golden age" whose values of self-discipline and individualism could cure manifold contemporary social ills if only somehow the nation could now as a whole imbibe them. Amid the conservative resurgence of the 1980s and 1990s, this reverence for the Puritan past has regained much popularity and now challenges the prevailing notion that Puritanism's cultural legacy has, in fact, caused the very social ills for which conservatives see Puritanism as an antidote.

A second and opposing view, generally associated with political and social liberalism, predominates still, and it regularly appears in cartoons, newspaper columns, and the rhetoric of the "culture wars." Mainstream popular intellectualism portrays the Puritan as a starched, repressed, nosy, and mean-spirited prude—an inveterate antagonist of fun, a burner of witches, and a hater of sex. In addition to the mainstream's litany of complaints about Puritan attitudes toward sex, alcohol, women, race, and the environment, Weber's argument for Puritanism's role in fostering capitalism has resulted, albeit far from Weber's intention or meaning, in the popular perception of the Puritan as the money-grubbing miser responsible for the worst abuses of the American capitalism. Indeed, this notion has not only persisted but flourished to become an inordinately powerful shibboleth in contemporary American cultural self-understanding. This "truth" is endlessly and blithely repeated, usually with the purpose of indicting the past as a ready scapegoat for current ills, which is a role that America's Puritan past has long served in American popular intellectualism. As such, the public image of probably no other group in American history is in greater need of revamping than that of the fabled and now usually ill-famed Puritans.

Despite the resurgence of a conservative nostalgia, the hostile stereotype of the New England Puritan still thrives, and its origins and development merit some historical explanation. It emerged first among professional historians as the profession as a whole moved in the 1920s and 1930s to embrace progressive economic theories of social and political development. In 1921, using an economic interpretive filter first set forth by historian Charles Beard in his work on the American Constitution, prominent historian James Truslow Adams declared in *The Founding of New England* that the primary motivation of the lay Puritan in coming to the New World was economic and political, the opportunity to do what one wished for oneself (121–22). Of the Puritan migration to New England, Adams held that the desire for free religious expression amounted at best to a secondary consideration (Anderson, "Migrants" 342). A few years later, in the first of three volumes on *Main Currents in American Thought*, historian Vernon Louis Parrington celebrated the triumph of American "democratic liberalism" over Puritanism's clerical tyranny and capitalistic fervor (13). For Parrington, a major figure in American historiography, religious ideas assumed value only insofar as they fostered, most often inadvertently, a Progressive political liberalism. From this perspective, the Puritans look regressive. Intellectually as well as politically, Puritans feared "the free spaces of thought," living instead in a "narrow and cold . . . prison" of intolerant "absolutist dogma" (12, 13). The sentiments of Adams, Parrington, and many other like-minded historians, now known collectively as the "Progressive" school, found in the

1920s and 1930s an indomitable popularizer in gadfly Baltimore journalist H. L. Mencken, whose nationally syndicated columns lampooned Puritan intelligence, charity, sexuality, and piety. In this climate, Weber's suggestion about the link between Puritanism and capitalism presented the final nail in the coffin of Puritanism—the combination of a pronounced, interpretive "climate of opinion" or ideological cast among professional historians and a talented popularizer firmly embedded the prevailing popular biases and caricatures of Puritan New England.

Caricatures of Puritanism have, over the decades, afforded much humor and political fodder, and they live still as convenient bugbears, culprits, and scapegoats. Unfortunately, as the preceding discussion suggests, this perception bears but faint connection to historical reality. Indeed, the problems with the liberal caricature are as great as with the skewed nostalgic images set forth by conservative proponents of self-help and economic individualism. Some scholars have gone so far as to suggest that realities of actual historical Puritanism provide exact mirror images of contemporary America's caricatures, whether from the Left or the Right. Indeed, it is no easy task to achieve a clear vision of Puritan historical reality, although historical scholarship in the last fifty years has taken enormous strides in revising the reigning stereotypes: in the place of the joyless and greedy, repressed and self-reliant Puritan, much contemporary scholarship pictures a robust, thoughtful, and full-blooded people who liked beer and making children and tried with their whole selves to see their individual and corporate lives as fragments of a larger loving intention for the world (Ryken 2–3). All indications are that Puritans possessed a healthy relish for life's pleasures, and while these might, to contemporary eyes, look to be of a rather austere variety, Puritans surely did not expect or want to live on prayer alone.

The person primarily responsible for this revaluation was the late Harvard historian Perry Miller (1905–1963). With exhaustive thoroughness, intellectual complexity, and literary passion, Miller undertook a decades-long foray into the Puritan mind and spirit, thereby initiating the current wave of historical curiosity. In five lengthy books, a total of roughly 2,000 pages, Miller retrieved a staggeringly full picture of the Puritan psyche. As historian Edmund Morgan has pointed out, Miller's work had a huge impact on how historians of his era understood the moving forces in history: Miller

related the settlement of New England not to the economic discontents or social ambitions of the emigrants but to the ecclesiastical ideas developed among English Puritans during the preceding fifty years. The result was to place both the ecclesiastical and the political history of New England in the context of intellectual history. (Miller 52)

For the dead-and-gone Puritans, Miller's lengthy history recovered the existential heft and drama of their lives and in the process bestowed on them a full measure of humanity. As one recent scholar of Miller has put it, Miller's study made the Puritans look strangely modern: the New England Puritans showed a "profound sense of man's smallness in a universe that was both mysterious and majestic, frightening and elating," wherein they "acutely felt the abyss that separated them from what they called God" (670). One of America's great historiographic achievements, it still constitutes a standard for scholarly sophistication and caution. Moreover, on Puritanism itself, Miller's description of Puritan intellectual, religious, and, to some extent, social reality has become the normative picture with which subsequent historians of early America have had to reckon. As one scholar has recently summarized, despite "decades of revisionist work, Miller's massive writings still dominate American Puritan studies, adding their considerable weight to the burden of anyone who wishes to engage the most recent scholarship in the field" (Peterson 13).

If Miller's lifelong study retrieved some intellectual respectability for the Puritans, in the last two decades the new field of social history has explored the life patterns and texture of social relations of the ordinary people of New England, many of whom were Puritans, and this new sort of historical investigation, too, has had a profound impact on popular portraitures of Puritan culture. With its conceptual origins in France, this new school of research methodology relies heavily on the use of almost any sort of extant data from long-gone social units, usually families, churches, and towns: genealogies, tax ledgers, court and municipal records, parish records, and, in some cases, company books. By painstakingly collating and then sifting vast amounts of data, the social historians have constructed startlingly full portraits of innumerable persons and families and of the larger social patterns their lives composed. With these techniques, we can now, with some empirical certainty, illumine what were either inaccessible or at best shadowy areas in the contours and texture of ordinary life several centuries ago. With the tools of social history at their disposal, historians have moved increasingly toward clarity on such factual matters, to name a few, as social and geographic mobility, marriage ages, fertility and mortality rates, family size, levels of family and community strife, and economic and trade practices. Previously, scholars' conclusions were necessarily more impressionistic, based as they were on surviving literary evidence, which itself could be highly subjective in its depictions. The data can still occasion rather eccentric interpretation, as we shall see later, but, on the whole, the new social history has both provided a fresh angle from which to view Puritan New England and yielded some surprising results. Indeed, as one prominent historian has noted, the recent community studies of pre-Revolutionary New England are in themselves "exciting, ingenious empirical research," but they have also made "the several hundred thousand souls who lived in this region one of the most studied human populations in the annals of history" (Nash, "Social" 233, 235).

This new wealth of information has, to some extent, occasioned a shift of historical interest from the lives and thought of a very small number of intellectual, political, and social elites, an "articulate few," as they are often called, to the experience and fate of the "folk," the ordinary and unheralded yeoman, wife, merchant, craftsman, or magistrate—by and large, common people who did not keep journals, who wrote few letters and no books, who never mounted a pulpit, or who in many cases could not read. While this still does not put the historian inside the mind of the folk, so to speak, information about towns, families, and individuals does afford a comparatively full glimpse of at least the surface or external shape of the experience of large numbers of people whose lives until now have remained almost fully obscure. Historian Michael Murrin has commented that with the new social history we come "as close to the lives of everyday men as the historians of the early modern era are ever likely to get" (227). Putting together Miller's sort of intellectual history and the new social history has led to a thorough revaluation of early New England that not only revises just about everyone's estimate of Puritanism but substantially challenges the validity of Weber's contention about Calvinism and the beginnings of capitalism and economic individualism. These conclusions directly pertain to questions about the origins of economic individualism and self-help in American history. The extent to which this is the case becomes evident in even a brief summary of the cultural history of the Puritans who came to New England: motives for immigration, community norms and ideals, attitudes toward work and wealth, the relation between religious practice and social achievement, and the forces of disintegration. Far from encouraging individual wealth-getting, the ethos of Puritan culture esteemed social concord and mutuality and, for the first decades of settlement, achieved social harmony to an extent that was unparalleled in any other part of the Western world.

WHAT BROUGHT THE PURITANS TO NEW ENGLAND

The European explorers and early settlers of North America formed but a small part of a vast westward movement of 50 million people in the last four and a half centuries of European life (Bailyn, *Peopling* 5). Through those centuries countless forgotten people made a long and perilous trek to North America, occupying lands from Nova Scotia to the West Indies and from the Carolinas to California. The conspicuous reasons for this enormous migration to the new land were political, social, economic, scientific, and religious. A new life in a new place surely held enormous appeal for many people and families, and attached to the lure of fresh beginnings were countless other factors. Rarely can we say that any one traveler chose to cross the Atlantic Ocean entirely for one reason or another. As is generally the case in human affairs, motives remain murky, mixed, and many in number, even for those who are supposedly the most rational and self-conscious of people. Given sometimes contradictory complexities, diverse contributing factors cannot be very readily separated or given an exact proportional weight or value. In short, in those coming to New England, motives were sometimes noble and were often remarkably crass, a quite normal admixture of altruism and self-interest. Moreover, European incentives for migration were neither uniform nor persistent but regularly differed from group to group, region to region, and time to time.

In short, the first immigrants to America were a diverse lot, just as was the long and unending migratory stream that followed. That bit of common sense and historical logic bears repeating at the outset. Very often, in both popular lore and much scholarly historical writing, these first European immigrants to America have ended up looking like either saints or pirates, democratic utopians or prototypes for robber barons. To insist that they carried around in their spiritual storehouses impulses both ignoble and humane may untidy the neatness of some ideological soapboxes in political camps and historical writing. In the aftermath of the crumble, however, we glimpse the historical possibility that traditional heroes and villains of this or that national mythology rarely fit into neat, preassigned categories.

Between the fifteenth and the sixteenth centuries, which was the zenith of geographical exploration of the globe, various hopes for social well-being, religious faith, and prosperity intertwined in complex ways to give impetus to exploration and settlement. For the explorers and missionaries, who were sometimes one and the same, finding new lands and laying claim for the king's possession offered attractive ways of advancing personal status. For the rulers came national glory and power and valuable scientific knowledge, and for the missionary came hope of expanding Christendom. Indeed, almost everywhere the causes of church and king were very often inseparable, for neither sponsor suffered from scientific glory and financial gain. Which motives predominated when and where, we cannot fully know, and many times the religious and economic motives struck a deal, as was the case with the Pilgrims of Plymouth Colony. We read documents and diaries and occasionally discern historical patterns, but, ultimately, human motives intertwine and burgeon in obscure ways that the best of historians and soothsayers cannot unpack.

In any case, what was true for explorers was also true for the first permanent European settlers of North America. With a large and sometimes heavy bundle of motives, the English, Dutch, French, and Spanish ventured to a vast new land that was simultaneously forbidding and promising. Always there was the allure of the new elsewhere, although it is probably unusually difficult for postmodern people to imagine it. As historian Bernard Bailyn has summarized:

in complex ways the American magnet exerted its force. For some, it was a distant but positive goal somehow to be reached; for others, it was a last resort, a refuge when all else failed; for still others, it was a mystery full of vague possibilities, to be explored, considered, realized, or rejected. But for everyone in this mobile world [of postmedieval Europe] it was an irreducible fact of life, ever present and ever potent. (*Peopling* 42–43)

Our focus here is necessarily on the fate of one large group within this vast westward movement, a collection of about 30,000 religious dissenters who left old England to come to New England, and those were, of course, the large contingent of so-called Puritans who crossed the Atlantic between 1630 and 1640. Their motives are important to examine because so much of their later history is popularly seen as merely an extension of the character that impelled them to migrate in the first place. So much of what we have come to assume about the Puritans rests upon their supposed motives in transplanting to New England, and this supposition, a dubious one at best, has occasioned, as one historian has described it, a "ferocious debate" among historians (Breen, *Puritans* 53). On this score, it is safe to say that historians have more and more come to conclude that regardless of whatever else one might wish to say about the Puritans, their intentions for migration set them quite apart from just about every other migratory group in those three centuries of global movement. The distinctiveness of Puritan motivation for coming to the New World appears in three clear and intertwined reasons, and together these reasons call into serious question the foundations of the Weber thesis and the Progressive historians' suspicions of economic incentives in immigration. Historian Joyce Appleby pointedly summarizes this shift in historical understanding: "The old story of individualism and free enterprise coming with the first boatloads of English colonists no longer is credible" ("Radical" 308).

One motive, very clearly, was religious. For the English Puritans who came to America, this religious impulse derived from their adoption of one vigorous strain of a broad religious revolution that in the sixteenth century shook Roman Catholicism and all of Europe. Brought to a boil by the dramatic actions of German monk Martin Luther, the reforming movement spread quickly from the writings and leadership of Luther, Zwingli, and French lawyer John Calvin. Mostly, these diverse theologians and their eager followers complained that over the centuries the Roman Catholic Church, of which they were sons and daughters, had gradually diluted and altered, perhaps to some extent unwittingly, the central teachings of Jesus and the apostle Paul. For the reformers, it was high time to address, no matter how they had crept in, the spiritual torpor, the theological error, and the institutional and moral chaos of the Roman Catholic Church. Thus, as church historian Sydney Ahlstrom has put it, "the Reformation, in the British Isles as elsewhere, was essentially a Christian revival in which the biblical understanding of man and history was forcefully proclaimed" (116).

This religious protest in behalf of religious reform was also in two ways political, and inevitably so given the setting and era in which it took place. The sixteenth century was a time of state churches and compulsory religious conformity. Church and state supported one another and intertwined. The crown supported the church, usually in exchange for the church's support of the crown, and vice versa. As such the domains of religion and politics could hardly be yanked apart. Consequently, dissent from the teachings or practices of the church was also dissent from the state that sponsored the church. In this regard, then, while the precipitating vision behind the cultural revolution that swept Europe in the sixteenth century was religious insofar as it directly challenged the theological correctness and ecclesiastical purity of the Roman Catholic Church, it simultaneously challenged the authority of the state. Thus, while the Reformation was to its core religious, within its political-ecclesiastical setting it was also inexorably political.

Whatever natural clash might arise between the reformers and the church-state alliance posed against them was aggravated by the fact that the broad movement reconceived the nature of the Christian life as a this-worldly enterprise whose proper sphere was not only the church but the rest of culture as well. While all the different major groups of the Reformation—Lutherans, Calvinists, and Anabaptists—differed on theological particulars and the extent of change necessary in the church and society, all concurred in urging, again in Ahlstrom's words, "a renewal of concern for this life, this world, and all their impinging problems, moral and social," an awareness that grew from "the prophetic demands of the Bible and its peculiar concern for the reversible course of history, in which men participate in the world as morally responsible persons." Among these groups, however, the Calvinist forebears of the Puritans generally tended to be the most troublesome politically with their insistence on reshaping not only theology but culture as a whole, from top to bottom and inside and out. More than just a spiritual awakening, the Calvinist religious vision carried within it a "rigorous and radical reconception of Christianity" that for one, as we shall see, "implied a whole new social order" (Ahlstrom 116). The believer was to esteem and transform all domains of human life, reforming not only churchly or spiritual matters but also political, social, and economic realms. In England, this stalwart insistence on change would eventually impel many Puritans to look for a haven of religious, political, and social renewal.

While the separate strands of the Reformation took different courses in different countries, in England by the turn of the sixteenth century neither the posture nor the rigor of Calvinism had diminished. Almost a century after Luther, the English heirs of Calvin continued to push for purification of the state Anglican Church, which separated from Roman Catholicism in 1534, when the pope refused British monarch Henry VIII a divorce so he might remarry and father a male heir. While this English Protestant state church had put some theological distance between itself and Rome, partic-

ularly on the issue of the papacy, it had not for the English Calvinists gone
nearly far enough. Much to the distaste of Calvinists, Anglicanism still retained a priestly hierarchy, sacramentalism, social elitism, and ample corruption in the control of its enormous wealth and power (Labaree 17). The
crown, on the other hand, was in no mood to accommodate the cranky
Calvinists, and moderate persecution followed. From this widespread discontent came New England's first small group of settlers, a radical, separatist, and untypical sect of Puritans, as Anglican archbishop Laud had
derisively named the larger movement of Calvinist agitation. For these radical dissenters, now known as the Pilgrims, both English society and its state
church were hopelessly corrupt. Given this state of hopeless calamity, the
logical choice was to withdraw and separate, choosing, in effect, to live apart
and in as much purity as possible until the final return and judgment of
Christ, which many among them believed to be imminent. Historical pes-
simists as they were, they sought religious refuge from the religious errors
and moral blindness of the English church, and for this they willingly risked
and suffered much. While they were extremists within the larger Puritan
movement, and their history proved unique, their motives were not greatly
different from those of more moderate Puritans who were to begin arriving
in 1630 as part of what became known as the Great Migration, an influx
that would last roughly ten years and bring to the area around Boston
20,000 Englishmen, the overwhelming number of them Puritans.

In 1608, long before the Great Migration, several hundred radical separatist Pilgrim Puritans followed their beliefs so far as to emigrate to the
Netherlands, where they hoped to escape the persecution their separatist
views met in England and find sufficient religious freedom "to practice an
austere form of 'congregational' piety purged of the various corruptions that
still (in their eyes) infested Anglicanism" (Demos 3). Much to their disappointment, the Dutch were also religiously restrictive, the times there were
financially hard, and, most of all, their children soon began to adopt profane
Dutch ways. Hoping to find a haven where the evil ways of the world would
not beguile their children, about a third of these English exiles began to
consider the possibility of moving away from European corruption to an
untainted North America. They hoped that there they might reestablish
"themselves in a land nominally English but effectively beyond the reach of
regular state and ecclesiastical power" of the British state (Demos 4). For
this purpose, a British charter was procured for Virginia, and in 1620,
aboard the fabled *Mayflower*, a contingent of about ninety strong landed,
very badly off-course, in Massachusetts Bay at Plymouth. There they set
about, as leader John Robinson enjoined them, to "entirely love and dili-
gently promote the common good" and to live communally (quoted in
McNeill 336). In this distant retreat from the world and its temptations,
the first winter about half died of chills and fever, and the community never
really prospered. By 1691 the later and far larger Puritan colony at Boston

officially absorbed the faltering Plymouth settlement. Through two decades of settlement at Plymouth, in a story to be oft-repeated in New England, population slowly dwindled as the children of the founders left in search of more and better land, a "large change whereby the community left behind the ideal of the first settlers" (Demos 11–12). In so doing, those restless settlers, in the words of aging Governor William Bradford, left the church in Plymouth "like an ancient mother grown old and forsaken of her children."

What apparently did not influence the movement of the large number of Puritans who followed the Pilgrims was the prospect of wealth, although this has become an explanatory shibboleth in popular renditions of early American history. The real settlement of New England began in 1630, when a large, more moderate contingent of Puritans began to arrive. Within a decade they would number 20,000. In contrast to the Pilgrims, these dissenters were generally of a milder and more hopeful sort. Religiously, they were nonseparatist, retaining at least a titular allegiance to the Anglican establishment. This conciliatory stance seemed to make little difference to either King Charles I or his archbishop Laud, who slowly increased pressure for religious conformity with economic and political discrimination as the penalty for nonconformity. Among these religious and political motives, which provided ample cause for moving, economic incentive did not apparently play a significant role. Close scrutiny of the personal histories of a sizable number of immigrants has allowed for some generalizations about the movement as a whole. Historian Virginia DeJohn Anderson has traced the histories of nearly 600 ordinary passengers who sailed for New England in seven different voyages between 1634 and 1637.

Scholars have previously conjectured that motives for migration were economic because so many of the known passengers had come from economically depressed areas, regions hit by crop failure or a slump in the textile market. Anderson's study of passengers from the seven ships indicates that while they came from economically depressed areas throughout England, they themselves had not suffered from the assorted economic crises in English cities or countryside, and therefore the prospect of economic betterment was very likely not a factor in their decision to migrate ("Migrants" 368–73). Even if they had suffered from the economic depressions of their time and region, she further concludes, New England was not a desirable place to go because reports from those who had moved or visited indicated that, in contrast to other English settlements in the Americas, New England was the least promising economically. New England was "no land of milk and honey," and the close study of those representative histories suggests that "[m]ost emigrants exchanged an economically viable present for a very uncertain future" ("Migrants" 373). Indeed, unlike the settlers of other English colonies in America, the Puritans "seem to have displayed fewer paradisiacal fantasies of a life of ease assisted by the natural abundance of a new Eden in America"; rather, the wilderness of the new land seemed to present considerable spiritual danger, for it was a place clearly in need of order and control (Greene, *Pursuits* 22). In vocation, most immigrants were farmers or artisans and were thus from "the more prosperous end of English society"; they on "the whole . . . were neither very high nor very low in social and economic status," a pattern that was repeated in their leadership in such people as John Winthrop (Anderson, "Migrants" 365–66). In fact, says Anderson, the appeal for emigration that was most emphasized by correspondents and publicists was the religious one: "Adherence to Puritan principles . . . became the common thread that stitched individual emigrants together into a larger movement" (376). Along with other factors such as age, marriage status, and relative social homogeneity, this common allegiance and shared experience in constructing what they thought of as a holy commonwealth explains much of the religious and social success of their venture to New England (382).

A third and last motive distinct from the religious and the political, although not finally separable from them, lies in the changing social world of seventeenth-century England. Rapid and drastic economic and social changes were irreparably damaging the texture of social relations in the English social fabric, and to Puritans in general and especially to leaders such as John Winthrop, future governor of Massachusetts, this occasioned a "profound disquiet" (Greene, *Pursuits* 21). Just as Charles I had moved with Laud to consolidate the throne's religious authority, he tried to do the same with political and economic power. Regular enclosures of land, for one, displaced great numbers of tenanted peasant farmers from life on the land. Very soon, cities and the countryside were beset by large numbers of begging and thieving poor. Moreover, privilege and honor seemed purchasable by those with money, and taxes on the gentry increased. Most of all, many Puritans sensed a change in the texture of the English social bond. Instead of the stability, order, and essential harmony of medieval society, from which England was at the time beginning to emerge, greed and ambition, pride and competition were rapidly shriveling the mutual respect inherent in the feudal social patterns of still largely medieval English society. By the late sixteenth century, "traditional" English society of agrarian interdependence was fast disappearing to become, as social historian Jack Greene has put it, a "mobile, fluid, rapidly changing society" that exhibited a "highly competitive, individualistic, and acquisitive 'modern' mentality" (*Pursuits* 34). Peasants, shopkeepers, and country gentry all had ample cause for alarm. To some extent, then, many of those who would become New Englanders departed with a sense of relief and expectation that the New England social order would not repeat the social disruptions that had lately soured English life. For assorted reasons, New England promised space for refuge and exile. Eventually, the move would look like a vital piece of God's miraculous providence and calling wherein New England would seem a beacon of faith and virtue to an erring world, "a city upon a hill," but initially at least, such expectations were not prominent in the minds of many settlers. From the deteriorating old world of England that seemed "increasingly chaotic and beleaguered," Winthrop hoped to establish in a new world, along with his Puritan fellow travelers, a society of "well-ordered communities knit together in Christian love and composed only of like-minded people with a common religious ideology and a strong sense of communal responsibility" (Greene, *Pursuits* 22, 23). In doing so, they sought "to avoid the most recent transformations" of life in England (Kishlansky 146).

How much this broad social deterioration in England figured in the choice to leave as opposed to religious or economic reasons we cannot finally know with precision. That it did play a significant role in the lives of many and that it, in part, fueled a particular social vision for New England seems clear. The story of one of the most prominent of the Puritans, a major spokesman and shaper of the Puritan social experiment in Massachusetts, offers ample evidence of its importance and gives some indication of what factors and hopes influenced the difficult decision to migrate. A middle-aged lawyer and Puritan member of the gentry and future governor of Massachusetts, John Winthrop only slowly and rather painfully arrived at the decision to emigrate. Leaving would involve giving up his place as lord of the manor at Groton, his ancestral estate, and his legal practice in the King's Court of Wards in London. Puritan friends implored him, however, telling him that the venture across the ocean could not succeed without his leadership. Admittedly, Winthrop's prospects in England seemed on the decline with the resurgence of a repressive Anglican conservatism. What ultimately seemed to tip the scales toward leaving was Winthrop's sense of growing social decay and chaos in old England. A crass and disruptive economic individualism bedeviled the people, with the rich driving down the poor. While pulpits talked of Christian brotherhood, the poor lived under the oppression of the rich, and, in Winthrop's eyes, the shrewd lawyers of the wealthy turned justice to wormwood. In the end, Winthrop protested this elite "misuse of property and position" by working to restore in New England a society, medieval in structure and Christian in intention, "in which men might subordinate themselves to their brothers' and community's good" (Rutman 8–21).

What exactly Winthrop had in mind for New England is made clear in the sermon he preached in 1630 on the flagship *Arabella* as she and three others carried to Boston the first large group of 1,000 moderate Puritans. As commonly agreed among scholars, Winthrop's "A Model of Christian Charity" is one of the most famous and important sermons in American history, for it restates a medieval social ideal of a God-ordained organic hierarchy of interdependent social and economic classes and functions. Its value in this account is that it conveys fully and precisely, better than any other document from the era, the full nature and scope of Winthrop's social-religious ideal for New England. What is perhaps striking in Winthrop's sermon, as its title suggests, is the centrality in this new social venture of what he calls "charity," a biblical notion into which scholars have since subsumed the notion of love. While Winthrop celebrates the stable class divisions in a medieval understanding of social structure, thinking that all people are "ranked into two sorts, rich and poor," he strenuously condemns, as one historian summarizes his attack, "calculating economic practices and competitive self-seeking" that overlook "the responsibility of the rich for the poor" (Henretta, "Ethic" 332). Put bluntly, the "rich and mighty should not eat up the poor." Rather, the New Testament Gospel of "justice and mercy" restrains and even transmutes natural instincts toward domination. To Winthrop, the rich must practice "extraordinary liberality" to the needy and bear in mind that "particular estates cannot subsist in the ruin of the Public at large," and conversely, the poor should not usurp the rights and tasks of their social superiors.

In short, without abolishing social demarcations, Winthrop stressed mutuality and interdependence, the obligations all have to one another, especially the rich to the poor. For all, regardless of social and economic status, the migrants must fret "not only upon our own things but also upon the things of our brethren." All must be "knit together in the bond of love" and "brotherly affection," always following the advice of the Old Testament prophet Micah: " 'to do justly, to love mercy, to walk humbly with our God.' . . . we must be willing to abridge ourselves of our superfluities, for supply of others' necessities; we must uphold a familiar commerce together in all meekness, gentleness, patience and liberality." So intense was Winthrop's longing for social harmony that he would push the civic body into fellowship or, more extremely still, into familyhood, where all would partake of each other's joy and travail: "We must delight in each other, make others' conditions our own, rejoice together, mourn together, labor and suffer together: always having before our selves our commission and community in the work, our community as members of the same body." If the Puritan settlers shirked the "unity of spirit in the bond of peace and embraced "carnal intentions, seeking great things and . . . prosperity," they would "shame" God's cause. On the other hand, at least in Winthrop's hopeful eyes, success would make them a beacon, "a city on a hill," whereby the rest of the fallen world might find the path to God and love. The moral and spiritual burdens, wild challenges both, were great indeed. For "orthodox puritan New England," as Jack Greene summarizes its history, Winthrop's social vision was widely and deeply shared and provided "an all-encompassing religious and social vision of the kind that restrained individualism and gave coherence, cohesion, and a larger sense of purpose to life" (*Pursuits* 46, 45). The extent to which orthodox Puritans achieved this vision was in the eyes of many historians "remarkable" and the Puritans' "greatest achievement" (Greene, *Pursuits* 80; Breen and Foster,

"Greatest"). It is important to examine this historical achievement because it substantively undercuts the common stereotypes of the Puritans and the Weber thesis in particular.

NEW ENGLAND PURITAN SOCIAL HISTORY

As articulated by Winthrop and broadly shared by his fellow migrants, the Puritan social vision at its core manifested both social and religious elements. Political freedom for their own distinctive religious belief and practice was surely a prominent feature of the Puritan enterprise in Massachusetts, but this quest for freedom for themselves, though not necessarily for any who disagreed with them, was inseparably tied up, as we have already seen, with a social purpose. In other words, in the case of the American Puritans, religious belief and its expression went beyond the pursuit for religious sanctuary to pervade in a very striking manner all the social relations and mores of their community. This was, then, as one scholar has summarized, an undertaking whose "primary purpose in coming to America" was "the establishment of a community dedicated to the fulfillment of God's will" for God and for the community (Labaree 40). Here there would be no disconnection between ecclesiastical life and ordinary life. In this melding of the religious and secular, the Puritans simply implemented a distinctive hallmark in Calvinist theology that affirmed the significance of all domains of human life, even those that had been disdained as secular by Roman Catholicism, such as government, banking, or husbandry. From this new integration naturally flowed, as Winthrop's sermon bears witness, "a model for society as a whole, not just for the religious institutions within society" (Labaree 72). In this regard, for the American Puritans, as for mentor John Calvin, "the glory of God and good of the community outweighed individual freedom in the marketplace" or anywhere else (Shi 9).

The practical fate of this social vision in the actual experience of the Puritan settlers and what it gave rise to has been, as suggested in the introduction to this chapter, of great interest to historians, and it has provided one of the more hotly debated topics in the whole of American historical research and discussion. Part of that interest derives from the fact that for historians, as for the Puritans themselves, New England functioned as a kind of crucible or laboratory for the testing of Puritan ideas, biases, ingenuity, and habits in a new and isolated world; rarely is such an opportunity afforded historical actors or the scholars that later examine their lives (Miller, *Colony* viii). Far from England's watchful eye, Puritans were relatively free to work out, sometimes under dire necessity, the practical implications of their theological and social commitments. While the Puritans were in relative concord in their religious and social vision, their circumstances and histories in the New World would vary, highly dependent as they were on quality of leadership, individual trade or profession, and place of settlement. For example, Stephen Innes has noted different social and economic structures in "three distinct settlement zones: an urbanized coastal region, typified by Boston and Salem; a subsistence farming region comprised of towns like Dedham and Andover; and an area of highly commercialized agriculture, such as the towns of the colony's breadbasket—the Connecticut River Valley" (*New Land* xvi). Recent careful studies of the social histories of these different sorts of communities indicate widely divergent patterns in social relationships, economic opportunity, and political behavior. Which pattern typified or dominated New England and reveals the inmost character of the Puritan experiment will remain a matter of some debate, but enough research into the social history of New England has taken place within the last two decades to provide the main contours of an answer. By and large, the complex social history of Massachusetts Bay Colony pointedly challenges the thesis that American Puritanism was significantly responsible for the growth of individualism and economic rationalism.

Even though historians have not yet produced social histories for all the towns of early New England, enough work has been accomplished to establish the main contours of life in early New England. Moreover, those studies suggest that the Puritanism of the first generations of New Englanders, leaders and common folk alike, impeded the emergence of what we today mean by economic individualism or capitalism. The social fabric of early New England, especially of Massachusetts, exhibited such equanimity and cohesion that two historians have called it "the Puritans' greatest achievement"—a "most startling accomplishment, fifty years of relative social peace" during a period that was in England and Europe characterized by turmoil and tumult (Breen and Foster, "Greatest" 5, 9). The chief features of this success lay in what social historian Jack Greene labels the "religious-based corporatism" of the "radically traditional world envisioned" by the founders and summarized in Winthrop's plea for social harmony (*Pursuits* 64, 80). With regard to the Weber thesis, this Puritan vision of the world proves markedly hostile to capitalist impulses of any sort, and the effects of this spiritual-moral ethos were pronounced. As Greene argues in his *Pursuits of Happiness*, an exhaustive comparative analysis of the social and economic orientations of the different British colonies from Barbados to Nova Scotia, early New England proved a marked exception to the norm insofar as it discouraged and effectively impeded "atomistic pursuit of wealth and self-interest" (64). Similarly, in a recent survey of the pace and texture of economic life in the first generations in Massachusetts, economic historian James Henretta argues, "The circumstances of life—spiritual and material—in early New England militated against the expansion of capitalist enterprise" ("Ethic" 335). Indeed, as Gary Nash summarizes, with the Weber thesis clearly in mind, a grudging "physical environment combined with the cultural restraints imposed by Puritanism to retard the advent of behavioral characteristics associated with the spread of the market economy" and set New England apart from the other British mainland colonies ("Social" 237).

As Henretta, Innes, and others have pointed out, this accomplishment was most obvious in numerous rural subsistence farming communities that sprang up during the initial huge migration of Englishmen in the first two decades, an influx that reached 20,000 in the first decade. As a whole, the Puritan experiment in New England was largely organized "around a series of tightly constructed and relatively independent settled permanent communities in which the inhabitants formally covenanted with each other to found unified social organisms," and throughout the seventeenth century ninety to ninety-five percent of the population lived in the rural towns (Greene, *Pursuits* 22, 56). New towns were planted; that is, groups of people—sometimes previously associated, sometimes not—gathered to found a village under a grant of land from the colonial authority. Typically, amid gathering together, on ship or upon landfall, a group of settlers would jointly formulate a contract or a covenant to undertake a town. Many of the attitudes and values contained in the contract were the same social mechanisms that characterized English peasant traditions. Historian Carl Bridenbaugh summarizes the ideal and the process:

In New England the community and social ideal . . . [were] present from the beginning. Groups of religious and socially like-minded families organized themselves into a "church and town," acquired a tract of land about six miles square, settled thereon according to definite rules and proceeded to work out for themselves an orderly agricultural community. The New England town was a carefully "planned society." (167)

Even before the formulation of a church congregation, town members formalized their covenant or contract with a verbal pledge and then set about the division of land, a potentially touchy process that was accomplished by a collection of factors. A committee of respected elders determined the size of a settler's grant on the basis of his previous economic or social status and his likely service to the community, as magistrate, minister, miller, constable, surveyor, and the like. Here, as in other domains of Puritan life, the notion of interdependence prevailed: the new Puritan Americans "envisioned a society of specialists bound together by mutual need and believed that any other arrangement would inevitably lead to chaos" (Foster, *Solitary* 14).

From the perspective of the late twentieth century, the Puritan social vision looks radically different. Puritan settlers imagined a society that would arise from an altogether different social ontology—a markedly different picture of the way a society should be put together and function. Distinctly medieval in origin, Puritan society sought to preserve hierarchical social distinctions not so much for privilege and power but for mutual service. This was hierarchy with a catch, as explained by historian Stephen Foster: "men of talent and virtue, deserved wealth and social status in proportion to the extent to which they contributed to the public good" (*Solitary* 20). In their experience, social usefulness usually preceded wealth and status. In a few towns, parceling committees also considered personal need as indicated by family size. Later distributions of land held commonly by the community relied on the same principles of service and reward, thus inhibiting the rapid accumulation of land in a given town. Town service and concord counted more than wealth or status, and the village green could not be bought up by the richest fellow on the block. Conversely, if a town member shirked community labor, he risked exclusion in later distributions. By and large, most town members were not only satisfied but pleasantly surprised. In England only half of the lesser farmers owned any land at all. Always, however, the weight of mutual obligation was such that owners of large areas of land were expected to "give almost unlimited time and service to the affairs of the town" (Powell 100, 136). Oft-elected colonial governor John Winthrop approached ruin several times when he was forced to entrust the management of his finances to an inept steward (Rutman, *Boston* 88). Satisfaction in individual ownership and in the practice of mutuality, service, and reward seemed to deflect contention while encouraging community awareness, interdependence, and obligation.

Numerous other and largely unexpected satisfactions helped create a fabric of harmony and mutuality. For one, political opportunity and efficiency contributed to contentment. Any upstanding adult landowner, even if not a church member, could vote for, and be elected to, town office, although it was unlikely he would be sent as town representative or deputy to the colony's legislative General Court. In Sudbury, a somewhat typical town, over an eighteen-year period slightly over one-half of all male landowners, about seventy-five in number, were elected to town office (Powell 100), although in some communities the percentage was considerably lower (Allen, "Englands"). Further, many churches chose their own ministers, and militia men could elect, at least until 1668, their own officers. Moreover, civil elections occurred often, giving dissatisfied citizens ample opportunity to make governmental changes (Breen and Foster, "Greatest" 13). While the average freeman usually deferred to the distribution of power inhering in the traditional social hierarchy—that is, to leaders of various sorts, whether civil or religious—political participation was not only possible but achievable, resulting by British standards in an "extraordinarily high" level of engagement and satisfaction (Greene, *Pursuits* 25).

To some extent the cause of harmony was aided by various aspects of the settlers' common predicament, a condition that in a number of ways fostered amicability and practical consensus. Put simply, villagers had to cooperate if they were at first merely to survive and eventually to achieve secure and durable physical and social environments. Surveying, roads, fences, defense, and meetinghouses required communal efforts. Private labors of homesteading and breaking and tilling the land provided additional shared concerns. Similarly, social and political circumstance bred largely unintended new measures of democratic process and participation, which were sometimes products of necessity far more than intention. Social authority here devolved upon the individual members of each community. While there were strong English traditions of social and religious authority located in the institutions of the crown and archbishop, these were for New Englanders happily distant, far across a very big ocean. Given the dispersion and isolation of the rural farming communities, a centralized leadership in Boston could hardly serve as an effective hand in establishing and maintaining social order. If the villagers were to prosper and live well, both physically and socially, they had to cooperate and live in concord; they had to do it themselves, together. Much as they necessarily divided responsibilities in accomplishing community tasks, they had to accomplish high levels of consensus in order to function socially. As historian Michael Zuckerman has argued, a "corporate ethos" of consensus consequently "governed the communities of provincial Massachusetts, and harmony and homogeneity were the regular—and required—realities of local life. Effective action necessitated a public opinion approaching if not attaining unanimity, and public policy was accordingly bent toward securing such unanimity" (Zuckerman, "Social" 544, 526). The foremost expression of this necessity was the now-famous town meeting, which "gave institutional expression to the imperatives of peace" (527).

The villagers were also yoked in common effort to establish church congregations and criteria for church membership. This intricate process demanded sensitivity, candor, and trust and often worked to coalesce strangers into an emotionally and religiously interdependent and committed social body. Only the framing of the town covenant surpassed church founding in demands for cooperation. The deep social trust forged in the founding town and church would sustain the vitality of the community for decades and allow for social stability and well-being. This social cohesion was further aided by the Puritans' good fortune in coming to a hospitable land and climate that differed little from English conditions, and in this they could rejoice together. While the land in New England was not as inviting as the colonies to the south, and while it was not generous, its productivity was nonetheless generally more than adequate, and New England was significantly less disease-prone than many of the southern settlements in the New World (Greene, *Pursuits* 25). Lastly, time itself was kind in the new land and allowed for the deepening of social bonds. Longevity greatly contributed to the stability of communities and the necessary transfer of values and mores from one generation to another. Moreover, families were large, and the first generations, because of the abundance of land, tended to remain in one locale, allowing for generational connection and the passing of values from the older to the younger (23).

Two intertwined inheritances from England benefited these immigrant farmers in their attempt to forge a congenial village. Historians call the first "localism," by which they mean centuries-old habits and customs of English village life. Social historian Kenneth Lockridge locates the foundation of localism in a "peasant ethos" that venerated utopian notions of a cooperative village life hedged about with security, stability, interdependence, and harmony (*Town* 16). It was the disruption of these "social folkways" by the drastic economic and social changes of sixteenth-century England that so threatened and angered Puritans like John Winthrop and other such diverse leaders as Thomas More and Captain John Smith. The spread of a new individualism in England under the aegis of kingly power, a burgeoning capitalism, and Renaissance self-confidence made traditionalists acutely aware of the value of customary social and political mores. In their move across the ocean, Puritan villages resolved to preserve in the New World what was almost lost in old England. Two concrete fruits of this localism were the famous town meeting and the fierce independence of Protestant congregationalism, which had its own theological and ecclesiastical rationales.

The Puritanism of the Puritans, so to speak, offers the second major contributor to their social weal. Religious zeal and devotion provided the fuel for the engine of social harmony. To be a Puritan meant rigorous and deep religious commitment, and with the Puritans that commitment was not abstract, ethereal, or tepid. Rather, as a group Puritans were decidedly this-worldly, intensely earnest, and energetically reverent of God, the church, morality, and humanity—all traits in "the Augustinian Strain of Piety" that Perry Miller understood to be the hallmark of the Puritan spirit (*Seventeenth* Ch. 1). While not lacking in humor, earthiness, or frivolity—what today we call normalcy—they took their belief, devotion, historical hopes, and social intentions with high seriousness. The broad currents of Puritanism, as perhaps best articulated in Winthrop's sermon, supplied the first generations with a significant ideological common ground, what today we might call a myth—"meaning for their present, a mission for their future, and, what was more, and perhaps most of all, a synthetic but compelling past" of spiritual heroism that would nourish them amid later travail and trouble, ranging from disease to Indian wars. These assorted English villagers joined, then, in a strong "unifying tradition" that provided not only meaning and inspiration but a full panoply of "rights and responsibilities" (Breen and Foster, "Greatest" 10). The Puritan cosmogony saw their daily lives infused with, and as a vehicle for, divine will, a holy presence whose social and ethical dictates culminated in the notion and practice of charity. This was true for almost the entire community. Jon Butler notes the marked difference between New England and other colonies, observing that "New England's surface and inner textures exemplified a deep Christian religiosity centered on an aggressive, reforming Protestantism." Moreover, Puritan commitments shaped almost everything they did: "immigration, settlement patterns, popular and learned religion, government, and secular liberties that included voting and land holding" (55).

In this practical realm of everyday living, the theology of the Puritan social vision combined with the traditions of English localism to foster a cohesive and generous spirit of mutuality and cooperation, attitudes that starkly oppose the economic self-concern that lies at the heart of the "spirit of capitalism." In his landmark study of Dedham, Massachusetts, *A New England Town: The First Hundred Years*, Kenneth Lockridge contends that Puritanism "actually perfected and sanctified the ideal of the peasant past," imbuing it with "a coherent social vision" whose hallmarks were "love, forbearance, cooperation, and peace" (4, 13). The high level of this Puritan social and moral commitment manifested itself in their stalwart efforts to avert and mediate contention. Breen and Foster report that in Puritan villages it was "incumbent upon all men to work out their disputes as peacefully as possible, thinking always of their greater obligation to the commonwealth as a whole and ultimately to God himself" ("Greatest" 12). On town questions, officials usually did "everything possible to force group agreement by discussion" (Powell 108). For disputes between neighbors over cows, fences, and the like, the Dedham town covenant provided an "effective system of mediation which largely supplanted the hierarchy of formal courts established by the colony," although as the colonies grew larger and more diverse, more and more matters ended in official litigation (Lockridge, *Town* 13). In the early decades, however, through the gentle mediation of neighbors, law courts and hostility were generally avoided. It is likely that the crucial shapers of this practice were a commonsense ingenuity, the folkways of localism, and Christian moral tradition. Whatever the case, it gels well with, if it did not indeed have much of its inspiration in, the spirit of Pauline teaching on social conduct (I Corinthians 6: 1–8). Believers should resolve conflicts among themselves rather than resort to the courts, a recourse that would only bring shame on the supposedly loving early Christians.

PURITAN COLLECTIVE CULTURE

That these Puritan outland communities were able to realize and then sustain this social equanimity as long as they did, until roughly 1700, has struck historians with an admixture of wonder, respect, and, at times, nostalgia that verges on sentimentality, as both Joyce Appleby and Anita and Darrett Rutman have suggested. Regardless of historians' attitudes toward Puritan social reality, it is indisputable that the recent scholarly work of social history constitutes one of the great successes of recent historiography (311). The historian's close inspection of the various human mechanisms—personal, social, and cultural—allows a glimpse of the functional realities of what academics call "collective culture," that is, how a group of people, whether family or society, gels or coheres and makes its way harmoniously in time. One benefit of this examination of Puritanism is the realization of the extent to which the much vaunted Puritan social cohesion arose from the inmost nature and character of Puritanism itself. As suggested earlier, the popular press has usually pictured Puritanism as a legalistic and heartless enterprise that was burdened with rules and repression, the subtle means of what historians have lately begun to call "social control." In fact, as Perry Miller long ago noted, the Puritan movement offered a psychically demanding and rich approach to perennial human burdens of selfhood and social relationship that engaged and shaped the deepest recesses of the self (*Seventeenth* 4). It is important, then, to understand something of Puritanism's various institutions and devotional habits that so deeply imbued their recipients with a dramatic and cogent way of interpreting individual experience and one's place in the flow of history, thereby inculcating purpose, meaning, ardor, and a high level of equanimity into personal and social life.

The extent to which Puritan New England was able to achieve ideological and social cohesion is suggested by John Butler, whose prizewinning *Awash in a Sea of Faith* chronicles the innumerable instances in which American religious belief departed from idealized, nostalgic portraits of religious unanimity. Neither orthodoxy nor conventional morality has ever had the hold on the American populace that popular nostalgia would suggest. Settlements on the eastern seaboard were characteristically rife with religious conflict, irreligion, and conventional paganism, except, that is, for the first decades of Puritan settlement in New England: "New England's surface and inner textures exemplified a deep Christian religiosity centered on an aggressive, reforming Protestantism" whose "commitments shaped immigration, settlement patterns, popular and learned religion, government, and secular liberties that included voting and land holding" (Butler 55).

Foremost among these commitments was its emphasis on Christian conversion, which for them and their evangelical descendants constituted the vital and indispensable bedrock of Christian experience. A decisive and complete turning to God and away from the corruption and confusion of one's life was simply the only way toward eternal salvation in heaven and, to use contemporary jargon, self-realization or wholeness. Central to this notion, as amply summarized by Charles Cohen in *God's Caress: The Psychology of Puritan Religious Experience*, were an understanding and scheme, as Puritan theology envisioned

an anthropology that dwelt on human frailty and a soteriology [idea of salvation] that strung together a sequence of steps through which the Holy Spirit turns the soul to God. So enfeebled by the Fall that one can never merit salvation by good works, the individual is liberated from sin's bondage only through the gratuitous gift of faith apprehending Christ the Redeemer and imputing his righteousness to the believer. Grace imparted by the Spirit regenerates the convert and issues forth in a lifetime of sanctified works. (7)

It is fair to say that the leadership of the Puritan movement in England and America struggled to create an environment, at once free and coercive, wherein the crucial encounter with God, a spiritual paradigm for the "good life," should and would transpire. Clergy and lay leadership, those like John Winthrop and John Cotton, formed a tireless and forceful collection of Puritan believers whose vision and personal qualities elicited high levels of support, although the New England Puritan populace was by no means lacking in intellectual or social independence, as even a cursory reading of their church and political wrangling indicates. To be sure, the clergy were indefatigable and earnest theological scholars and preachers who exerted enormous influence over their flocks, which is the alignment traditional historical research has pictured, but they were not aloof divines with no time or care for the pain and elation of either parishioners or the reprobate.

A study of the pastoral work of the New England clergy by George Selement shows that "in diaries, letters, and solid histories . . . pastors—even those like Increase and Cotton Mather—were abroad in their communities, involving themselves in every aspect of New England life," documenting "the extent to which pastors personally led parishioners to grace, comforted the afflicted, helped the sick, aided the needy, and reproved sinners" (*Keepers* 15). The first generation of New England Puritan clergy, contrary to popular stereotype, "were an earthy lot and close to their people" and not "cloistered savants" invoking judgment, control, and hellfire upon their people (103, 23). Rather, they regularly undertook domestic and community reconciliation, visited the sick, the grieving, the poor, supervised local commonplace charity, and evangelized criminals, backsliders, and indigenous Americans. Further, they wrote, preached, and published countless sermons that were eagerly consumed by their public. Clergy-authored devotional guides were similarly popular, indicating the regard in which they and their message were held. Contrary to the stereotype, the "ministers were not scholars writing for elite colleagues but popular writers striving to win commoners" who, indeed, "reached the masses and influenced their thinking" (74–75). Pastoral work of ministers among all segments of the population enabled them to influence significantly the religious, social, and political culture of New England. To be sure, for a variety of reasons, with the passage of time more and more people rejected the clergy and opted for either folk traditions, new religions, or avant-garde philosophies in lieu of Puritanism. Or more typically, they mixed them all together (Butler 61). Nonetheless, because Puritan ministers did so often come into close, often daily contact with almost all New Englanders, it is likely that many laypeople accepted in varying degrees ministerial ideas. To that unquantifiable extent, New Englanders shared a collective Puritan culture, sustaining it until about the end of the seventeenth century (Selement, *Keepers* 35–36).

Still, regardless of ministerial immersion into the common life and trials of New England farmers, businessmen, and housewives, the clergy's major agent of influence was very likely Puritan New England's preeminent vehicle for transmitting religious and cultural values. In *The New England Soul: Preaching and Religious Culture in Colonial New England*, historian Harry S. Stout has argued that the preacher possessed a medium

whose topical range and social influence were so powerful in shaping cultural values, meanings, and a sense of corporate purpose that even television pales in comparison. . . . Seldom, if ever before, did so many people hear the same message of purpose and direction over so long a period of time as did the New England "Puritans."

Nor was its focus narrowly religious; its subject matter and influence extended "to all significant facets of life—social and political, as well as religious" (3). The average Puritan life heard something like 7,000 sermons totaling approximately 15,000 hours of concentrated listening, and this was, unlike the multivocal pluralism of contemporary culture, the only regular voice of authority in the culture (3–4).

In New England there would be no competing voices or rituals, and the sermon would become as important for social meaning as for spiritual enlightenment. It not only interpreted God's plan and told the people how they must live as a church but also defined and legitimated the meaning of their lives as citizen and magistrate, superior and inferior, soldier, parent, child, and laborer. Sermons were authority incarnate. (23)

As another historian well summarizes,

Only in New England did the sermon enjoy such a powerful role in directing thought. And so, the reader can see in colonial New England a model—as clear as any that exists in American history—of the way in which religion came to permeate a national identity at its deepest cultural and intellectual levels. (Hambrick-Stowe 10)

At the heart of the sermonic enterprise, always, was the effort at conversion, but close on its heels—part and parcel and the purpose and end of conversion, the destination of the self in its spiritual journey—was the sanctified or holy life of the redeemed, the "saints." As the loathsomeness of sin pressed upon the individual, in moments of deepest self-condemnation, "the soul grasped the reality of God's grace" to continue thereafter "a life of obedience out of sheer gratitude and thanksgiving" (Stout, *Soul* 39–40). The linchpin and catalyst on New England theology and experience, the integuments of selfhood, were the motions of grace in spirit and conscience, meaning the forgiveness of sin and a life of grateful response to God, the giver of mercy (35). Salvation constituted the existential acceptance of the real and ever-mysterious action of God in the inmost self and the subsequent lifelong practice of loving gratitude to God and his creatures.

In response to the gift of saving faith, God's law taught individuals how to live their lives in the present according to the rule of charity or love. For the Puritans, this divine love was . . . a practical commitment to obey God's law and teaching in all aspects of their life. Such "sanctified" obedience could never be motivated by self-righteousness but had to proceed from a deep sense of gratitude for what Christ had done on the cross. (33)

Thus came into being what Stout aptly dubs the "sin-salvation-service formula" (43).

Regular Sunday sermons concentrated on the matters of the soul and its eternal destination—the sin-and-salvation nexus that composed the existential core of Puritan personal identity. In addressing such matters, ministers were then "gospel heralds proclaiming the way of personal salvation through faith in Christ" (27). With the regular Sunday exhortations soon developed another stripe of sermon that came to focus wholly on the "service" or social-ethical dimensions of the Puritan quest. Periodically, sermons were delivered in town squares on occasions of public importance, usually elections or days designated for repentant fasting, and these contrasted markedly in content to Sunday sermonizing. These public orations addressed to the whole community dealt centrally with the moral and social conditions within God's experiment in the New World. In speaking their mind publicly on moral and social conditions in New England, ministers took on the added responsibility of prophethood, employing "a rhetoric and mode of persuasion different from the evangelical message [of conversion]. . . . As social and cultural custodians . . . their primary focus shifted from God's mercy to man's responsibility to honor the conditional terms of God's national covenant." Thus, the preacher came to comment on "social order, conditional obedience, and corporate mission" to remind the "nation who they were and what they must do to retain God's special covenant interest" (24, 27). Fearing that New England might yet "degenerate into another Sodom," the social critique in these community sermons was meant, as were chastisements from God, to correct and not to damn or demoralize an oft-wandering public (Bercovitch, *Jeremiad* 5, 8). Characteristically, such sermons, which have come to be called jeremiads after the nay-saying Old Testament prophet, specified community sins ranging from foppery to greed.

Undergirding the congregational and public push for religious assent and personal and social rectitude was the Puritan practice of piety, the reinvigorated and democratized Christian tradition of personal devotion. The Reformation had declared all believers to be priests, and roughly speaking, popular Puritanism embraced the notion with thoroughness and fervor. As such, Puritanism was but a part of the larger religious awakening that swept Europe in the Protestant Reformation and Roman Catholic Counter-Reformation. A mainstay of Puritan religiosity was the earnest and disciplined devotional life of prayer and meditation, and while peculiarly American, it nonetheless constituted a broad, popular expansion of traditional Roman Catholic spirituality (Hambrick-Stowe 25). In sixteenth-century Catholicism and Anglicanism, there had been some distance between clerical knowledge and devotion and the attitudes and habits of the folk who attended parishes and understood sermons and liturgy at best episodically (Reay). In contrast, those who became Puritan combined the life of adoration with rigorous and regular spiritual and moral introspection. The Bible was both the prime catalyst for this practice and a sourcebook for how devotion and self-searching should be undertaken.

In addition, there flourished in England and America a burgeoning library of devotional guides designed to prosper believers in their religious quest. If editions and printings are any indication, these were widely and constantly used throughout the seventeenth century by New England Puritans of all social levels (Hambrick-Stowe ix, 4). In assisting the spiritual life of Puritans, they joined the regular torrent of printed sermons, which the literate Puritan community eagerly devoured. Such manuals to spiritual exercise and growth, which were, in effect, America's first religious self-help books, detailed "the patterns, techniques, and themes of worship, meditation, and prayer" whereby the soul might find its path to God (20). The Augustinian spiritual tradition, a paradigm well described by Perry Miller, found repeated articulation in numerous books, including Lewis Bayly's *The Practice of Piety*, which went through sixty editions by the end of the seventeenth century (49). The dominant motif within the guides and a prominent metaphor within Puritanism as a whole for understanding one's own life was pilgrimage. Indeed, Puritans found the notion of a personal religious journey within the world to be "a powerful instrument for interpreting their individual and communal lives" (63). Their mentor in the venture at self-understanding was English Puritan John Bunyan, whose *Pilgrim's Progress* became the paradigm for the personal journey to holiness and heaven. The devotional manuals took note of the fact that the Puritan was a believer who lived in the world, and thus the manuals were all "devised for people 'in the world,' engaged in secular pursuits" (47). There is perhaps some irony in the fact that America's first self-help books were manuals that counseled the loss or denial of self.

For roughly two generations, then, the small farming villages of early New England were so successful in sustaining social harmony and mutuality that Kenneth Lockridge has described them as "a Christian Utopian Closed Corporate Community" (*Town* 16). The social vision that informed, shaped, and sustained them was "common to the founders of nearly all the towns in the first waves of New England settlers," and, as such, that vision formed "the mainstream of a wide and enduring New England tradition" that would be felt through the nineteenth century, although with ever-diminishing force (167). As Lockridge notes, to some extent the settlers were aided by the fact that New England's agricultural riches, while abundant, were not so great as to allow for quick or large personal accumulation (167; Greene, *Pursuits* 25). Favorable cultural, historical, religious, and geographic forces combined to foster small, insulated social organisms that frowned upon and restrained an inordinate self-seeking that disregarded the bonds and welfare of the host community. Clearly, the Puritans worked hard, but labor, especially for the wealthy, did not stop with self-enrichment. As long as land was plentiful and distribution fair, providing what David Shi calls "a prudent sufficiency," competition, self-aggrandizement, and contention were largely unknown (11). The linchpin of the enterprise and success, as Michael Zuckerman concluded in his survey of fifteen Massachusetts towns, was "a broadly diffused desire for consensual communalism as the operative premise of group life" (*Peaceable* 4). Harry Stout concludes in *The New England Soul* that "New England towns achieved extraordinarily high levels of persistence and social cohesion. Townspeople endured disagreements and bickerings to be sure, but compared to other seventeenth-century societies the New England Way was remarkable for its record of internal peace, order, and uniformity" (23). Its "communal ethic," as James Henretta has called it, sharply distinguishes it from the social and economic interchange that very soon came to dominate New England's major trading centers ("Ethic" 337). In short, American economic individualism did not start on the village farmsteads of the first settlers of New England; the religious ethos of those first settlers, if anything, exerted retrograde or inhibitory force against self-seeking. As we shall see in the case of Boston, the founders of Massachusetts Bay resisted as best they could, and futilely, the forces of economic individualism.

BOSTON AND ECONOMIC DIVERSIFICATION

Boston's leaders also were eager to erect an ideal commonwealth, but the challenge before them demanded far more than that presented to the small, isolated farming villages. For one, Boston Puritans faced the special challenges of a mixed population instead of the homogeneous true believers of the largely static country towns. Because of its location as a port and thus as an economic center for the colony, it drew diverse sorts of people into the community—sailors, laborers, wanderers—who were not necessarily in the least sympathetic to the Puritan cause. The leaders then confronted the problems of how to create and manage a holy community that included unholy participants. As Darret Rutman points out in *Winthrop's Boston*, leader Winthrop faced "the paradox of anticipating a society of saints and sinners held together by a quality available only to the saints" (13–14): how to have, in other words, a collective of love if some within its supposed bounds cared not at all for the notion. The problem grew more acute with increased immigration and, before long, prosperity, and as the colony's governor in its most prominent town, Winthrop confronted a major Puritan dilemma, to borrow the title of Edmund Morgan's book, of maintaining social unity in a pluralistic and prosperous state.

The heterogeneity of Boston grew because it simply became ever more successful as a trading center and port. Goods and money flowed through its businesses. It soon became the logical terminus of the roads that scattered to the Massachusetts villages. Further, its bay proved to be best suited for foreign ships and import and export traffic. By 1641, local markets produced an excess of grain that could then be sent abroad, along with livestock, wood, and fish (Rutman, *Boston* 185–91). More exports brought more people and more cash. A "bustling, vibrant, energetic, prosperous" atmosphere "of quick profits" came to dominate as people "traded, speculated, gambled . . . along the coast north and south, and on the sea lanes of the Atlantic" (198–99). The commercial allure proved too great. By the time of Winthrop's death in 1649, barely two decades after settlement, Boston citizens, churched and unchurched alike, were "generally failing in their duty to community, seeking their own aggrandizement in the rich opportunities afforded by land, commerce, crafts, and speculations, to the detriment of the community" (243). In a way that its founders could not have anticipated, Boston was placed squarely in the path of what would come to be an enormously productive regional economy. In the end, as we briefly discuss here, the charity and the resolution of the saints were a poor match for the wealth of the land and a diverse citizenry interested in making the most of its commercial potential.

The tension between piety and wealth arose not only between the Puritans and "outsiders" but within the Puritan contingent itself. The Puritan leaders had intended to found, especially in economic matters, an "authoritarian state, a holy commonwealth on the model of Calvin's Geneva," which some historians have described as a sixteenth-century welfare state (Henretta, "Ethic" 333). Because of this resolve, the Puritan leadership through the first decades regularly found themselves in the position of having to negotiate complex economic grievances, including the prosecution of prominent Puritan merchants for greed and chicanery. A strong antagonism quickly grew up between the Puritan leadership, with its medieval mentality, and the entrepreneurship of the rapidly emerging merchant class. In church and court alike, the leadership acted consistently to restrain, partly out of conviction and partly from public pressure, the improvident and asocial acquisitiveness of the merchants. The contention even infiltrated the most famous theological controversy of the early decades. In the case of Anne Hutchinson, many powerful merchants aligned themselves with Hutchinson, who had been accused of antinomian heresy. Her doctrine of the primacy of private revelation and personal scriptural interpretation apparently proved attractive to those interested in undercutting the leadership's conservative economic practice: "free grace above the legalistic restrictions of the moral law meant freer enterprise beyond the specific regulation of the state" (Ziff 75). Ever religiously scrupulous, the pious merchants wanted theological justification for their innovative and thirsty practices.

The economic views of the leaders appeared in other conspicuous ways as well. In a study of *The New England Merchants of the Seventeenth Century*, Bernard Bailyn reports that by the late 1630s Boston saw frequent "public condemnations for malpractice of trade, particularly of overcharging, usury, taking advantage of a neighbor's need" (41). According to Rutman, court and church actions "most frequently" had to do with violations in the marketplace (*Boston* 243). In short, financial greed seemed a greater moral problem for the Puritans than their supposed preoccupations with alcohol, sex, and gaming. The most famous effort at economic control came in 1639 in the court prosecution and church discipline of wealthy merchant Robert Keayne for extortionist pricing, a stark violation of the medieval concept of a just price. The Bay Colony General Court fined Keayne a hefty 200 pounds, a sum later reduced by half, and the First Church of Boston nearly excommunicated him but finally contented itself with severe admonishment and Keayne's public apology (Henretta, "Ethic" 330). Others guilty of economic offenses were in fact excommunicated. A year later, in 1640, when the economy faltered, the General Court acted again, this time to impede the merchants from exacting the full measure of debt from the small farmers who owed them money. Debts were to be mediated by a disinterested panel and could be paid in commodities such as cattle or fish, and the value of the payments could be adjusted from market value by the court. Clearly, Winthrop's admonition that the rich should not eat up the poor and that debts should be forgiven outright was taken with utmost seriousness in the first decades of settlement (333).

Struggle as they might against the wiles of prosperity and the blandishments of wealth-getting, the Puritan leadership fought an increasingly rearguard battle against overeager merchants and a general thirst for wealth and its display. Gradual economic expansion in the port cities of Salem and Boston provided for the possibility of prosperity for all those who would labor with intelligence and perseverance. In Boston, for example, a general labor shortage permitted even manual laborers to prosper. Recognizing that they could not keep people from making money and fearing the moral decay that often accompanied it, the leadership moved to stem the tawdry and sometimes bawdy effects of general prosperity. In 1651 Boston saw its first sumptuary laws. As their title indicates, the laws were aimed at habits of consumption, from quantities of alcohol to the display of lace (Rutman, *Boston* 243). Both medieval and Calvinistic in their mind-set, the leaders believed that ostentation, conspicuous adornments, frivolous leisure, impiety, and irreverence subverted and fragmented commonality of purpose through vanity, envy, triviality, and strife. Such laws were commonplace in

European medievalism, the localism of old England, and especially Calvin's welfare state in Geneva, but not until two decades into their social experiment did the New England Puritans deem them necessary.

The same diversification took place in isolated inland pockets of New England, although these were comparatively infrequent. In addition to the inland subsistence farming communities and urbanized coastal towns like Boston and Salem, there was in Puritan New England a zone of highly commercialized agriculture in the Connecticut River Valley, and this consisted of a unique kind of social-economic arrangement (Innes, *New Land* xvi). Towns like Springfield, founded on the frontier for commercial exploitation by William Pynchon, differed from Boston and still more radically from the cooperative farming village, looking mostly like a modern-day company town. For other towns along the Connecticut River the record conflicts, depending on what social historian is reading the data. Where one has seen harmony akin to Massachusetts (Bushman), another has detected strife and acrimony from the start, often involving clerical domination (Lucas). On and on the list might go, as studies of local communities have come forth. It is fair to say, however, that most communities started with similar high visions. More difficult interpretive questions intrude when scholars question to what extent those visions were realized and how soon and why they began to lose their cogency, and those questions do, indeed, occasion a whole host of diverse responses.

DECLENSION IN NEW ENGLAND

An array of analyses has been given for the causes and extent of what historians call "declension," meaning erosion or decline, in the Puritan experiment, both religious and social, specifically in New England's loss of social cohesion and harmony. So diverse have been the interpretations of the where, who, when, extent, and how of New England's decline that one historian has recently declared the lack of unanimity an "advancing embarrassment" to the historical profession (Zuckerman, "Fabrication" 183). Such disagreement does prove useful, however, insofar as the assorted explanations amply display a range of cultural pressures that bore upon the Puritan experiment and precipitated whatever change took place. This variety of perspective and theory about the origins and mechanisms of decline does allow for a fullness of analytic explanation, approaching what Clifford Geertz calls a "thick description," of cultural function and change.

The decay itself seems to surface in two large, but not unrelated, realms of Puritan life, specifically, religious zeal and social morality. As a great number of extant sermons, tracts, and letters suggest, there seemed to be a widespread decrease in religious zeal and devotion, a steady diminishing of spiritual energy. The traditional view of New England decline, which is regularly called into question and then reasserted, pictures "a period of increasing religious apathy" characterized by "a spiritual deadness and loss of piety." The proportion of church members in the larger society diminished, and the steady "stream of new saints envisioned by the founding generation simply failed to materialize in the free air of the new world" (Pope 97). But as some critics of this view have pointed out, the impressionistic evidence of contemporary participants is open to varied interpretation, and a few critics go so far as to suggest that instead of decline there was an increase in religious rigor. The suggestion is that church membership declined because criteria for membership became more stringent. The other chief manifestation of decay, which is more readily quantifiable, appeared in the changing tone of private interest and social relations. Second, instead of the harmony experienced by the founders and the first rural generations, gradually from "all over the colonies . . . came complaints about a growing contentiousness in all areas of colonial life, insubordination and declining deference among social inferiors, rankly antisocial individualism, neglect of calling and of public duty, deceit, avarice, extravagance and pursuit of pleasure" (Greene, "Identities" 194). For whatever reasons, "ordinary men became absorbed in secular pursuits and factionalism set in." And as might be expected, the Puritan clergy, as "guardians of tradition, came to bewail the turn of events," both social and religious (Butts 669). Clearly, something did happen in New England because both the religious and social complexion of that world pretty much disappeared by the middle of the eighteenth century and much earlier in urban areas like Boston. For this decline, the new social history has breathed considerable life into an old thesis, offering a "plausible framework" for what the preachers of the jeremiads bemoaned (Greene, *Pursuits* 80). The changing patterns and texture of social interaction suggest, at the very least, that Puritan ideology and devotion were not sufficient to impede forever the forces of individualism set loose by both the necessity and romance of money-getting. As social historian Jack Greene has recently argued, not only did "religion become less central to the lives of its people," but "the strength of the corporate impulse that had been so powerfully manifest during the first and second generations of settlement was sapped and the old puritan social order greatly loosened" (*Pursuits* 79).

Often overlooked and not to be underestimated is the weight of time itself. Together, that and the limits of imagination took a high toll on the original resolve. The founders faced the perennial human problem of how to instill in their children the fullness and vigor of their radical vision of a holy commonwealth. After all, the first American Puritans, especially their leadership, were voluntary exiles from the heat of English religious and political warfare. They came to the new land hardened by fire, their imaginations fueled in the contest between light and darkness. Ardent and determined, they saw their new world of a "city on a hill," as John Winthrop termed it, as personally and historically necessary, an instrument whereby others might attend to the saving message of God. By the third and fourth generations, however, the hotbed of English religious politics that had shaped the crisis that fired the founding generation and even the memory thereof had cooled. What was left of the founders' sense of vital religious conflict necessarily faded still more by 1684, when the crown took control of the colony and mandated religious tolerance. Moreover, the New Englanders faced abundant enough challenges to occupy them in their new homeland. In another way, the goal of religious autonomy no longer seemed to matter because, in essence, the Puritans had achieved it. Puritanism itself had become the predominant belief, and save for theological squabbles within its own community, it soon became routinized and predictable. The zealot's heat is hard to pass undiminished to offspring, especially when the original warming conflagration has virtually extinguished (Greene, *Pursuits* 60).

The first concern about the colony's spiritual health surfaced when the founding generations demanded that applicants for church membership recount tales of conversion and zeal sufficient to match their own intense experience of religious drama and fervor, even though these climactic personal events were by then decades past. Distant from the fires of English political struggle, the children had a difficult time emulating the passion and light that seemed to the parents indispensable signs of true conversion to Christianity. As a result of what some historians have come to see as an overscrupulous expectation that was peculiar to American Puritanism, church membership and religious confidence sagged, a condition that led indirectly to the famous Half-Way covenant, which allowed church membership to the baptized but still unconfessing children of full members. The parents and grandparents either did not anticipate the problem or lacked the strategies of nurture with which to impart their attitudes. It seemed, consequently, that the descendants in the second and third New England generations lacked the imagination to know and feel the forerunners' experience and urgency. Nor was this fate peculiar to the Puritan community; this pattern of generational deflation of zeal resembles the fate of many insurgent religious movements, as H. Richard Niebuhr showed in his classic study of *The Social Sources of Denominationalism* ([1929] 1957). Churchgoing and piety per se did not necessarily fall off markedly, but the ardor and conviction that fueled migration suffered dilution.

The effects of this situation were numerous. Parents and children alike pondered the absence of clear intrusions of the divine in the emphatic experience of conversion in individual lives. Instead, religious aspirants perhaps led somewhat fretful religious lives marked by introspection and uncertainty. A second problem came in the failure of the church to sustain influence over successive generations who felt distant and bewildered at their nonacceptance into the church. A last consequence posed difficulties for the social texture of New England life. The founders held that the success of their "holy experiment" depended on mature Christian behavior, whose foremost mark was love. Yet, according to Puritan theology, such superior conduct and attitude could be expected only from the saints, the converted and sanctified, and by no means whatever were the founders' children experientially ready for church membership. While the "visible saints," as Edmund Morgan has called them, might be expected to radiate brotherly love and concern, not all the Puritans or their children were converted. A large minority, at the very least, were either earnest seekers, for whom the church held a respected place, or passive subscribers who attended from social or legal coercion. Because humankind generally lacks a great capacity for foresight and empathy, the failure to pass on one's ideals or commitments to the younger generations regularly occurs, and that happens quite apart from ideology or context.

Of greater impact still were other natural conditions, unforeseeable and crucial, that befell the Puritans in their new land, specifically, "the moderate acceleration and changing character of the economy during the last half of the seventeenth century" (Greene, *Pursuits* 61). Of prime importance is the fact that the Puritans prospered, sometimes far more than they had expected. Despite "a relatively stingy physical environment," farmers, merchants, and traders prospered, although the urban-centered latter two realized far more wealth far faster than their rural country folk. The less prosperous the area, the more likely were the inhabitants to hold onto their Puritan communitarianism. For farmers, "[a] harsh climate, hilly terrain, and poor soil limited production of valuable staple crops, and its ever-growing population pressed constantly on living standards" (Henretta, "Ethic" 338). While there was always adequate food, and most freemen owned land, it would be a long time before rural Massachusetts would prosper nearly as much as regional trading centers like Salem and Boston. In any case, for all, the necessity of survival demanded the hard work of settlement and establishing trading practices to acquire supplies for the rudiments of living. Through the decades of this necessary work, as Perry Miller explains, by "slow and insensible degrees," colonial society lost the trappings of a mercantile agrarian order and took on "the now familiar outlines of a commercial and capitalist society" (*Nature's* 33). The "sacred cod" sprang from the seas, and the land gave sufficiently of its goods for most farmers to move beyond mere subsistence to the raising of cash crops and a "subsistence-plus economy" (Henretta, "Ethic" 340). Merchants harvested fur, and when those supplies were exhausted, they began to level the forests to provide lumber for the construction needs of other British colonies (Greene, *Pursuits* 62). Compared with other British colonies, New England was notably the poorest, the wealth holdings of free white people a quarter of what they were in the southern colonies and sixty percent of those in the middle colonies (Henretta, "Ethic" 338). While neither ascetic nor greedy, the Puritans and their leaders soon had to contend, especially in commercial centers like Boston and Salem, with the lures, blandishments, pleasures, and satisfactions of wealth. As Miller puts it, for the Puritan the problem lay in getting "profits without succumbing to the seductions" and sensuality of wealth (_Nature's_ 35).

Their collective economic good fortune offered their greatest challenge, for which several aspects of their theology—namely, those dealing with vocation and history—were perhaps ill suited. As Miller and others have contended, the Puritans' own theology got them into a prosperity predicament in two ways. First off, if they followed the general mood of their theology, they could hardly help acquiring some means. Calvinism did not specifically encourage the making of money, except as a means of serving others, but it did affirm the dignity of work in any sphere so long as it was moral. That is, Puritans embraced worldly work because Calvinism, unlike its Catholic precursor, not only sanctioned but, in its doctrine of vocation, encouraged worldly pursuit. Medieval monasticism had divided the world into two distinct spheres of sacred and secular, with any life but of holy orders deemed markedly inferior. In contrast, Calvin and his Puritan disciples followed Luther in noting two equally necessary and legitimate callings. Each person had both a "general calling" to the Christian faith and, beyond that, a "specific calling" to a particular kind of task or employment that was to serve the community and God. As Perry Miller has summarized, not all worldly work or its fruits were proper: "[A] man might not make all the money he could or spend it as he chose, for he was bound to serve the good of the whole, else he was an unclean beast" (_Nature's_ 35). Wealth itself was permitted so long as it was obtained fairly and was meant, as with everything, to serve the society and did not result from avarice or deceit. This standard did, indeed, prevail insofar as in the early generations prosperous merchants won the respect from the community only if they were philanthropically and humbly generous (Henretta, "Ethic" 335).

The consequence of these views of work and wealth was to thrust American Puritans into an ambiguous, perhaps irresolvable tension. If they worked, they prospered, and the pride and pursuit of wealth seemed to be sundering the commonwealth. Puritan theology in New England put its prosperous adherents in a double predicament. The Puritan was burdened with a vocational earnestness that would, if pursued, yield potentially disastrous social temptations. With money-making came "class antagonisms" and the wearing of "expensive apparel." However, if individual Puritans had forsaken their obligation to reap the fruits of the wilderness, they would have ceased to fulfill their religious duty as Puritans, losing both religiously and economically. Rather, the question was how to be a Puritan, given their understanding of vocation, and how to remain poor. According to Miller, New England Puritanism instilled attitudes that made grace-full poverty difficult. "The code of Puritanism itself" prompted its followers "to do exactly those things that were spoiling the Puritan commonwealth" (_Nature's_ 48).

In response to the economic success that seemed to bring with it sundry sins, the Puritan clergy began to bewail the sins of the community. As early as the 1630s and increasingly until 1700, the clergy took almost every public occasion apart from their regular Sunday sermonizing to lament the clear loss of the founders' vision of mutuality and charity. With these prophetic warnings, called jeremiads after the Old Testament prophet Jeremiah, their hope was to abate the tide of secularism and acquisitiveness. Characteristically, their tone was one of dismay at New England's fickleness, which was portrayed by them to be extreme. A special gathering of clergy in 1679 indicted the citizenry for just about everything: spiritual torpor, vanity, worldliness, gambling, heresy, Sabbath-breaking, contentiousness, family discord, and business fraud. Whether the common folk were quite as bad as the ministers made them out to be, or whether the clergy were simply trying to keep themselves in business remains somewhat murky. Nor can we discern very clearly the popular response to either the economic success or the clerical warnings, although Miller contends that the increasing gap between an older style of humility, deference, and piety and a new power and pride of wealth brought on "profound anxiety, some apprehension of the heart that needed constant and repeated assuaging" (*Nature's* 43).

Discernible pressures on the founding ethos first emerged in urban areas such as Boston, and its moral and religious fate amid steady economic growth foreshadowed what would eventually also transpire in the hinterlands, although much later and for different reasons. The variety of moral and legal challenges the leadership faced in the early years, such as those posed by the trial of merchant Robert Keayne, betrayed a markedly different mind-set that only gathered force as the urban trading economy gathered steam. So marked were the differences between the rural and urban cultures that economic historian James Henretta sees the first as shaped and sustained by a communitarian or "communal ethic" and the second by, using Weber's term, the "Protestant Ethic" ("Ethic" 337). Despite a colony leadership that consistently, through the early decades, supported the interests of farmers against the merchants—in 1640, only two of the colony's twenty-two magistrates were merchants—merchants themselves continued to prosper and gain power within the community. For one, the children of merchants and the clergy intermarried, and sons of the ministers became merchants, just as the sons of the merchants entered the ministry (335–36). This social melding effectively blurred the heretofore clear demarcations between one group and another, working to destigmatize each in the other's eyes.

More important still, perhaps, is the fact that the merchants had made considerable money, and with that prosperity came power. "As early as 1670, thirty Boston merchants had estates of ten to thirty thousand pounds, and by the time of the revolution ten percent of the population controlled fifty-seven percent of the wealth of New England" (Henretta, "Ethic" 336, 338). In 1686, when King James II revoked the charter, the "merchants seized control of the government, awarding vast tracts of frontier lands and dozens of government offices to themselves and their supporters." Two years later, when it suited their needs, they became anticrown, supporting the overthrow of the new Dominion of New England in order to protect their holdings from the greed of Royal Governor Edmund Andros (336). From that point on, the merchant class seemed to have the ascendancy, and efforts to achieve a communitarian ethos in the cities simply stopped, although the preachers would regularly bewail the circumstance in their jeremiads.

Religiously, the merchants tended to identify with the more liberal theological impulses in the colony that promised to subvert the moral authority of the communitarian founders, just as Anne Hutchinson's antinomianism had in the first decade. As Daniel Walker Howe has pointed out, "The optimistic, energetic, 'merchant princes' of Boston did not take it kindly when Calvinist clergymen informed them they were miserable sinners, worms, or spiders kept from dropping into the fires of Hell only by the whim of an inscrutable God" ("Decline" 317). Such language demeaned the merchants' worldly accomplishments, mocked their power, and questioned their moral legitimacy. Later on, in the first decades of the eighteenth century, they would gravitate toward the rational protodeism of ministers like Jonathan Mayhew, Benjamin Colman, and Charles Chauncy, all of whom, to some extent, served as apologists for the business ethos. Chauncy, for example, arduously opposing the efforts of Edwards and others during the Great Awakening, admonished Edwards for the emotionalism and irrationality of a revivalism that was especially hard on wealth-getting and its pomp. The countryside, however, was quite a different matter, for there, for diverse reasons, Puritan religious vitality and the communal ethos persisted long beyond the decline of the urban centers. Partly due to their isolation, their homogeneity, the village–church interdependence, their meager prosperity, and their stalwart anticapitalism, the villages of Massachusetts sustained their Puritan localism well into the eighteenth century. From that world came the fire of religious revival that would propel the First Great Awakening.

When the rural world did finally lose its hard-won harmony, it was seemingly for notably different reasons than those that affected Boston. Here social historians have pointed to a markedly different set of agents and mechanisms disconnected from the influence of theologies of vocation or history. When change did finally happen, it resulted far more from economic necessity than from the thirst for wealth or even a modest prosperity, specifically, the pressures of population growth. As early as 1660, depending on specific locale, the fabric of largely rural Puritan society began to fray because there simply got to be too many people for the available land. Until that time, predominantly rural New England had exhibited comparative harmony in small homogeneous and tightly knit villages. For better or worse, New Englanders proved remarkably prolific, and the population grew rapidly. After several generations in the oldest settlements, the pressure of this expanding population "led to the dispersal of people out from the early clusters of settlements" (Greene, *Pursuits* 56–57).

The first consequence of population increase was on village cohesion. As land became scarce, those villages whose original land distribution was in long, thin strips extending out from the town center ended up pushing farmers to the far perimeters of the village. Scarcity forced hard-pressed sons and grandsons to cultivate the fringes of the original grant of land, and these were often six miles from family and village. Efficiency forced them to live on these outlands, even though this weakened ties to the community and church.

As towns expanded, owing to natural increase and in-migration, a rising proportion of outlivers lost touch with the central church. Distance and bad weather made travel to Sabbath services so hazardous that outlying males frequently were granted 'winter privileges,' or the right to conduct their own services under lay direction. (Bonomi 88)

Not only did religious coherence, a vital glue in Puritan life, suffer, but such outliving practices "diminished the cohesive force of the community and augmented the significance of the individual family settled on its own lands at an appreciable distance from other neighbors" (Greven 57). In Dedham in the 1660s, the desire to live on outlying lands was punished with fines. Such efforts were, however, but slight retardants to the centripetal growth of the villages: by 1680 the residential center of the town had shifted to the south and away from the original village center (Lockridge, *Town* 56). Understandably, this pattern worked to subvert the designs of the original Puritan leaders and threatened the unity of the town, bonds within neighborhoods, and the authority of political and social institutions. From the last third of the seventeenth century to the Revolution, the process only accelerated and in its early stages corresponded with the ministers' indictments of increasing worldliness and individualism (Greene, *Pursuits* 57–58).

One historian concludes that the outliers who had chosen "to promote their economic interests at the expense of their spiritual welfare . . . valued land or cattle more than church worship or participation in community life" (Bushman 58). While this is a convenient judgment, oftentimes a thin margin stands between choice and necessity. With the emergence of two separate communities, one in the original settlement with its meetinghouse and the other on the boundaries, small-scale sectional competition emerged for social and economic control of the splintered towns. Frequently, outliers wished for their own meetinghouse or separate parish, as much for increased property values as for convenience or piety. Economic and sectional animosities often infected a determined congregation as well as town politics.

For several generations the original grants supported as many sons and grandsons and families as the land could bear. Outliers and the allotment of new lands in grants merely forestalled the inevitable, and land pressure continued to mount. As one scholar of intergenerational land transfer summarizes,

When families sought to provide livelihoods and settlements for their sons, as their parents had done for them, they often felt the pressures which the demographic growth . . . put upon the land and the economic resources that they had inherited. The parceling of the original estates of the first-generation settlers created problems for the second generation when the time came for them to consider the divisions of their estates and the establishment of their sons upon the land. (Greven 125–26)

Fearing the growing pressure on available land and hoping to provide for future generations, Andover in the 1660s went so far as to distribute large quantities of the remaining common holdings of the town (Greven 62). The time came, however, when numerous families had to face penury, a vocational shift from farming, or pushing westward to find new land and form new communities (Henretta, "Ethic" 339–40). Only families of owners of large areas of land, usually from original grants, were able to absorb and sustain their progeny without diminishing status or wealth.

Eventually, despite their best efforts, two distinct classes emerged to damage the homogeneity, "economic and social, of the community" (Bushman 53). In many New England towns, wealth and power tended to move toward the most powerful, who were in the position to gain the biggest subsequent allotments and to buy out the struggling and failing freeholder. Contention and factionalism often characterized community formation as new lands opened. As the Connecticut Assembly, for example, allowed for new towns in uninhabited areas, competition and speculation arose for those new holdings. Once established, a change in village design reduced possibilities for communal bonding. New villages were most often plotted for large, separate, and evenly proportioned farming tracts with no common center. This new practice effectively did away with the possibility of a community center and a certain degree of familiarity and cohesion. With this new design, "all residents lived at a distance from one another, no longer meeting regularly, and able if they wished to draw into some untravelled corner of the town" (82). Economic necessity and opportunity thus detracted in multiple ways from the social and religious cohesion that had been the strength of the old order. Before long, then, the medieval communitarian impulse behind this scheme of calling and wealth—that all work and wealth were to serve society—was gradually overshadowed, first, by the necessities of survival and then, eventually, by graspingness and greed.

The cultural history of Puritanism in its first decades in Massachusetts argues powerfully for the continued usefulness of a model of religious and social declension, and this model speaks directly to those who would contend that colonial Puritanism constituted a significant catalyst for the growth of the capitalist spirit in North America. The deeply intertwined religious and social visions of Massachusetts Calvinism created a cultural world whose central currents deeply opposed the calculating, rationalized individualism that many see as the psychological and moral precondition for the development of modern economic practices. The exceptional character of New England stands out dramatically when contrasted with the social milieus of both old England and the other British colonies in North America. As discussed earlier, old England had undergone rapid and substantial change, and by the start of the seventeenth century, its atmosphere was contentious and chaotic, driven by increasing competitive individualism. From this the New England Puritans sought refuge and sought, with all of their considerable spiritual and moral energies, to create a "holy commonwealth" that not only would retrieve what they thought was fast disappearing from old England but would imbue their new society with a rigorously Christian, moral self-consciousness that centered on a notion of love that promised to infuse and sustain the social fabric.

In the end, it is fair to say that Puritan New England simply became like all the other colonies, which were, from the start, individualistic and competitive in the extreme. Originally, Puritan New England stood out, and in contrast to the others, the full measure of the Puritan accomplishment stands out. In his concise survey of the social histories of early Colonial America, social historian Jack Greene singles out Massachusetts as the exception to the norm that characterized both old England and the British settlements from Bermuda to Barbados. Old England, says Greene, had become a "dynamic, mobile, loose, open, individualistic, competitive, conflicted, acquisitive, highly stratified, and market-based society undergoing rapid economic and social change" (*Pursuits* 35). Over the Atlantic, the colonies were characterized, with the exception of New England, by the same, and of these the Chesapeake was typical. The description is sweeping, to say the least: "lack of social cohesion, weak social institutions, slowly-developing community spirit, religious pluralism, secular orientation, competitiveness, acquisitiveness, high levels of property concentration, rapidly circulating elite, reliance upon dependent servant labor, treatment of labor as a disposable commodity, mobility," and the list continues (36). In short, the other colonies suffered because they lacked "an all-encompassing religious and social vision of the kind that restrained individualism and gave coherence, cohesion, and a larger sense of purpose to life" (45). In this vacuum rampant individualism flourished, and from it emerges the competitive economic ethos of America. The self came to labor solely for itself, although it lived still within an encompassing social unit. No longer was the end of labor God, the church, or the social body. The shift is from labor and service for others to pursuit of the well-being of the self, and that pursuit is subsequently valued and enshrined to sanction personal well-being and wealth-getting as appropriate norms for human behavior.

Historians have long debated how Puritan New England in the late seventeenth and early eighteenth centuries adjusted to the reality of prosperity and increasing individualism. Although it has been often questioned, the predominant view has been that of Perry Miller, who found Puritan theologians accommodating and rationalizing the acquisition of wealth. Miller saw the seeds for this justification in aspects of the theology that the Puritans brought with them to New England. For Miller, just as New England Puritanism gave work a theological justification, its historical vision eventually provided theological justification for wealth, although this was very likely undreamed of by its first spokesmen. In addition to arguing for charity in his Arabella sermon, John Winthrop contended that the Puritan venture was special insofar as its success as "a city upon a hill" could determine Christian, if not world, history. With "naive egotism," in Perry Miller's phrase, they had thought themselves a latter-day chosen Israel with a special destiny (*Seventeenth* 485). Given this sense, they thought themselves justified in posing a special contract—or, to use the biblical term, covenant—with God. Winthrop understood their covenant to be approved and pledged by God if he brought them safely over the Atlantic. Further, he understood that if the New England saints lived by faith and enacted their medieval vision of social charity, God would favor them with grace and prosperity, at least spiritually if not materially.

While this suggestion of reward did not compose a major dimension in American Puritan theology, it did raise the possibility of some causal connection between special piety and obedience and personal well-being, whether interpreted materially or religiously. It is doubtful that this suggestion received much emphasis during the early decades, especially in light of the communitarian hostility toward individual acquisition. At what point Winthrop's convenantal formulation was first raised as a trustworthy theological principle applicable to personal financial improvement we cannot be sure. However, says Miller, by the end of the seventeenth century and during a period of considerable trial for Puritanism, New England clergy apparently invoked the piety-and-riches formula with some frequency: "[M]any long pages in New England sermons were devoted to exhorting the people to reform in order to gain material blessing, or to pointing out that their physical castigations had resulted from their wilful defaultings." (*Seventeenth* 489). As Sacvan Bercovitch summarizes in his *American Jeremiad*, the biblical promises of blessing that other Puritans understood to have only spiritual import, the New England group, in a radical departure, interpreted to be material: in New England, "the wheel of grace and the wheel of fortune revolved in harmony" (47). What the ministerial conclave of 1673 would condemn as the chief subverter of piety—the lure and pleasures of riches—came to be used popularly as a lever to woo vagrants back into the church. The Puritan had to grapple with the strange and contradictory phenomenon of an apparent fruit of the covenant turning out to be a source of subversion. In any case, the transcendent, inscrutable, and moral God of the founders had become, in Perry Miller's fine phrase, "an economic schoolmaster, rewarding His good pupils for their model deportment and punishing His bad ones for neglect of their lessons" (*Colony* 485). That is, nonetheless, a debate that continues on into considerations of such figures of eighteenth-century America as Ben Franklin, whom sociologist Max Weber cast as the fruition of the Puritan ethos.

PURITAN LITERATURE AND THE WEBER THESIS

One major area of dispute in the Weber thesis has focused on the presence in Puritan theology, sermons, and popular literature of those elements that Max Weber identified as the contributing religious agents in the creation of the Protestant Ethic. Weber cited prominent English Puritan theologians as encouraging wealth-getting, and ever since, historians have hotly and voluminously contested on how to read the literary evidence in both old and New England. As might be predicted, those who favor economic interpretations that stress the collusion of religion and wealth-getting find ample evidence of Puritan greed, and still others of assorted theoretical persuasions dissent vigorously. The controversy runs something like this: if Weber was right, some notable religious parts of the Puritan world—theology, preaching, and popular books—should, with some regularity, accentuate predestination, assurance of salvation, calling, diligence, and wealth-getting. After all, Weber contended that Puritan anxiety about the believers' eternal fate— an uncertainty sufficiently widespread to create a pervasive "spirit" for the growth of capitalism—threw them into fervent pursuit of their calling in order to get sufficient riches to constitute indisputable tangible proof that God favored them, a liking that was a sure sign of eternal salvation. The focus of inquiry has been upon what lies in Puritan literature of the seventeenth century and how that is to be interpreted in its own right and from the perspective of its original listeners, specifically, the artisans and merchants who composed a good portion of the Puritan movement. The conclusion of numerous authors who have looked closely at the different kinds of literary influence upon seventeenth-century Puritans is that the postulations of Weber and others who followed his lead on the relation of Puritanism to capitalism had gotten the linkage exactly wrong.

The first strong dissent from the model set forth by Weber came in an early essay by T. H. Breen, who has since gone on to become a prominent historian of Colonial America. In "The Non-Existent Controversy: Puritan and Anglican Attitudes on Work and Wealth" (1966), Breen seeks to test the hypotheses set forth by British historian Christopher Hill in his *Puri-*

tanism and Revolution: Studies in the Interpretation of the English Revolution of the 17th Century (1958) that Puritanism supplied the middle class with a rationale for economic pursuit that diverged sharply from the medieval ethos that condemned the labor for the acquisition of riches and urged charity for the poor. Moreover, Hill placed Anglicanism on the side of feudalism, as a retardant on acquisitive impulses. Breen gently concludes from his reading of primary materials that Hill and other modern historians have over-emphasized the relation of Calvinism to capitalism (274). Not only was there nothing distinctive in Puritan attitudes on calling, the condemnation of idleness, and wealth, but the Puritans proved to be notably more conservatively anticapitalistic on these matters than the Anglicans (275). Both Puritans and Anglicans envisioned two callings, the first to labor to the glory of God in the care of one's family and the second for welfare of all people. The Puritans went so far as to warn against overwork (276). Both groups distinguished idle from deserving poor, who merited charity. While one Puritan allowed that sometimes poverty might be sent by God, one Anglican went to the opposite extreme in deeming poverty a failure of character (281). The Puritans were emphatic that any wealth beyond the necessities was to be spent for the kingdom, church, and the needy, and many Anglicans seemed comparatively stingy. "Contrary to Hill's beliefs we find that at least one major Anglican adopted a hard line toward the poor and at times sounded much more bourgeois than the bourgeois themselves" (282). Puritans strictly forbade labor that had as its intent the accumulation of wealth, while Anglicans tended to indulge both covetousness and ambition. While Breen concludes that it is "difficult to find evidence on either side of a new morality blessing the increase of riches" (283), it is clear that Puritans were far more emphatic in insisting that wealth was a gift from God that imposed enormous moral obligations in attempting to better the welfare of all. The gist of the interpretation is to seriously undermine Hill's association of Puritanism with the encouragement of wealth-getting attitudes.

Something of the same conclusion is reached in Laura O'Connell's examination of "Anti-Entrepreneurial Attitudes in Elizabethan Sermons and Popular Literature" (1976). As Breen reacted to Christopher Hill, O'Connell reacts to the habit of historians of reading back into English history the conclusions drawn by R. H. Tawney in his *Religion and Rise of Capitalism* (1926), a book that argued that Puritanism in post-Restoration England ended up sanctifying economic expediency and accumulation. As a test case for the conclusions of several prominent historians, O'Connell undertakes a close reading of Elizabethan Puritan sermons and secular popular literature. On the question of diligence, labor, and wealth, she finds that the Puritan divines "defined as the *only* legitimate diligence . . . that which provided for the necessities of life and status, and the *only* legitimate wealth was that which was given by God." In trying to become rich, a person "disobeyed God's commandments and became a slave of Mammon"

(5). Greater emphasis fell upon the necessity of those with money to devote themselves to dispensing it in charity to the poor and the needy (6). She concludes, "Sixteenth-century Puritans neither admired nor encouraged work which was done to enrich the worker. The kind of labor they encouraged was . . . a vigorous social energy turned to the good of the commonwealth," specifically, "justice, temperance, liberality, and charity" (8).

In "The Anti-Puritan Work Ethic" (1981), John Sommerville argues that Puritan understandings of work and wealth had not notably changed by the Restoration (1660–1711). To some extent Sommerville reexamines the territory viewed by Breen fifteen years before, except that Sommerville's research is far more extensive and detailed insofar as it entails "a rigorously quantitative content analysis of the most popular religious books of Restoration England" (70). Sommerville's work examines the ideas of Puritans and Anglicans on a wide range of theological and ethical matters, of which attitudes toward wealth and labor are only a small part. Like Breen, Sommerville finds that Anglicans were far more likely to encourage wealth-getting attitudes than were Puritans (73). In an inquiry not undertaken by Breen or O'Connell, Sommerville looks at levels of religious anxiety in Puritan and Anglican writers, and while he concludes that the Puritans did, in general, manifest more anxiety in religious matters than Anglicans, they did not do so on the vital predestinarian question of "assurance" of one's salvation, which is the psychological element that Weber had argued was the engine that drove Puritans into ardent pursuit of their calling. More than that, Puritans seemed rather overconfident to the extent that it was a matter of concern to Puritan writers. Nor was there any indication anywhere that Puritan authors ever saw "intense activity in one's worldly calling as a sign of God grace, much less an infallible test" (75). Those most interested in worldly activity were, in fact, Anglicans, as Sommerville points out in this essay and in his book-length study of *Popular Religion in Restoration England* (1977). Against the usual expectations of the economic theorists, "those who were the most insistent upon work as a religious duty were those who emphasized human freedom, and not those who believed in God's election," as did the Puritans (*Popular* 104). On the whole, Puritan writers "were entirely scornful of reputation and material prosperity as motives in religious duty," but some Anglican writers went so far as to view wealth and religion instrumentally as means to happiness in this life (106). Like previous writers, Sommerville finds that the religious and social attitudes economic historians have most often identified as requisites for the getting of wealth not only do not appear within the Puritan cosmos but are actively discouraged within that world. It is important to note, too, the Sommerville's studies look at the relatively late Puritanism of the Restoration, the very period in which historians such as Tawney see Puritanism going to seed.

The question of how the wisdom of the divines in preaching and in books was received by ordinary common laity is addressed by Paul Seaver in his examination of the extensive personal journal of Nehemiah Wallington (1580–1658), an artisan "turner" or woodworker who spent his Puritan adulthood in London. In "The Puritan Work Ethic Revisited" (1980), Seaver seeks to respond to Christopher Hill's attempt to save the Weber thesis by suggesting that Puritan merchants listened selectively to their preachers, ignoring the uncomfortable parts and taking away only those that seemed to bless their wealth-getting desires and habits. The only difficulty for Hill's thesis "lies in proving that such selectivity was indeed the case, for few men are likely to leave us unambiguous evidence that they only heard or read what it was socially or economically convenient for them to hear or read" (38). A second possibility is that Puritan merchants were just simply hypocrites, so great was the appetite for wealth. Or there is a third possibility, one apparently not considered by economic theorists. As Seaver puts it at some length,

Londoners may have heard the Puritan message in its fullness, have accepted its strictures regarding the temptations and dangers of economic enterprise, and have perceived no contradiction between the values preached and their business practices, because what was in fact preached was supportive of, rather than at variance with, their way of life.

All three attitudes may have existed simultaneously, but the journals of Wallington, some 2,000 pages kept intermittently over a twenty-year period, "the best documented life of a London artisan in the early modern period," seem to support the last option (40).

In light of the preaching and books analyzed above, Wallington was strikingly normal in that he was aware of the possibility of immorality in his trade practices and of lack of diligence in his labors. Seaver writes that Wallington understood that the "point of a calling was not to gain riches, but to be profitable and useful to oneself, one's family, church, and commonwealth," and any real wealth entailed obligation, for it was a gift from God and was to be given to the poor (43). Further, there was the risk that wealth might result from dishonest business practices. Seaver summarizes that Wallington's "values and attitudes are not medieval, but neither did they aid and abet the entrepreneurial spirit" (44). While Wallington's aspirations were fitting for his time, bound as he was by town and guild, it is evident that his "consciousness of being numbered among the godly, of being a member of the Puritan community, inhibited sharp practice and profiteering" (46). For Puritans of Wallington's time and for Wallington, too, "economic enterprise was never seen as an end in itself," and during Wallington's lifetime, "Puritan precept and artisan practice seemed to go hand in hand" (48, 52). After laying out his portrait of Wallington and his Puritan world, Seaver responds to Christopher Hill with the admission that such "evidence as Wallington provides may be a slender foundation on which to base any large conclusions" but also with the assertion that "for the great mass of honest householders who filled the City churches" there were no selective hearing, hypocrisy, or anxious charity to compensate for one's greed (52). Finally, the evidence of Wallington's journal and spirit suggests that historians have been mistaken "to assume that what the Puritan urban laity wanted was the sanctification of entrepreneurial energy and profits; it seems more likely that most Puritans sought assurance that a good conscience in hard times was blessing enough" (53).

A BRIEF HISTORY OF THE HISTORIES OF PURITAN NEW ENGLAND

In 1964, intellectual historian Henry May announced in a now-famous essay the beginning of "The Recovery of American Religious History." May has since recalled that his claim was greeted with skepticism (*Ideas* 66). The subsequent record, however, has proven him more than right. In hindsight it is fair to say that May's essay heralded only the first trickle of what soon became a continuous flood of historical scholarship on American religion. Numerous new emphases and approaches, such as those, respectively, on popular religion and social history and virtually no theme, movement, tradition, group, or era have escaped attention: revivalism, esoterica, civil religion, indigenous populations, women, new religions, ethnic imports, and just about every denomination twice-over.

One movement in particular, the Puritans of colonial New England, have received enormous amounts of investigation and analysis. So great has been the flood of scholarship that, as one history pundit has suggested, at least one book of "Puritan studies" has been written for every ten original Puritans. We now seem to be near the threshold of knowing more about the Puritans than anyone should properly want to know about anybody (Morgan, "Historians" 41). Indeed, no group of mostly ordinary people, save maybe for the ancient Israelites, has ever been so closely inspected, analyzed, and interpreted (Murrin 226). In spite of schools and mountains of past and present scrutiny, or maybe because of it, no stable image of the nature of Puritanism or its American settlement has emerged. Rather, we have seen in the last half century large-scale shifts of perspective and emphasis that have depended largely on the individual historian's interpretive goggles— the perceptual dispositions and biases the historian inevitably brings to questions of why and how humans and events occur as they do. The discussion that follows briefly surveys the beginnings and general contours of the major historical analyses of American Puritan culture. By examining the changing approaches and judgments of Puritan culture, we can perhaps derive a useful and accurate image of Puritan culture and of what ways it relates to our own.

Those first New England settlers, ministers and layfolk alike, were themselves acutely conscious of historical meaning. They had, after all, passed through some historical fire and crisis in Reformation, persecution, and, in England, revolution. While those who migrated to the wild and largely uncharted North American continent surely possessed a mix of motives for doing so, ample evidence exists to support the claim that the Christian religion and its personal and social values played a substantial part in their reasoning. Notions of a guiding providence in whom they could trust and who cared desperately about the fate of the world shaped the individual and collective sense of their venture and its historical significance. History mattered because of a divine loving presence, and they as a people seeking holiness mattered. Preoccupation is not too strong a word to characterize Puritan concern with history and its directions and meanings. Thus, the first to probe and reflect upon the Puritan experiment were Puritans themselves—wondering all the while on the strange and demanding ways of God's love and care. The diary-memoir of William Bradford, the leader of the Pilgrim Plymouth settlement, told Pilgrim history through a filter of providential significance, that is, selecting and meditating upon events for their potential to reveal the kindnesses and judgments in the thick of ordinary events. Empirical evidence was thus marshaled to support the reality of covenantal bond between God and his particular people.

The same covenantal wrestlings shaped the historical vision of John Winthrop, who served as governor of Massachusetts Bay for almost all his three decades in the New World. While on the ship *Arabella*, before setting ashore, lawyer Winthrop preached his famous "A Model of Christian Charity," which, in effect, threw down the gauntlet to his shipmates to live as God beckoned them to if they wished his favor. The means to, and fruit of, God's blessing would be the life of corporate love, and by that holy accomplishment the Puritan foothold in America could serve as a beacon—again an empirical evidence—of the abiding love and care of God as manifest in his people. By upholding the covenant in a life of love, New England might become a "city upon a hill" that might dispel and retrieve the darkness then besetting Europe. These well-known works by founders offer conspicuous examples of an impulse that pervaded colonial Puritanism. Poetess Ann Bradstreet brooded on the ways of God in work after work and in private journal and correspondence. Massachusetts regularly inspected its historical course on virtually every public occasion with sermons and orations focused on how the venture fared spiritually and morally. Countless journals, diaries, and letters—many dutifully preserved for posterity—attest to the vitality of historical questions. Before very long, more formal histories sought to spell out providential design and vindication. In 1654, Edward Johnson published *The Wonder-Working Providence of Sions Savior in New England*, and Nathaniel Norton followed in 1669 with *New Englands Memoriall*. Moreover, the histories were popularly oriented, serving to remind, persuade, and inspire. The prolific minister Cotton Mather produced his monumental *Magnalia Christi Americana*, in part, to summon his contemporaries to the fervor and courage of their forebears, and Michael Wigglesworth attempted the same on a cosmic scale in conjuring the eschatological climax of history for his best-selling *Day of Doom*.

An honored and mythologized past, revered as the seedbed of democracy and civic virtue, the highly esteemed Puritan culture was endorsed by early nineteenth-century historian George Bancroft. In his ten-volume *History of the United States*, whose composition spanned forty years (1834–1874), Bancroft esteemed the Puritans for their political and religious innovation and freedom. John Gorham Palfrey's five-volume *History of New England during the Stuart Dynasty* (1858–1890) adopted the same point of view, adding powerful support for Puritan cultural enshrinement. The emergence of a Massachusetts blue-blooded historical and genealogical establishment in the revered Massachusetts Historical Society gave long-lasting official sanction through visible archives and scholarly journals.

The first notable divergences from Puritan hagiolatry did not come until the late nineteenth century and then gathered to a storm of assault by the 1930s. From a famous Puritan lineage came the first substantive assaults. The three grandsons of John Quincy Adams all wrote lengthy studies of early America. Brother Brooks Adams began the revision with *The Emancipation of Massachusetts* (1887). In *Three Episodes of Massachusetts History* (1892) and *Massachusetts: Its Historians and Its History* (1893), Charles Francis Adams continued the indictment of Puritan culture for religious intolerance in expelling and executing opponents, Quaker and witch indiscriminately. Politics rather than theology and morality loomed large in these treatments. When the third Adams brother, Henry, came to write his history of early America, he chose to applaud the contributions of the Enlightenment figure Thomas Jefferson. While the contributions of the Adams family to historical scholarship and revision are immense, one must wonder how much of the impulse underlying their work arose from the old pattern of the sons of esteemed fathers rejecting a constraining family lore to forge a fresh and self-made identity.

The reputation of the American Puritans has undergone two major revisions in the twentieth century, especially in what we might call popular intellectualism. However much the broad, religious middle class of the United States has venerated the pious and sentimental image of Plymouth Rock and Thanksgiving, the Puritans' fate among the liberally educated and urbane "new class" has been decidedly less complimentary. The regnant stereotype in popular intellectual lore, old and vigorous still and as skewed in its own way as the sentimental image, pictures stern, repressive, and nosy black-suited ogres whose legacy consists of pious fanaticism, clerical tyranny, gross superstition, obsessive guilt, sexual denial, and heedless capitalism (the latest charge is environmental despoliation). While many academic historians have long since largely discarded this caricature, that fact has not daunted innumerable media sages. Journalists galore, columnist upon commentator, Left and Right alike continue to manhandle the ill-famed Puritans as scapegoat, whipping boy, and bugbear for just about everything wrong with American culture. What it might finally take to dislodge this woeful distortion from pop intellectualism remains one of the eternal mysteries.

The beginnings and history of the mounting negative estimate are not difficult to trace. The significant interpretive reorientation provided by the Adams brothers was overshadowed by larger, new cultural emphases on the shaping role of economic, political, and social factors in historical motivation. The first substantive criticism of American Puritanism came in the 1920s and 1930s. In 1913, Charles A. Beard argued in *An Economic Interpretation of the Constitution* that the founders' religious and political rhetoric about liberty only masked oligarchic economic interest. Using Beard's economic interpretive filter, James Truslow Adams declared in *The Founding of New England* (1921) that the primary motivation of the lay Puritan in coming to the New World was economic and political, the opportunity to do what one wished for oneself (121–22); religion was a secondary consideration at best. The theology and mores of Puritanism held sway because its ethos was the spiritual articulation for middle-class acquisitiveness. A few years later, in the first of three volumes on the *Main Currents in American Thought*, historian Vernon Parrington celebrated the triumph of American "democratic liberalism" over Puritanism's clerical tyranny and capitalistic fervor (13). For Parrington, a major figure in American historiography, religious ideas assumed value only insofar as they fostered, most often inadvertently, a Progressive political liberalism. Intellectually as well as politically, the American Puritans feared "the free spaces of thought," living in a "narrow and cold . . . prison" of intolerant "absolutist dogma" (12, 13). In the 1920s and 1930s, however, the sentiments of Adams, Parrington, and many other like-minded historians, generally known as the Progressive school, prevailed and found an indomitable popularizer in gadfly journalist H. L. Mencken, whose syndicated columns lampooned Puritan intelligence, charity, sexuality, and piety. The combination of a pronounced anti-Puritan interpretive "climate of opinion" or ideological cast among professional historians and a talented popularizer fairly well entrenched the still-dominant popular biases and caricatures of the Puritan past.

As might be expected, liberal economic theory as the only resource for the explanation of history drew ample fire because the conviction with which its proponents embraced it seemed to block out other explanatory factors. The persistence of the Progressive explanation is difficult to underestimate. In 1980 in his *American Historical Explanations*, historiographer Gene Wise contends that the sociopolitical aspirations of the Progressive historians of the 1920s and 1930s were so dearly and commonly shared that it remained legitimate to designate it as still the "dominant explanation form in twentieth-century American historical scholarship" (216). In that judgment Wise followed the lead of the Progressive school's most careful analyst, Richard Hofstadter, who suggested that the group formed by Beard, Turner, and Parrington gave the profession "the pivotal ideas of the first half of the twentieth century" (xii). On Parrington specifically, Lionel Trilling in 1950 described Parrington's *Main Currents in American Thought* as having "an influence on our conception of American culture which is not equaled by that of any other writer of the last two decades" (1). The limits of the school were identified in the 1960s by prominent colonial historian Edmund Morgan, who took the economic school to task because its ideological commitments predetermined their conclusions. Their approach "became less a spur to investigation of economic history than a way of interpreting the past without investigating it." For Morgan, the economic interpretation, as practiced,

too often accepted, substituted intuition for research. If the written record was a snare for the unwary, if what men said could not be trusted, there was no urgency to study what they said. When you are sure that a man who says x really means y, there is no point in pausing over the value of x. ("Historians" 47)

The seemingly final nail in the coffin of Puritanism came not from America or the historical profession but from Germany and the emerging discipline of sociology. In 1904–1905 German sociologist Max Weber published two articles that would become, in English translation in 1930, *The Protestant Ethic and the Spirit of Capitalism*. In that classic work, Weber set forth the notion that the practical rational and organizational processes necessary for the emergence of modern industrial capitalism were dramatically furthered by a single central facet of Puritan theology. According to Weber, the Calvinistic insistence on predestination imposed enormous psychological anxiety upon the believer. Uncertain of one's eternal fate, the believer sought desperately for earthly signs of God's election. The very urgency of the search impelled the seeker to interpret any good occurrence, especially material prosperity, as an indication of divine favor. With the prospect of vindicating one's salvation as an impetus, the Puritans threw themselves into the pursuit of wealth. The religious mind-set, then, fostered a new efficiency in the marketplace; after all, the stakes were high—a life of grim uncertainty or sweet repose. The effect of Weber's formulation was to further the notion of the Puritan as intellectually impoverished and, because of that, economically resolute or, put more bluntly, plain greedy. Moved by a powerful idea, predestination, Weber's Puritans initiated the modern world.

One of the central and most hotly contested cultural theories about the nature of modern life, Weber's work exerted an enormous, lasting influence on the image of Puritan culture. Two rather large ironies emerge in this regard. On one hand, Weber clearly intended his work to be a refutation of economic determinism, that interpretive filter that sees all activity and ideation as products of economic self-interest, whether acknowledged or not. In short, Weber wished to assert the primacy of religious ideas over economic causation. He perhaps, in part, accomplished his purpose but with a sizable toll upon the image of the Puritans. Whatever ideas religion had, they weren't very good, either in themselves or in their social effects. Weber's work jelled with the mood of the Progressive historians and became a major intellectual cliché. A second irony lies in the fact that while much of Weber's historical understanding of Puritanism has been called into serious question, if not outright disproven, his notion of a selfish work ethic and a mercenary religious sect persists.

The first assaults on the Progressive school questioned both its historical method and its philosophic basis for judgment. Its first major critic, Samuel Eliot Morison, himself a descendant of the Puritans, published *Builders of the Bay Colony* (1930), a work that consciously set out to challenge the facts and conjectures of Adams's groundbreaking study. For him, the Puritans were more or less who they said they were, both politically and religiously; in short, he gave them the benefit of the doubt and supposed that their rhetoric did, in fact, approximate their actual motives and circumstances. His success lies in making the dread Puritans not only into plausible human beings but into stalwart, brave souls who struggled morally and philosophically to tame a wilderness and to live and make sense of their belief. In effect, then, Morison denied a central tenet of the Progressive school: that religious ideas, unless socially radical, function mostly as ingenious cloaks for social and economic control.

In the decade that followed Morison's book, the Puritans found their most cogent and prolific defender in Perry Miller, a young Harvard historian. With exhaustive thoroughness, intellectual complexity, and literary passion, Miller undertook a decades-long foray into the Puritan mind and spirit, thereby initiating the current momentum of historical curiosity. In five different, lengthy books, a total of roughly 2,000 pages, Miller retrieved a staggeringly full picture of the Puritan psyche. One of America's great historiographic achievements, it still constitutes a standard for historical sophistication and caution, regardless of subject area. Moreover, on Puritanism itself, Miller's description of Puritan intellectual, religious, and, to some extent, social reality has become the normative picture with which subsequent historians of early America have had to reckon. That is no easy process, for Miller's thoroughness, taste for nuance, and intellectual complexity make his books demanding reading. More than one historian, having launched "the attack" on where Miller was wrong, has been found guilty of not reading Miller closely enough. Indeed, with his capacious and subtle rendering of the Puritan past, Miller has almost become as finally unknowable as the voluble and now distant Puritans.

Miller's first volume, *Orthodoxy in Massachusetts* (1933), surveyed the re-

lationship of the theology of English Puritanism to the creation of the ecclesiastical and governmental forms of New England society. Again Edmund
Morgan, the current dean of scholars of early America, best points to the
nature of Miller's challenge to the Progressive school:

He considered the actions of the founders to be the product of their ideas and not
vice versa. He related the settlement of New England not to the economic discontents or social ambitions of the emigrants but to the ecclesiastical ideas developed
among English Puritans during the preceding fifty years. The result was to place both
the ecclesiastical and the political history of New England in the context of intellectual history. ("Miller" 52)

Miller followed in a few years with *The New England Mind: The Seventeenth
Century* ([1939] 1961), an extensive examination of the crucial and complex
theological and experiential core of Puritanism. Interrupted by World War
II, Miller's next study did not appear until 1949. *Jonathan Edwards* advocated that its subject was not only the greatest of Puritan theologians but
also the bold precursor of the toughest modern intellectual dilemmas. In
1956 Miller collected various essays on the New England Puritans into *Errand into the Wilderness*. Three years later, he concluded his venture with
the second volume of the *New England Mind: From Colony to Province*
(1953), which traced the fate of the Puritans' ideology through time in the
wilderness setting.

The nature of Miller's contribution has prompted a good deal of discussion among historians. The most frequent criticism of his work has focused
on his approach to history. In the first volume of *The New England Mind*,
Miller unabashedly confessed to avoiding "giving more than passing notice
to social or economic influence" in order to concentrate on "the importance
of ideas in American history" (xii), especially with reference to "the integrity
and profundity of the Puritan character," which was "one of the major
expressions of the Western intellect" and "the most powerful single factor
in the early history of America" (viii). That being the case, Miller "sought
to discover what it held, what spirit and what thoughts inspired it and to
what it aspired, what combinations it made of older ideas and what it added
of its own, and what finally . . . it can be said to have meant or still means
as a living force" (viii). This venture evidenced a radical departure for the
practice of history, for Miller had made bold, as Edmund Morgan has put
it, to "understand the past not through its contributions to political liberty,
and not through sympathy with common or uncommon men, but through
a study of the way men understood themselves" ("Miller" 53).

Miller's attention to what he called "mind" went beyond intellectual or
doctrinal matters to plunge into the intricacies and depths of the Puritan
psyche. For him, the glory of Puritanism lay in its hardheaded analysis of
the somber "plight of humanity" (8). Calvinism, then, was but "one more

instance of a recurrent spiritual answer to interrogations eternally posed by human existence" (4). The theology and deep piety of Puritanism "came from an urgent sense of man's predicament, from a mood so deep that it could never be completely articulated" (4); from a recognition, that is, "of the natural emptiness of the heart and its consuming desire for fullness" (22). Such realism fascinated Miller and, in his eyes, throughout history has appealed "irresistibly to large numbers of exceptionally vigorous spirits" (4). The consequence was a theology that sought desperately to understand and mediate between a yearning and deeply flawed self and an essentially mysterious and forbidding world, one more akin to those of Ecclesiastes, Job, and Augustine than to the visions of latter-day optimists, whether Unitarian or New Deal. Miller's Puritans shared, in the words of Francis Butts, a "profound sense of man's smallness in a universe that was both mysterious and majestic, frightening and elating" wherein they "acutely felt the abyss that separated them from what they called God" (670). What stands out, then, as their accomplishment, which Miller respected, was their "drive for an intelligible universe" (Hollinger 160). Their task was, in the words of Henry May, "to make an intellectual system out of the mystery and terror of the Universe" (*Ideas* 215).

If in the first volume of *The New England Mind* Miller confined his focus to "the architecture of the intellect brought to America by the founders of New England," in its second volume, *From Colony to Province*, Miller examined the fate that befell that intellect as it necessarily accommodated itself to an American setting (*Colony* vii). As such Miller sought to generalize "about the relation of thought or ideas to community experience" (viii). There Miller traced the passing of the first generation and the strategies with which the second tried to sustain the religious fervor and purity of the forebears. His story was not a happy one, even though that, too, has now become a matter of debate. He detected subtle shifts of religious mood and tone more than overt changes in theology and doctrine, although those, too, did transpire, as with the famous Half-Way Covenant. The formal content of New England theology did not cause so much change as it did a softening or diversion of the private soul's sense of belief, what the spirit and imagination made of notions like sin, redemption, and holiness. Miller labeled this process declension or decline, and the Puritans themselves seemed to have judged it to be so, for they regularly inveighed in sermons known as jeremiads. In any case, the culprit seems to have been how richly God blessed Puritan efforts in the New World. Hard work "was mandated as a way to glorify God, yet the fruit of industry [wealth] distracted the Saints from their initial errand. Success bred failure" (Butts 683). The blandishments of an even modest prosperity amply diverted and distracted the culture from the wholehearted pursuit of God. The texture of piety had changed: one could still believe the old doctrines, but God had imperceptibly become less the end of the Puritan venture than the guarantor of its well-being.

Miller's grand edifice has undergone a steady and useful critique since his death in 1964, especially with regard to his unflinching emphasis on ideas as opposed to social factors as shaping forces in cultural history. While that allegiance was, to some extent, corrected by the second volume of *The New England Mind*, many later historians have seen there as well a large measure of insensitivity to the significance and complexity of psychological, class, or economic realities in conditioning various sorts of religious expression, be they ecclesiastical, theological, or devotional. While surely Miller erred in countless ways, especially in some emphases and occasional fuzziness (given not the least his own existentialist sympathies and accompanying perceptual biases), the boldness, freshness, and cogency of his rendering of Puritanism stand as the major historiographical accomplishment of the last half century. Miller not only reasserted the historical significance of ideas but initiated among historians the refurbishing of the image of religion as a potentially credible and rigorous psychological and intellectual enterprise. Subsequent historians have most often looked at the adequacy of Miller's data or the soundness of his interpretations.

Roughly the last three decades of Puritan studies have benefited greatly from the emergence of a whole new methodological school of historical research. With its conceptual origins in France, the first applications of what is called the new social history to Puritanism were to English settings. In 1963 Sumner Chilton Powell published his Pulitzer Prize-winning *Puritan Village: The Formation of a New England Town*, a study that attempted to trace the transfer of cultural patterns from old England to New England. English scholar Peter Laslett's *The World We Have Lost: England before the Industrial Age* (1965) provided a detailed portrait of the last phases of medieval society before the onset of industrialization. Both studies were as remarkable for their methods as for their content. As a methodology, the new social history has relied heavily on the use of almost any sort of extant data from long-gone social units, usually families, churches, and towns: genealogies, tax ledgers, court and municipal records, parish records, and, in some cases, company books. By painstakingly collating and then sifting vast amounts of data, the social historians have constructed startlingly full portraits of innumerable persons and family and the larger social patterns their lives compose. With these techniques, we can now with some empirical certainty illumine what were either inaccessible or at best shadowy areas in the contours and texture of ordinary life several centuries ago. Historians have moved increasingly toward clarity on such factual matters, to name a few, as social and geographic mobility, marriage ages, fertility and mortality rates, family size, levels of family and community strife, and economic and trade practices. Previously, scholars' conclusions were necessarily more impressionistic, based as they were on surviving literary evidence, which itself could be highly subjective in its depictions. The data can still occasion rather eccentric interpretation, as we shall see later, but, on the whole, the new social history has both provided a fresh angle from which to view Puritan New England and yielded some surprising results.

This new wealth and kind of information have, to some extent, occasioned a shift of historical interest from the lives and thought of very small intellectual, political, and social elites, what is usually referred to as an "articulate few," to the experience and fate of the ordinary and unheralded yeoman, wife, merchant, craftsman, or magistrate—by and large, common people who did not keep journals, who wrote few letters and no books, who never mounted a pulpit, or who in many cases could not read. While this still does not put the historian inside the mind of the folk, so to speak, information about towns, families, and individuals does afford a comparatively full glimpse of at least the surface or external shape of the experience of large numbers of people whose lives until now have remained almost fully obscure. As historian J. Michael Murrin as commented, with the new social history, we come "as close to the lives of everyday men as the historians of the early modern era are ever likely to get" (227).

To some extent, at least in terms of the writing of religious history, this shift of study from elite to popular subjects—"popular" meaning, in this instance, ordinary or common—was already under way. Most religious history in America has been what we call church history or, put simply, the fates of denominations, the chronicle of ecclesiastical, doctrinal, and institutional change. The larger culture in which the denomination finds itself has been considered only insofar as it gave a setting for, or influenced, the denomination. Beginning with the Progressive historians, whose interests were other than writing a holy history, at least of the traditional, religious kind, historians have wondered more and more about the role of religion in the formation of American culture and history. As historian William Clebsch has suggested, historians must write a very different story if they ask "to what uses American history has put its religion" or look at the "function of religion and religious ideas in the common life of Americans" (3, ix). That possibility has introduced a secularist perspective in the writing of religious history that has brought enormous amounts of attention to bear on the history and nature of the religious life, even though much of that has not been sympathetic.

One of the accomplishments of the new social history has been to expand our understanding of the role of religion and its prominence in Puritan society, especially of the centrality of its social vision and the extent to which it often translated into communal reality. For example, the work of Perry Miller duly emphasized Puritan hopes for a free and "pure" religious and spiritual environment—a kind of utopia of holiness—far, indeed, from the repressive thumb of crown and state church. When New England seemed to decline, Miller rightly highlighted the preachers' concerns over the fraying of what we today call "personal piety." In part because its methodology dictates its focus and the questions it asks, social history has allowed us to see to what extent Puritan piety was indeed also and perhaps foremost a social piety, which for them ideologically and practically meant a whole lot more than looking into their neighbor's business. Put simply, because of the work of the social historians in a veritable multitude of what have come to be called "town studies" of villages throughout New England, we now have a clearer picture of what Puritanism was all about and how well Puritans accomplished their goals.

The preceding narrative of the history of Puritan New England as it bears upon the plausibility of the Weber thesis relies on a wide variety of works, social and literary, and these need not be repeated in this brief survey other than to point briefly to a few central directions and conclusions. A sufficient number of "town studies" in the new social history had appeared by 1973 for one pair of scholars, T. H. Breen and Stephen Foster, to conclude in an important summary article that American Puritanism's "greatest achievement," its "most startling accomplishment," came in "fifty years of relative social peace" ("Greatest" 5). This came, as they point out, during a period of general turmoil and strife in England and Europe. In accounting for this phenomenon, Breen and Foster point to a series of factors, not the least of which was the social vision promulgated by Puritan leaders such as John Winthrop, whose "A Model of Christian Charity" summoned all voyagers to New England to be "knit together in the bond of love" and "brotherly affection" and to live together "in all meekness, gentleness, patience, and liberality." Such an attitude infused New England's medieval hierarchical class structure with remarkable degrees of cooperation, interdependence, and charity. Nor has subsequent research significantly changed that conclusion. A mounting number of accounts of small inland New England villages strongly suggest that Winthrop's vision, spoken as it was by an elite leader, actually filtered down to a local lay level. So successful were some of the small inland subsistence farming villages that in 1970 Kenneth Lockridge in his landmark study of Dedham, Massachusetts, described it, perhaps somewhat lavishly, as a "Christian Utopian Closed Corporate Community" (*Town* 16). While by no means not all New England towns shared this harmony and stability, the social vision that animated them was, says Lockridge, "common to the founders of nearly all the towns in the first waves of New England settlers" and, as such, initiated "the mainstream of a wide and enduring New England tradition" that would be felt through the nineteenth century (167).

The drive that fueled whatever degree of social accomplishment the Puritans pulled off came no doubt from the very Puritanism of the Puritans, so to speak. Puritanism was, to be sure, theologically "precise and fervent" intellectually (Marty, *Pilgrims* 63). It also entailed a vigorous and deep religious commitment. They were beset by a particular disposition or temperament, a complexion of spirit that made them decidedly this-worldly, intensely earnest, and energetically reverent of God, the church, morality, and humanity—all traits in "the Augustinian Strain of Piety" that Perry Miller called the hallmark of the Puritan spirit. Most who came in the early years were this sort of Puritan. As studies of motives for migration have shown, their desire and motives in coming to the New World seem to have been primarily religious, and once in New England "they imbued their society with a deeply spiritual significance" (Anderson, "Migrants" 382). The "peasant ethos" of medieval English localism that venerated utopian ideals of a cooperative village life of security, stability, interdependence, and harmony was fired anew by Puritan zeal. The extent to which this was the case for most of New England has recently been highlighted by Jack Greene in his *Pursuits of Happiness*, a comparative study that compares the social histories of New England and those in other regions along the Atlantic seaboard.

In the midst of emphasizing the success of New England, it is important to note, however, that not all parts of Puritan New England enjoyed such well-being as the outland villages. In addition to the inland subsistence farming communities described earlier, there were an urbanized coastal region, towns like Boston and Salem, and a zone of highly commercialized agriculture, as in the Connecticut River Valley (Innes, *New Land* xvi). Less isolated and more commercial, Boston only briefly, if ever, shared in the sort of cohesive social vision of the agricultural towns (Rutman; Henretta, "Ethic"). By the time of Winthrop's death in 1649, barely two decades after settlement, Boston citizens, churched and unchurched alike, were "generally failing in their duty to community, seeking their own aggrandizement in the rich opportunities afforded by land, commerce, crafts, and speculations, to the detriment of the community" (Rutman, *Boston* 243). Other towns, like Springfield, founded on the frontier for commercial exploitation by William Pynchon, differed still more radically from the cooperative farming village, looking mostly like a modern-day company town (Innes, *New Land*). For still other towns along the Connecticut River the record conflicts, depending on what social historian is reading the data. Where one has seen harmony akin to Massachusetts (Bushman), another has detected strife and acrimony from the start, often involving clerical domination (Lucas). On and on the list might go, as studies of local communities have come forth. It is fair to say, however, that most communities started with similar high visions. More difficult interpretive questions intrude when scholars question to what extent those visions were realized and how soon and why they began to loose their cogency, and those questions do, indeed, occasion a whole host of diverse and fascinating responses. As there are many accounts of the social achievements of New England, historians have also reckoned with the origins and sources of its "declension" or decline religiously and socially, and there is again a variety of explanatory models, most of which point to the fading zeal of the founders' generations and the pressure of ever-increasing population on limited quantities of land.

In addition, scholars of Puritan America have continued to undertake the intellectual history modeled by Perry Miller, and several of those studies have contributed to understanding the "collective culture" of New England Puritan life that shaped and supported their relatively harmonious social mores. Notable in this regard is Harry S. Stout's *The New England Soul: Preaching and Religious Culture in Colonial New England* (1986) which offers a thorough examination of the substance and powerful role of preaching in New England culture. Similarly, George Selement's *Keepers of the Vineyard: The Puritan Ministry and Collective Culture in Colonial New England* (1984) records the often remarkable engagement and influence of New England clergy in the fabric of the small communities in which they usually found themselves. Charles Cohen's *God's Caress: The Psychology of Puritan Religious Experience* (1986) examines the religious sensibility that composes the psychological and emotional backdrop for the public life of Puritan communities. Of particular interest in Cohen's work is the apparent, resolute Puritan focus upon divine love both in the drama of the soul and in the life of the community. Charles Hambrick-Stowe's *The Practice of Piety: Puritan Devotional Disciplines in Seventeenth-Century New England* (1982) looks at the role of devotional literature in the religious life of Puritan New England. The work of C. John Sommerville, particularly his content analysis of religious best-sellers in *Popular Religion in Restoration England* (1977), reveals the surprising absence of either predestinarian, "work ethic," or wealth admonitions in English Puritan best-sellers, especially in contrast to frequent Anglican encouragements to labor. The same is true for Paul Seaver's analysis in "The Puritan Work Ethic Revisited" of the extensive journals of London Puritan artisan Nehemiah Wallington (1598–1558), who showed no signs of an entrepreneurial appetite and who wrestled with the methods and meaning of obtaining money, even within the limits of barely sufficient income.

For better or worse, Puritanism made a sizable and indelible impression upon the culture and political history of the United States. That is where interesting historical disputes begin, with the "better or worse"—in this case, on the questions of the nature of Puritanism and how it has affected, and still does, the shape and texture of American culture. A long, venerable tradition of scholarly work on Puritanism has illumined much of the genesis and heritage of innumerable American practices, political, economic, religious, and, lately and especially, social. More research constantly appears on popular religion and Puritan intellectual culture, social life, and historical influence. Clearly, these questions have more than antiquarian value. These historical estimates have immediate pertinence in much current public policy debate. Both liberals and conservatives have encouraged a politics of recollection—the effort to recall America to an elusive set of attitudes, customs, and mores, often referred to as distinctively Protestant or Christian, that some time back, at some unnoticed juncture, the country as a whole seems to have abandoned. The most prominent of these recollections has been the resurgence of an energetic Christian cultural and political conservatism. Much the same sort of recollection of an exemplary past informs the work of prominent religious sociologist Robert Bellah in his influential 1975 book, *The Broken Covenant: American Civil Religion in a Time of Trial.* With Winthrop's social vision in mind, Bellah lamented America's neglect of a Puritan communitarian social vision or, for that matter, any social cohesive national vision. The same concern pervades Bellah's latest project, coauthored with four others, *The Habits of the Heart: Individualism and Commitment in American Life.* In that book, Bellah et al. try to identify a commonly held coalescent center of value, other than individualism, that informs contemporary American life. Their search does not meet with much success. A similar search for a usable past informs Barry Alan Shain's *The Myth of American Individualism: The Protestant Origins of American Political Thought* (1994), in which Shain recalls the Puritan social vision and cohesive social bonds as prescriptions for the breakdown of traditional American liberalism. Apparently, the New England Puritans are still saying their piece.

Chapter 4

Benjamin Franklin, Cotton Mather, and Individualism

Few figures in American history have carried so much mythic weight, so many dimensions and overtones, so much controversy as Benjamin Franklin—diplomat, politician, businessman, scientist, philosopher, inventor, public servant, author, and, in all these accomplishments, self-made man par excellence. Indeed, the conjunction of these feats put Franklin in a unique category in American history, a niche occupied by Franklin alone. The uniqueness of that niche is partly indicated in the lasting popularity of his books. While no remotely precise sales figures are available, the consistent production over the centuries of Franklin's *Poor Richard's Almanac, The Way to Wealth*, and the *Autobiography* very probably makes him the best-selling author in American history (if this is not true for all genres, it surely applies to the sales of nonfiction). If Franklin's publishing success has been dwarfed by the prolific sales of contemporary romance writer Barbara Cartland or, to cite a latter-day self-help proponent, Norman Vincent Peale, neither of these popular authors nor any self-help proselytizer has paralleled Franklin's mammoth influence upon the length and breadth of American culture. While Franklin's own books have remained popular, the person and his life have in their own right over the centuries attracted enormous attention, sustaining the lively legend of Ben Franklin. Over 4,000 scholarly and popular articles on Franklin have appeared since 1721, a number probably unmatched by any other figure in American history (see Melvin Buxbaum's two-volume, annotated reference guide).

The mainspring and core of Franklin's perduring message as writer and cultural icon have been his counsel of self-help, and that advice appears even in his fabled kite-flying proof of the existence of electricity. In the ingenuity and bravado of his experiment Franklin witnesses to the heroic determination and capacities of the solitary inquirer. In his life as in his preachments, Franklin epitomized the self-made man, and in the telling of his own story in his *Autobiography of Benjamin Franklin*, Franklin has had a still unmatched impact on American culture. Abraham Lincoln, Horatio Alger, and Jay Gatsby surely follow in Franklin's wake in the popular imagination, but even as each is variously indebted to the tradition to which Franklin gave so much impetus, none go beyond Franklin's role in promulgating the lure and influence of a philosophy of individualistic self-help as an abiding referent in American self-understanding. Moreover, Franklin's philosophy and self-portrait initiate, in the words of John Cawelti, the vocational pattern that gave rise to "a new hero" who would come to be the "model," the very "archetypal" definition of personal success in America (9). This "new ideal of human excellence and virtue" would entail, as it inevitably must, "a correspondingly new concept of the social order" (12). As more than one historian has commented, Franklin's example and his work remain the "classic statement of the American Dream of material success" (Silverman, "From" 106; Lemay, "Autobiography" 201).

The clearest and most immediate measure of Franklin's influence appears in the number of his aphorisms on wealth-getting and life in general from *Poor Richard's Almanac*, a best-selling almanac he cowrote and produced for nearly twenty years, that still reverberate far into the faceless mass conformity of twentieth-century America. With such living evidence of Franklin's lasting influence, questions about past and present popularity and influence are relatively easy to settle and depict. Clearly, Franklin's life and writing have exerted enormous power in shaping habits and mores as well as perceptions of self and society. Questions about the nature and means of that influence have, however, occasioned considerable debate among Franklin scholars and historians of American culture. Of primary interest here are those questions about the nature and value of Franklin's self-help ethic. This larger question breaks down into four separate, but interdependent, questions: the nature of Franklin's prudential morality; the differences between the public and private persons; Franklin's self-help ethic's consequences for American social harmony; and finally, its relations to the Puritan past, of which Franklin is often seen to be a direct, though secularized, descendant.

AN IMPOSING LIFE

Franklin was born in Boston in 1706, just a few years after the birth of another famous American with whom he is often contrasted, Puritan theologian and evangelist Jonathan Edwards, and in scholarly books and essays the two continue to be contrasted as a way in which to highlight different traditions and directions in American culture (Oberg and Stout 4–5). Appropriately enough for their son's future as America's foremost promulgator of sturdy independence, Franklin's parents were candlemakers of industrious and scrupulous tradesman stock. As a conscientious Presbyterian, Franklin's own father viewed the world far more with the eyes of the Puritan past than with the confident and very secular empiricism his famous son would adopt and celebrate. The father intended Benjamin for the ministry until he came to recognize the high financial cost of preparing his son for the profession. Instead, following in his father's vocational model of small tradesman, Franklin apprenticed at age twelve to his brother James, who had earlier established himself as a printer and journalist. Through five rather stormy years with his brother, Franklin anonymously published his first satirical pieces and America's first series of journalistic essays, the Silence Dogood papers, in the *New England Courant* (1721–1726), a newspaper published and printed by his brother (Lemay, *Reappraising* 19). As Franklin tells it, a decisive spat with his brother—probably as much due to the feisty spirit of the apprentice as to the overbearing temper of the employer-brother—prompted the younger brother to run off to the anonymity of Philadelphia, which was then the second largest city in the colonies. Franklin's description in the *Autobiography* of his raggle-taggle first entry into Philadelphia and his encounter with the woman he would marry stands out as "the most artful paragraph" in the work and has become one of the most famous vignettes in American literature, one which is, from one recent critic's perspective, both "cunning and effective" for Franklin's construction of his own self-mythology (Wilson 24, 25). In Philadelphia, Franklin supported himself for over a year as a printer's assistant. With the promise of letters of credit from colonial governor William Keith, Franklin ventured off to London to buy equipment with which to start his own printing business, but the promised letters never materialized. Indeed, young Franklin's time in England proved one long misadventure. He returned to Philadelphia in 1726, where he worked for two years as a printer's assistant before starting his own business.

After this rather unpromising early history of failed beginnings, Franklin seemingly set himself to the mundane task of making his way in the world by living the life of discipline and service that would make him world-famous as the archetypal American. He launched his own printing business in 1728, married Deborah Read in 1730, and began his series of *Poor Richard's Almanacs* two years later amid a competitive field of six other Philadelphia published almanacs (Granger 129). Both the *Pennsylvania Gazette*, a newspaper he bought from Robert Keimer in 1729, and *Poor Richard* soon became under Franklin's guidance the best-selling periodicals in colonial America (Lemay, *Reappraising* 20). Franklin continued the almanac series for nearly two decades, eventually averaging 10,000 copies a year in sales. In his early thirties, Franklin was appointed postmaster of Philadelphia and then elected to serve in the colony's assembly. By his late thirties, he had turned increasingly away from business to public service—instituting the American Philosophical Society, planning for the University of Pennsylvania,

and, in a more practical sphere, inventing the Franklin stove. So successful
was Franklin in his newspaper and almanac ventures that by 1748 four-fifths
of his sizable annual income came directly from his writing (Wilson 56–57).
As such, Franklin would become the first American "working outside the
ministry and not depending primarily on either private wealth or public
sinecure" to gain "both wealth and celebrity from his writing" (65). Indeed,
at age forty-two in 1748, Franklin was sufficiently wealthy to retire altogether from business and devote all his energy to public service. For the
next nine years, until he was sent to England to plead Pennsylvania's economic cause, Franklin worked with his famous electricity experiments, and
their success won him an appointment to the prestigious British Royal Society. At the same time, his record as Pennsylvania postal director won him
appointment as deputy postmaster general for the whole of the colonies.
For the eighteen years following 1757, Franklin was mostly in England,
where he served as Pennsylvania's ambassador to the throne, a post in which
his success won him similar appointments from other colonies in search of
effective representation. By the time he returned from England in 1775, he
had unquestionably become the most famous and powerful American in
England, if not in all of Europe.

In 1775, again back in America and entering the final phase of his career,
Franklin was chosen a delegate to the second Continental Congress. In the
climactic following year, he took part in drafting the Declaration of Independence and was appointed to be one of three ambassadors to France
whose chief purpose was to seek aid for the North American rebels. Bril-
liantly successful, Franklin won the French to American support and a defensive alliance. At the end of the Revolution, as the most significant
American in Europe, Franklin signed the peace treaty between England and
the new United States. When he finally returned to America in 1785, he
was promptly elected to the presidency of the state of Pennsylvania. He also
played a prominent role in framing the Constitution. Two years before his
death at age eighty-four in 1790, he completed the *Autobiography*, a project
he had begun almost two decades before and which would become, in the
words of one historian, "the most popular and influential American autobiography of all time" (Zuckerman, *Chosen* 146). His funeral would draw
20,000 mourners, a fact that by itself offers ample testimony to the notoriety
of Franklin's life and public career. His national reputation was, of course,
enormous, and in addition, Philadelphians could hardly turn around without
noting Franklin's many innovations for their public welfare—everything
from lightning rods to paved streets, street lamps, fire departments, and
circulating libraries. The *Autobiography* gives Franklin's version of his life, a
moving and mythic story told, as Kenneth Silverman comments, "from the
point of view of his own legend" (Silverman, "Introduction" ix). The poor
and footloose lad from Boston had made good in terms that would become
the measure of success in the American future: he won the girl who had

mocked him, served his country well, and became wealthy—all on his own. Estimates of his personal wealth at the time of his death valued his estate at one-half million colonial dollars.

Franklin "straddled his century like a colossus," and by the time of his death he had been widely "acclaimed the representative American of his age" (Zuckerman, *Chosen* 145). A large part of that stature derived from that fact that while Franklin had become a successful writer, he had also achieved stature as a "serious writer," and no others of the kind in America and only a few in England had thus far "enjoyed anything like Franklin's success at reaching large audiences" (Wilson 56). By any standard, then— political, economic, social, literary, or ethical—Franklin's was an extraordinary life, the very prototype for rags-to-riches mobility. To be sure, Franklin did not grow up in the rags of poverty. Rather, he started in the shop-keeper's plain cloth, but that hardly suggested the full measure of authentic fame he would achieve by devoting his energy first to his own pecuniary betterment and then, once that wealth was attained, to the welfare of his region and his would-be nation. The full measure of Franklin's success, con-tribution, and influence, even in a relatively fluid and mobile society, can hardly be underestimated. Science, civil engineering, government, diplo-macy, administration, publishing, real estate, and popular writing—in each of these areas Franklin made unique contributions, and never since has America encountered a person who mastered so much in so many areas.

BEN FRANKLIN AND POOR RICHARD

While there is little doubt about the great range of Franklin's interests and accomplishments—probably the closest America has ever come to a genuine Renaissance man—no such quick certainty is possible with regard to the actual character and ideas of the man himself. There exists, in other words, long-standing ambiguity in key areas of Franklin's thought and leg-acy, enough so that critics have often talked about the difficulty of locating the "real" Franklin, and disagreement still persists among historians about crucial elements in Franklin's personality, life, writing, and thought. For example, it is often suggested that the actual Franklin stands some distance from the numerous personae or variably fictional voices he utilized in a great portion of his writing, including *Poor Richard's Almanac*, the *Autobiogra-phy*, and even many of his personal letters. The variety and subtlety of these many voices have often been so great that interpretations of individual sec-tions of some of his works, especially in the *Autobiography*, have diverged widely. It is generally acknowledged, even by Franklin's most vehement pro-ponents, that it was Franklin's habit to tailor his remarks and modes of presentation to his reader, whether that audience was the thousands who imbibed Poor Richard's homely wisdom or a personal correspondent Frank-lin wrote on a specific issue.

The matter of how much Franklin concealed himself in any one piece, whether by persona or irony, remains unresolved to this day, and that question speaks to the problem of locating the actual Franklin. One stance, taken up in the extreme by modern British novelist D. H. Lawrence, accepts a straightforward portrait of the man who wrote them. The result is to see Franklin as the pioneer of modern Babbitry, of greed and smugness, of a trite, status-mongering acquisitiveness. For Lawrence and others like Herman Melville, Franklin constituted the prototype for the stunted mental and emotional range of the modern, middle-class American whose end in life is the pursuit of the petty and trivial (Gilmore 122–24). Many of Franklin's defenders would concede the partial accuracy of such harsh assessments of the image conveyed in Franklin's popular writings. These defenders seek, however, to balance the negative moral thrust of the popular writings by reinterpreting them, either by setting them within the context of Franklin's total canon or by revising understandings of the way they were received by his audience. Others would dilute their possibly bad effects by attempting to understand their role within an exacting historical context. A last group, the more literally inclined, asserts that Franklin's popular works have simply been victim to a long tradition of misreading that has overlooked Franklin's frequent use of irony and self-deprecating humor.

Among the various areas of dispute about Franklin, none are more important for the history of self-help than his advice for the pursuit of wealth, an inquiry that quickly opens to larger questions about the nature and import of Franklin's philosophy of ethics. The important topic of wealth-getting appears prominently in his popular writings and has drawn a variety of interpretations. The major note of criticism of Franklin in the getting of wealth has been his advocacy of what might be called a prudential ethic that makes material and social status morality's chief end. Certainly, this strain seems to characterize many of the maxims contained in *Poor Richard's Almanac* and all those that were collected in *The Way to Wealth* and have since been passed on orally for many generations and now form a part of America's folk wisdom. Franklin did not originate most of the advice contained in the full run of the *Almanac*, but he was directly responsible for most of the *Almanac*'s early contents, borrowing freely from many ancient and modern sources and improvising much material himself (Granger 139–45). As time went on, and Franklin devoted himself to other interests, his associates took over much of the labor of composition, although Franklin retained final editorial control.

Poor Richard's Almanac was but one of many almanacs and self-help guides in Colonial America, and its success helped make Franklin a rich man. In it, Franklin gave advice on a whole range of matters, from choosing a mate, to excess drinking, to how long relatives might stay without causing domestic strife. Also included with Franklin's pungent and witty formulation on the conduct of life were matters of astrological and zoological curiosity.

The most consistent concern, however, a preoccupation shared by Franklin and his public, was the means of getting wealth, and the centrality of this interest has bothered Franklin's critics for centuries. Throughout the twenty-five years of publication, the almanac's narrator, poor Richard Saunders, counseled a careful and calculated management of all of one's resources, both tangible and intangible. Time, energy, money, and friendship are hoarded and cautiously directed toward the goal of raising one's status economically and socially. From the perspective of this self-interested prudence, as it is often called, certain sorts of behavior could be advocated quite apart from their intrinsic religious or moral worth and were subsequently justified according to their effectiveness in attaining personal security—in other words, how well they worked. The most famous of these maxims was the advice that "honesty is the best policy." Here honesty is wise because dishonesty is likely to bring more trouble than ease; disadvantages for the self outweigh advantages if dishonesty is discovered. Similarly, pride is condemned not because it is intrinsically wrong but because it leads to personal bad fortune in the loss of friends and diversion from necessary tasks. In short, it is not useful for building up material well-being, and its expression often pushes on into material excess and thus into debt.

A second complaint against Poor Richard's economic counsel was that his advice on wealth paid little heed to the social consequences of individual wealth-getting. A narrow and relentless concern with one's own estate in life is reiterated throughout. Occasional items bid avoidance of excess in wealth, but in those suggestions the dangers are vaguely stated and are always termed dangerous for potential injury to the self, such as excess in food and drink. Such entreaties, though, are far outnumbered by the frequency of admonitions on the specific means of establishing one's own prosperity. Franklin's caution against wealth warns not against wealth itself but only against its distorting blandishments, which often lead to its loss. Poor Richard's advice tends more toward making sure the wealthy keep their wealth instead of frittering it away in finery or even in excess charity. "Get what you can, and what you get hold" is not a doctrine to encourage lavishness in anything save work and hoarding. Indeed, "if you would have a faithful servant, and one that you like, serve yourself," says Poor Richard. Such notions cannot be credited with furthering trust between people generally, let alone between servants and masters. Moreover, they argue strongly for a moral posture of exclusive self-concern. Regardless of their flavor, however, in the rhetorical marketplace of ideas, the very wit and pithiness of such mottoes go a long way toward vindicating the sentiment conveyed. Their style partakes of the very efficiency and shrewdness that the saying advocates.

That Franklin and his audience took this all very seriously is well indicated by the fact that in 1758, when Franklin chose to end his quarter-century run of *Poor Richard's Almanac*, he did so with a collection of Poor Richard's previous twenty-some years of guidance on accruing wealth. "The Advice of Father Abraham" or, in its later pamphlet title, *The Way to Wealth*, became a best-selling work in the colonies and abroad. Its many aphorisms have lived on to the present, although their users usually do not know their origin. In this special last valedictory edition, Poor Richard hears an old man, Father Abraham, lecturing a group of people (Michael Gilmore sees the use of this biblical allusion for the central character as a "clever attack on the Calvinist clergy" [120]). The entire lecture consists of quotations on wealth from previous issues of the *Almanac*. The most notable feature of the rendition of *Poor Richard* given by Father Abraham is the lecture's climactic reference to the relationship between providence and wealth, and here, true to form, Franklin places religion within his utilitarian frame of reference. In this concluding and seemingly obligatory nod to piety, gratitude, and humility, Father Abraham warns against depending "too much" on "Industry, and Frugality, and Prudence." We are told that "the blessing of Heaven" is also necessary. In the total context of *Poor Richard's Almanac*, piety and humility are now seen as requisites to wealth and not as worthy ends in themselves, which constitutes a marked departure from traditional Puritanism. If wealth is a blessing for piety, the poor and humble should not be scorned, for they, too, may possess virtue in the making, even as "Job suffered, and was afterwards prosperous." In any case, human worth and virtue are assessed and valued only in their relation to present or future wealth. All in all, it is very difficult to see the run of *Poor Richard's Almanac*, especially its distillation in *The Way to Wealth*, in any other light than an unremitting advocacy of the individual pursuit of wealth by means that are selfishly prudential, if not altogether expedient.

Some historians argue against this line of critique by distinguishing between narrator Poor Richard Saunders's individualistic work ethic and writer Franklin's purposes in writing. For them, Poor Richard's views are an intentionally homely expression of Franklin's very sophisticated view of human nature, and in themselves Richard's opinions possess a good deal of cogency. This perspective contends that Franklin's work ethic was expressly and sensibly geared to the needs of the times. America was largely an agricultural, frontier society. Even in its more settled communities, the demands of domestic agriculture were great and hard, and sloth and carelessness readily led to personal failure. Farm life would long continue to be so, as Hamlin Garland's tales of the rural life in the northern plains during the late nineteenth century so well illustrate. Here, out on the hard-scrabble frontier, the demands of circumstance did not allow settlers to fret over purity of motivation or social altruism. The more immediate and probably higher matter of urgency was plain physical survival and modest material improvement, ends that in themselves can hardly be labeled excessive or greedy. The critic needs to be careful, as Louis Wright has cautioned, not to see in the colonial period the same sort of use of *Poor Richard* and the *Autobiography* that became prevalent in the Gilded Age—that is, the easy justification for a rather heartless work ethic. If Franklin's ethic of labor and prudence seemed to emphasize the practical routes to economic well-being, such a model was well and, one might say, humanly suited to quite specific and pressing social exigencies (I. Cohen 61–62). Franklin wished to make life on the agricultural frontier possible by inculcating habits necessary for survival, habits that by their necessity became virtues.

Another perspective that justifies Franklin's prudential ethical counsel argues that it followed quite naturally from Franklin's vision of an ideal frontier society. A prominent strain in Franklin's thought foresaw life on the small farm as normative and satisfactory in the New World, the foundation for achievement of personal and social health in a new culture. While diligence and frugality were necessary for frontier farm life, the same virtues constituted routes to personal and civic virtue. Given a seemingly endless frontier and the agricultural basis of life in the New World, Franklin struggled to fashion a moral code that would accommodate these facts. As Charles Sanford has commented, Franklin's "moral vision was colored by the presence of the frontier" and shaped its substance (68). For Franklin, who could not have envisioned Gilded Age industrialism or modern agribusiness, the modest prosperity of farm life was adequate for personal physical well-being, and since great wealth from the farm was unlikely, it was also a benign barrier against the excess and opulence that had corrupted the European social order, a condition of which Franklin was acutely aware. In contrast to the European model, a free and moderately prosperous population would very likely find a new degree of contentment and happiness and thereby establish a new American social reality. Whether a product of economic jealousy or a remnant of the Puritan Ethic, as Edmund Morgan has argued, moral aversion to European social and economic inequality, especially to aristocratic exorbitance, greatly influenced American resolve to avoid European practices, to fight the British during the Revolution, and to shape a society that would have a unique future (Cawelti 15–16). The didactic intent behind Poor Richard's methods and attitudes of hard work was not only to provide a way to wealth, at least on a modest scale, but to foster an agricultural pattern for a new society of seemingly endless frontier. In short, say Franklin's defenders, Franklin could not foresee the extent to which his ethic for the yeoman would also be a model for the tradesman and entrepreneur.

A third line of interpretation of Poor Richard's economic ethics seeks to diminish its prominence in Franklin's original intentions for the *Almanac*. John Ross has noted that the character of narrator Richard Saunders markedly changed through the twenty years of the *Almanac*. Through roughly the first six or seven years, he is only slightly the economic adviser and far more the genial buffoon—an "entertaining philomath," student of curiosities, and "comic astrologer" (35, 36). Only with time does the maker of economic proverbs begin to displace the character of the humorous, star-gazing lover of learning. Thus, one of Franklin's original main purposes in the *Almanac*, entertainment, lost ground to his other goal, which was in-struction. Ross further argues that the character of Poor Richard changed because Franklin was often pressed by deadlines in getting the annual in-stallment of the *Almanac* to the presses. Under such pressure it was easier for Franklin to let Richard become a natural extension of Franklin's own attitudes. There would have been far more work involved in sustaining a persona whose comic character was far removed from his own. By this line of logic, Ross strives to question the image of Franklin and Poor Richard as always being one and the same and by that means calls attention to the "real" Franklin, whose popular icon is at best a partial representation of the whole social vision and Morgan's portrait of colonial antimaterialism. Bruce Granger agrees with Ross but thinks that whatever change in portraiture occurred happened unconsciously (135). On the other hand, in light of the views in the preceding discussion, it seems likely that Franklin fully intended the change from humor to economic education in his almanac, for he clearly felt the need to promulgate the virtues of frugality and diligence that he thought lay at the core of the pastoral egalitarian society he envisioned. That this might have been the case is indicated by Franklin's decision to end the series of almanacs with the collection of economic proverbs that made up *The Way to Wealth*. A prudential economic morality might at times be in the best interest of the individual and the social body of which that person is a part.

Similarly, biographer Carl Van Doren contends that for *Poor Richard* to be justly understood, the prudential, utilitarian proverbs must be seen within Franklin's larger ethical vision, even though that vision is not fully revealed within the *Almanac*. Franklin's economic maxims constitute but a small portion of a huge array of comment on a host of various subjects (96–98). While this may be true, it should be noted that even those that deal with self, marriage, or sin carry a distinctively utilitarian air of self-interest. A stronger case for less focus on Poor Richard as even a proximate reflection of Franklin's full ethical system is made by John Cawelti and, with regard to the *Autobiography*, David Larson. Like others who write of the impor-tance of the frontier for Franklin, Cawelti sees Poor Richard's wisdom as part of a frontier ethos that created a practical and empirical temper. Cawelti extends this logic, however, to suggest that Franklin held out wealth as a lure to civic virtue, which was coincidental with diligence, frugality, and seriousness: "how better stimulate man to practice this bait than by showing that wealth and comfort could be achieved by this means? This was the role of Poor Richard" (15). The primary, though hidden, end was personal and social rectitude, with the first leading to the second. In the agrarian setting, the virtues necessary for obtaining wealth coincided with the path to social rectitude; it was consequently possible to hold forth the promise of wealth and still anticipate positive societal development.

FRANKLIN AND THE *AUTOBIOGRAPHY*

This same sort of discussion over the meaning and intention in the *Almanac* is only amplified in interpretations of the *Autobiography*, especially as they relate to crucial and famous passages. Cawelti, for example, finds an enormous difference between *Poor Richard* and the *Autobiography*. If the former were read as a primer on wealth-getting, the memoir "presented a broad and humane ideal of self improvement" which assumed "responsibility towards one's fellow man" (16). Still, as many novelists and historians have pointed out, the *Autobiography* has not, on a popular level, been interpreted in this benign manner. Often, sympathetic interpreters have been moved to exonerate Franklin of a popular message that, however much the public likes, they clearly do not. Franklin's defenders suggest that the *Autobiography* has been taken too seriously, has been consistently read without noting the "humorous self-criticism," if not thorough irony, that Franklin intended (Levin, "Autobiography" 55). The more judicious apologists do admit that Franklin is not without guilt in contriving a character or persona, much as in the later *Almanac*, whose primary task is more instruction that self-revelation. Franklin chooses to feature certain elements of his career in order to accomplish a didactic, dramatic purpose that is not much different from that behind Poor Richard. Once again Franklin wishes to inculcate certain values, only here the method is changed. Instead of pithy advice on how to become financially prosperous, the reader receives a narrative in which the narrator, in complex ways, is the hero of his own tale; instead of maxims, the reader is given dramatized illustrations of the truth of those maxims from Franklin's own life. In a way, one might say that the debate over Franklin has been over whether Franklin was haughty, foolish, deceptive, or manipulative in undertaking such projects as *Poor Richard's Almanac* and his own instructional life story as told in the *Autobiography*.

Three episodes, the most frequently cited from the *Autobiography*, serve to indicate the gist of the narrative and ensuing debate over its meanings. The first and most famous recounts Franklin's first entrance into Philadelphia as a penniless young man eating a large loaf of bread with two others tucked under his free arm. Dirty and ragged from a rough boat trip, his plight is worsened when he is laughed at by a young woman standing in a doorway. Seven years later, we are told, a now prosperous and respected Franklin marries the very same girl who had scorned him on his bedraggled arrival in Philadelphia. In this sequence, the American archetype for rags-to-riches prosperity and marrying the boss's daughter is born. A second familiar event is the manner by which Franklin attained his initial success as

a printer in Philadelphia. Here he describes his efforts to appear always respectable and industrious before his neighbors, even if such an appearance
was all a charade enacted only to impress those neighbors. Here and in other
like incidents, we have a return to the advocacy of the prudential ethic that
informs much of *Poor Richard's Almanac*. The last such episode details
Franklin's attempt to construct what he called an "art of Virtue," which
was an attempt to design a pathway to moral perfection. Franklin isolated
thirteen personal virtues for the purpose of prolonged ethical development:
temperance, silence, order, resolution, frugality, industry, sincerity, justice,
moderation, cleanliness, tranquillity, chastity, and humility. The intention
was to create the habit of each virtue by concentrating on one per week,
thus allowing for four repetitions of the complete list each year. The project
has been attacked as naive, arrogant, socially myopic, and self-serving.

For better or worse, because of their unusual vividness of description or
intellectual novelty, these instances have stood out in Franklin's account
with the effect of obscuring or overshadowing most other parts of the *Autobiography*. The entrance to Philadelphia is usually interpreted to set the
tone and the shape of the work as a whole, the progress of the young man
not only from poverty to riches but also from foolishness to wisdom and
from selfishness to service. In adopting this scheme some see Franklin's clear
intention to mimic Christian literary forms that see life as pilgrimage or
conversion. The first half of the biography, it is generally admitted, is devoted to the journey toward wealth. As Franklin suggests, the accomplishment of wisdom and service is simultaneous upon the accomplishment of
wealth; virtue leads to wealth. "It was . . . everyone's interest to be virtuous
who wished to be happy in this world," material possession being a part of
wealth and happiness. Franklin can conclude that "no qualities were so likely
to make a poor man's future as those of probity and integrity." Within such
a scheme of virtue, as critics of Franklin have been quick to point out, virtue
becomes both instrumental and utilitarian. In the first instance, as with religious faith that expects blessing, virtue might be used to get something
else, which would be material betterment. Virtue is sought for some goal
other than itself and not for the love of virtue. So also with the utilitarian
stance. Here virtue is pursued out of self-interest or, one might say, even
self-love, since the virtue is understood to be no more than one's own enlightened self-interest. Some critics, such as J. A. Leo Lemay or Norman
Fiering, see in Franklin a clear anticipation of American pragmatism and
Victorian utilitarianism.

Many defenders of Franklin see the gist of the *Autobiography* as an uncharacteristic or a partial expression of Franklin's ethical thought and seek
to place its negative implications, as do the defenders of the *Almanac*, within
a larger and more tolerant scheme. Some admit that Franklin was, in part,
responsible for conveying a mistaken impression in the *Autobiography*. While
his intention was different and more complex than what appeared, there was

a "great error in communication" (Levin, "Autobiography" 53). Admitting this gap between intention and effect, David Levin tempers Franklin's utilitarianism by placing it in the context of the new wave of scientific inquiry that had steadily gained momentum since the Renaissance. Living in "an age of experiments, an age of empirical enlightenment," Franklin tends to discount tradition and abstruse metaphysics (49). One feature of utilitarianism is its susceptibility to methodological trial and error, to the experimental testing of theories and assumptions. With such a temperament, Franklin was prompted "always to consider major questions in terms of simple practical experience." Levin further argues that Franklin applied this empirical bias to testing the correctness of moral ideas. This stance, combined with a mild distrust of human nature, persuaded Franklin of the necessity of "demonstrating the usefulness of virtue" (53). Similarly, I. Bernard Cohen finds in Franklin a blend of frontier realism and a scientific bent that results in an ethical experimentalism. In ethics as in science, "an experimental test" proved "more important in evaluating the worth of concepts than their logical consistency or their mutual relatedness in a system" of philosophy (63). An allegiance to empirical verification could, for Franklin, only work to put personal ethics and social goodness on surer ground. In demonstrating an empirical base for the wisdom and effectiveness of an ethical system, he had hoped to shore up general rectitude.

If the empirical temper of the Enlightenment made practicality an effective criterion for formulating ethical standards, the age's vision of human creatures as rational also gave added impetus to a prudential morality. Critics have differed widely over Franklin's view of humankind's moral nature. One party sees deistic optimism about people and their ability to know God and goodness and to do the latter. The opposing side looks to many private comments by Franklin to suggest that Franklin was either a growing or thorough pessimist concerning the native tendencies of the species in knowing or caring about the good. It is probably reasonable, though, to follow a recent suggestion by David Larson that Franklin varied somewhat in his opinions but most often held a middle ground about a person's moral state. Whatever the case may be, however, Larson does make clear that Franklin's ethical appeals, as in the *Autobiography*, most often utilized a two-leveled approach that partook of both confidence and caution about humanity's eagerness to pursue the good. Rather, Franklin appeals both to love and sympathy for others and to personal self-interest. Franklin insisted "that moral behavior is profitable as well as intrinsically virtuous because he wanted to make good use of man's selfish as well as selfless impulses" (118). Franklin believed goodness itself was obvious or self-evident to the sensible person, but apparently in cases where sensible folk were not plentiful, he would leave nothing to chance. If humankind did, indeed, not carry an inborn or innate goodness within, the individual was at least rational enough to assess logically personal interest, and if seen clearly and rationally, that self-interest would necessitate opting for the larger social good. Within this social vision, then, self-interest became crucial for the well-being of society as a whole.

These interpretations of Franklin's ethical thought go some way toward clarifying the shaping vision of the *Autobiography of Benjamin Franklin*. Still there remains the problem of gauging the impact of the lessons its strong didacticism wishes to teach. The intention and the accomplished act, which is the intention's tangible product, are, after all, two different entities. As David Levin, one of the most astute and cogent defenders of Franklin, acknowledges, Franklin's "decision to portray himself as an inquisitive empiricist, the very success of his effort to exemplify rural virtues in accounts of practical experience, his doctrine of enlightened self interest—all these combine to make him seem philosophically more naive, and practically more materialistic, than he is" (Levin, "Autobiography" 57). While Levin sees the content and effect of the *Autobiography* as unfortunate and perhaps unintended or at least unreflective of the true Franklin, a less sympathetic historian, Melvin Buxbaum, views Franklin's venture as all the more unfortunate because it was quite intended by, and indicative of, the true Franklin. In his *Benjamin Franklin and the Zealous Presbyterians* (1975), Buxbaum argues that Franklin's narrator was a self-flattering distortion of the actual Franklin, his history, and the American national character. As Buxbaum views Franklin, the scientist-diplomat was inordinately concerned with his place in history. The *Autobiography* constitutes Franklin's most significant attempt to create the personal image of himself that he wanted to leave behind (10). For his own historical legacy, Franklin created "defensive and positive images" at the cost of numerous historical distortions and untruths, concerning everything from his role in the post office, to the founding of the University of Pennsylvania, to incidents of religious bigotry, and to colonial politics (17). Generally, throughout his memoir, Franklin is "less interested in strict historical accuracy than in defending himself against damaging attacks on his character by inventing a plausible, delightful, and very useful but imaginative protagonist . . . who, especially in the future, would stand for the actual man" (28). Moreover, Franklin not only fostered "a defensive myth of Franklin" but also strove to make his memoirs "a national document, albeit a propagandistic one" (27, 31). In making himself likable and scrupulous, he exonerated his conduct and provided an admirable portrait of a country where Franklinesque virtues were acknowledged and rewarded. The scientist, teacher, and all-around helper became the prototype for what should be in America, a country on whose cause and future Franklin had staked his reputation and hopes.

FRANKLIN AND THE PURITAN ETHOS

Surely one of the more unhelpful habits of historians of early American culture and ideas has been the constant practice of labeling Franklin and his ethic as Puritan in spirit and origin. This historiographical usage, for long virtually an intellectual custom, now seems to be undergoing some critical scrutiny or is at least acquiring some greater precision in the use of the label Puritan. Its persistent, wholesale application has been at the expense of considerable historical clarity about, as one historian has put it, "the intellectual forces in early America" (Fiering 200). The cost has been especially great in attaining rudimentary understandings of both Puritan history and Franklin's biography. Of course, a good deal of this interpretive tradition has derived from a consciously broad interpretation of the ethos associated or emerging from American Puritan history; the term Puritan could label any idea or social practice that had but the faintest relationship to the realities of historic Puritanism. By and large, then, references to Puritanism have failed to distinguish between Puritanism early or late or, for that matter, English or American. Further, the supposed Puritan influence on Franklin has been cited to account for the undesirable, individualistic aspects of his ethic, while the influence of Enlightenment rationalism has been seen to have prompted this thought toward more democratic and "Progressive" stances.

Max Weber, the founder of modern sociology, began this historiographical convention of broad use in his famous *Protestant Ethic and the Spirit of Capitalism*, whose relation to the history of Puritan New England is discussed in the preceding chapter. Weber thought he saw in Franklin the fruition of a Puritan impulse toward the sanctification of money-getting through the exaltation of particular rationalized values and attitudes. While Weber suggested the initial tie between Puritanism and Franklin, he left the specific historical conduit for the values of Puritanism into Franklin relatively uncharted in his discussion. In the early 1930s in America, in what has probably been America's most anthologized and cited article on the self-help tradition, A. Whitney Griswold, who was much later to become president of Yale University, sought to make the supposed linkage more apparent. Still, his mistakes are the same as Weber's. In "Three Puritans on Prosperity," Griswold asserts that Franklin was "the soul of Puritanism" or "authentic Puritanism" (45, 47). He bothersomely leaves that essential core of Puritanism that Franklin embodied largely undefined other than to point to Franklin's avowed indebtedness to Cotton Mather's *Bonifacius: or Essays to Do Good* and to characterize Puritanism as "the piety of individual prosperity" (46). The elusive center of Puritanism, at least of Mather's late sort, was, then, the tendency to let religion sanction "the customs of society," which in Puritanism was for Griswold an inordinate concern with money-making (43). Griswold looks to Puritan teachings on vocation and calling and Mather's encouragements on economic discipline for the source of Franklin's emphasis on the methodology of getting rich. He fails to engage the more complex question of how Franklin, whose religious opinions might at best be called deistical, might still sensibly be called a Puritan in any historically meaningful sense of the term. Nor are the lines of transmission into Franklin of the full and "authentic" Puritanism explored. Griswold is nonetheless sure of Franklin's status as Puritan, which itself is but most vaguely and unsatisfactorily suggested. Lastly, Griswold knew nothing of the findings of recent social historians that establish that Puritan American was very largely communalistic and stringently anticapitalist. Moreover, in a recent essay upon the bicentennial of Franklin's death, A. Owen Aldridge, the foremost scholar of Franklin's religious attitudes, has vehemently protested the practice of dubbing Franklin a Puritan, although some suggest he protested too loudly ("Alleged Puritanism").

Despite deficiencies in both Weber and Griswold, the frequent practice of referring to Franklin as a Puritan, especially in his work ethic, has become a historical convention. The tendency has been to identify the unsavory aspects of his practice, person, and persona with the Puritan past and to designate his democratic and more liberal social views as having their origins in the Enlightenment. While there might be some truth in this causative formulation, it has become a tiresome and unquestioned refrain. As recently as the national bicentennial, church historian Karl Weintraub reiterated the Weber thesis on the connection between Puritanism and Franklin's work ethic (1976). Although Weintraub offered a superb short rendition of Weber's thesis, especially in its fostering of modernization, the essay fails to take any account of decades-old critiques of Weber. The notion of predestination as a catalytic agent for the Protestant Ethic—an idea that even Griswold rejects as "over-subtle"—is elaborately detailed. Even though Weintraub is more fully reasoned and clearer than Weber himself, the essay falters for its lack of historical grounding. There is little doubt that Franklin is an example of early "stress on pragmatic rationality, on utilitarian ethics, on individualism, on rational management and organization, on the 'purpose-rationality' inherent in industrial capitalism, and on legal constitutionalism" (225). However, Weintraub's case for the Puritan origins of these elements falters for lack of specific reference insofar as he cites only two American sources, Mather's *Bonifacius* and an obscure diary. Franklin apparently imbibed the Puritan past by osmosis: "the work ethos . . . *must* have entered the very bones of the young Franklin. . . . He developed it further, and . . . systematized it with immense rational consistency" (233; emphasis added). The critic must wonder, as in the case of Griswold, how a personality can be Puritan, as Weintraub himself phrases the question, "without the Puritan motivation or the Puritan objective" (231). Franklin accepted his inherited Puritan values because they seemed wise and useful apart from their religious origin, and Franklin's supposed deism stressed moral order and purpose in the universe (233, 236). While a weak support, argues Weintraub, the deism nonetheless did serve as a minimal, but adequate, prop in Franklin's essentially nonreligious sensibility. If the internal logic and contours of Puritanism so changed by the time they reached Franklin, it can only be wondered what is gained either semantically or historically by continued reference to Franklin's ethics as being in any reasonable way genuinely or even tangentially Puritan.

Similarly, an essay on Franklin by David Levin calls Franklin in its subtitle "the Puritan Experimenter in Life and Art." Again, the wisdom of this descriptive tact must be questioned. Levin argues that the interpreter could not overestimate the importance of Franklin's Puritan heritage, but perhaps that comment effectively works to diminish the significance of other youthful influences of a deistical slant, particularly Franklin's own reading in Locke and Shaftesbury and adolescent association with his deist brother. Levin bases his argument for labeling Franklin a Puritan experimenter on the conspicuous presence of Puritan virtues of personal discipline, as does Weintraub, of Puritan notions of public service, and of the Puritan and especially Bunyanesque literary model of pilgrimage that Franklin adopts for the structure of the *Autobiography* (45–46). As significant as these associations are, one must wonder how much Levin's criteria for Puritanhood measure up to any criteria actual Puritans themselves would devise. Levin acknowledges that the Puritan pilgrim was concerned with "doing right for the glory of God" (45). Yet, a hallmark to Franklin's approach to ethics, as to science, was, again as Levin argues, a taste for experimental proof, which itself reflected the rational and inquiring spirit of Franklin's time, "when every freeman might, if wary and lucky, learn by experience and test for himself" (49). Hardly an American Puritan from Winthrop to Cotton Mather could rest easy with this sort of experimentalism in significant ethical questions, as the histories of Ann Hutchinson and Roger Williams well attest. To submit the ethical to the caprice and whim of personal inclination and circumstance, no matter how grounded in self-evident rationality, would be to overlook Puritan insistence on a fallen human nature and an objective, transcendent moral authority. To experiment with, and test, the moral dictates of God as, by and large, clearly displayed in Scripture constituted, in effect, a questioning of the metaphysical stature of God. Surely reason and experience were important aspects of the Puritan mode of negotiating the earthly pilgrimage, but the interpretive frame for their legitimate activity was always narrowly prescribed. To plunge beyond these constraints was to forsake the ship of orthodoxy and be set adrift in a sea of subjectivism and delusion, even if the latter did bear the name of reason. The label Puritan can stretch only so far, and, reasonably, the psychic landscape must form a crucial line of demarcation between Puritanism and what follows.

Melvin Buxbaum dislikes the practice of dubbing as Puritan Franklin's attempt to achieve moral perfection. Buxbaum suggests that not even the most religious Puritan would have trouble with the list of virtues Franklin wishes to master. There is, in other words, some continuity in form in the emphasis on practical virtues. However, the Puritan would see the enterprise as inadequate and foolhardy, as lacking a mainspring, which would be faith and piety. Any strict Calvinist, says Buxbaum, "would be horrified by the framework of the project, the atomistic approach to reform, and by assuming that men could achieve anything like perfection without having first undergone the conversion experience" (*Presbyterians* 90). In short, the whole conception of Franklin's ethical project discards in wholesale fashion the inner core of Puritanism, even in its often supposed late diluted and temporizing remnant. Franklin's confidence in the ability of the individual, sensible person to discover and enact goodness constitutes a gargantuan shift in consciousness or orientation. While Franklin emphasized many Puritan traits—diligence, sobriety, and frugality—in the process of making these values prudential, self-justifying, and self-serving, he emptied Puritanism of its religious catalyst and replaced it with a different agent altogether.

On the question of the Puritanism of Ben Franklin, a host of recent scholars have weighed in on the question in a collection of essays comparing Franklin and Jonathan Edwards: *Benjamin Franklin, Jonathan Edwards, and the Representation of American Culture*, edited by Barbara Oberg and Harry Stout (1993). None of the pertinent essays on possible kinship between the two subjects link the two together on the basis of shared Puritanism, even so far as citing influence of their common past on Franklin. Rather, essay after essay develops the significant differences between Puritan Edwards and whatever it is that Franklin had become. On the question of what sort of ethics his understanding of human nature dictated, Daniel Walker Howe contends that Franklin emphasized a morality that featured "tangible temporal rewards" and saw virtue as "a good bargain" ("Franklin" 80). In contrast, Edwards bluntly rejected Franklin's prudential self-interest, instead seeing Christianity as the only way to tame the intense "self-preoccupation that corrupted the human heart" and to initiate a selfless or true virtue that contained at its center "benevolence to Being in general" (85, 89). Church historian Edwin S. Gaustad argues that the foundations of Franklin's ethics lay more in anthropology, works, and consequences than a Puritan could countenance (46). Franklin and Edwards brought to belief and ethics "sharply different cosmologies and theologies," although they both agreed that genuine virtue was spontaneous, volitional, and fruitful and took notice of the role of self-interest; the route to these and substance of these traits greatly differed, however (49). Similarly, Elizabeth Dunn argues that an insurmountable "wall" stood between "Edwards' theocentrism and Franklin's humanism" (63). Edwards and Franklin shared interests in both science and religion, but their understandings of, and work within, those fields were opposite of one another. As Dunn summarizes, "Edwards viewed revivalism, science, and reason as means to an inherently valuable end, the glorification of God." For Franklin, however, "means had become ends in themselves, and he applied his usual standard of utility to every case" (70).

Finally, the inadequacy of citing a Puritan background for explaining Franklin's utilitarian prudential ethic has been rather fully shown by Norman

S. Fiering's essay on "Benjamin Franklin and the Way to Virtue" (1978). Through extensive historical and logical analyses, Fiering identifies the origins of Franklin's moral theory with seventeenth-century adaptations of Aristotelian moral tradition, a heritage that stressed the acquisition of moral behavior through practice and habit. This perspective stood apart from two other prominent traditions in the West: the Platonic, which stressed virtue as the product of right knowledge, and the Judeo-Christian, which emphasized conversion of a person's inmost moral disposition. Throughout his examination, Fiering is careful to indicate the "profound division between Franklin's thinking and that of the Puritans" (202). Once the intellectual sources of Franklin's thought are investigated—from Plutarch to Locke—it becomes amply clear that his moral theory derived "from a particular and rather mechanistic eighteenth-century form of the Aristotelian tradition" and "was antithetical to any meaningful idea of Puritanism." With an approach that was "essentially neo-pagan," Franklin "placed almost exclusive emphasis on slow, incremental modification of external behavior," much in the manner of today's psychological behavioralism (206, 223). Fiering contends that the theory of virtue through habit was very much a part of Franklin's time, eventually coming to dominate "the Western imagination as a means of progress" (207).

The Puritan vision, on the other hand, contended that any virtue worth having emanated from a "divine infusion" that effected "a decisive change of heart resulting in a reorientation of the appetites or affections" (221, 222). Fully missing from Franklin's understanding of life, as Mitchell Breitweiser comments, is the " 'organic turmoil' of 'conversion' during which the particular man is transformed" (228). The practice of real virtue, then, could only be "infused rather than acquired" (Fiering 205). The primary mode of Puritan moral psychology—what Fiering calls "scrupulosity" or "that intense self-examination" for "purity of intention"—is entirely missing from Franklin's moral reflection (207). Not only is the inmost wellspring of Franklin's moral life markedly different from that of his Puritan forebears, lacking in religious impetus, but the very tenor of the moral imagination and venture lacks the rigor of Puritan self-inquiry. While Franklin admitted significant moral failures early in life, his eventual habit was to "call them errata, a compositor's slips of the hand, a metaphor that will greatly reduce the implication of any intense participation of the self in the commission of mistakes" (Breitweiser 237–38).

Moreover, if Franklin lacked the temper of Puritan moral passion, he differed as well in matter-of-fact moral strictness. In ways that Puritans would consider inconceivable, Franklin could tolerate some prudential hypocrisy as long as its effects were either personally or socially benign, such as was the case with his seeking to appear the industrious youth or the humble do-gooder when he had no real inclination for either quality. There is no doubting the success of the often positive social benefits of Franklin's pretense.

However, even as a means of accomplishing a good cause, dissembling would have been greeted as "contamination" by the Puritans (Fiering 217). Fiering even doubts the Puritan character of the famous thirteen virtues, whose acquisition is the end of Franklin's moral experiment. Almost all the virtues can be attributed to a tradition, especially Greco-Roman, other than Puritan. When seemingly "Puritan virtues do appear, such as frugality and industry, their inclusion results not from religious inhibitions" but from their instrumental role as supports of economic and social order (Fiering 221).

THE CASE OF COTTON MATHER: PURITANISM, SELF-HELP, AND HISTORICAL INFLUENCE

It has been the historiographic habit to equate the worst of Franklin's morality with the legacy of Puritan minister Cotton Mather, a towering figure in his own time who has become something of a gargoyle in American popular culture. To understand this contention fully, it is necessary to review briefly the foundation for the claim that Mather prepares the way for Franklin. That begins, of course, with particular understandings of the nature of Puritan culture.

With its roots in England and before that in the European Reformation, Puritanism's visions of religion and culture had imbibed the Calvinistic spiritual dialectic between humankind's radical fallenness and God's gift of grace and salvation. The result was an acute consciousness of the moral insufficiency of the natural person. This sense of unworthiness led to a rigoristic ethic in pursuit of sanctification—the acquisition of holiness or godliness, which was a long process of righting the self in fulfilling the promise and reality of grace, of making oneself Christlike or fit for God. In this enterprise of conversion and nurture, the English Puritans, like the Protestant Reformation as a whole, fully employed the new technologies of printing, a resource that can hardly be underestimated (Bercovitch, "Vision" 34). Books were everywhere, being cheap and varied, and the British public was surprisingly literate, rising to roughly one-third of the adult male population by the mid-seventeenth century (Sommerville, *Popular* 20). The first how-to books, which were also the first best-sellers, were religious and moral in origin and intention.

The creative reaches of Puritanism's fervent religious imagination no doubt found its popular and artistic fruition in Englishman John Bunyan's *A Pilgrim's Progress* (1678), an immensely popular tale of worldly temptation, spiritual struggle, and redemption—a fictional how-to rendering of the earthly sojourner's path to salvation. While Bunyan's novelistic allegory was a somewhat unusual form for its day—perhaps bridging the distance between the medieval morality tale and the emergence of the novel—the same impulse for offering practical help and inspiration was by no means uncommon. Englishman Lewis Bayly's *The Practice of Piety* (1612), a devotional guide of advice on the route to godliness, appeared in over twenty editions, and Joseph Alleine's *The Sure Guide to Heaven* (1672) sold 50,000 copies in the colonies. Between 1660 and 1711, *The Whole Duty of Man* (1657; traditionally ascribed to John Rawlet, it was probably written by Richard Allestree) went through forty-five editions and totaled 135,000 copies, one for every ten families in England (Sommerville, *Popular* 29). Emphases within such guides varied from spiritual development to resisting temptation and, in one of the genre's more controversial topics, the duty of daily practical charity and doing good. At their most popular these guides became a significant current of popular religious influence and reflect a significant appetite in their English public, loyalist and dissenter alike, for religious counsel and personal direction (Hambrick-Stowe 279).

Most of these books found their way to New England, and their successes were more or less repeated in the colonies. Before long, however, New Englanders were producing such for themselves. Surely, the most controversial and influential American author of the genre was also one of the most controversial and famous of Puritans, in his own time and ever since in the eyes of historians. Puritan minister Cotton Mather (1663–1727) was the grandson of two revered Puritan founders—the English Puritan ministers Richard Mather and John Cotton—and son of the famed New England minister Increase Mather. A man of brilliance and tremendous energy, Mather preached at the distinguished Boston North Church for some forty-five years. Moreover, he was active in contemporary politics, science, medicine, and evangelization—most notably as a judge at the Salem witchcraft trials and as an advocate of smallpox inoculation. He buried thirteen of his fifteen children and lived with the disappointment of a prominently reprobate son. Within such a full life, he published 388 works and left the components of many more in his diaries and notebooks. His literary and historical reputation rests securely on his *Magnalia Christi Americana*, the first full-blown interpretation of American history and destiny. In spite of these accomplishments, or perhaps because of them, historians of New England have not until recently looked kindly upon Mather. Even those who have esteemed Puritanism as a whole, such as Perry Miller, have recoiled from Mather's personality and have charged Mather to have been bigoted and seriously neurotic, something of a "national gargoyle" (Silverman, *Life* 425). As David Levin has recounted, Mather has become an ogre in American cultural history, being labeled a "monster" or the "Puritan everybody loves to hate" by those who should know better (*Forms* 163). The accuracy of such portraits has, in recent years, gone under significant revision in biographies by historians David Levin and Kenneth Silverman.

Mather's significance in the history of religion and self-help in America emerges from the small, but popular, portion of his writing that dealt with questions of vocation and social ethics. It has been supposed by some his-

torians and commentators that Mather represented, encouraged, and sanctioned wealth-getting and what has become known as the Protestant Ethic,
as delineated by German sociologist Max Weber. That frequent claim rests
primarily on two works, *The Christian at His Calling* (1701) and *Bonifacius:
An Essay upon the Good*, popularly known as *Essays to Do Good* (1710), which
went through eighteen editions by 1940. In the earlier work Mather stressed
a two-faceted vocation for the believer, which had become a commonplace
in Lutheran and Calvinist sectors of the Reformation. The first, or general,
calling entailed conversion and allegiance to Jesus Christ. The second
stressed worldly vocation, wherein the Christian was called to engage in
practical employment for the benefit of society. In both callings whatever
the Christian undertook was not primarily for personal gain but done in
grateful praise to God and for the good of his fellows. For historians the
importance of Mather's formulation lay in its emphasis on the obligation of
gainful activity and its justification of secular pursuits. Neither of these had
been strong themes in pre-Reformation theology. The duty to undertake
an energetic vocation to supply others and oneself with necessities and good
repudiated any lingering tendency toward quietism or monastic withdrawal.

The impulse behind Mather's worldly activism is made clearer in the more
controversial *Bonifacius: An Essay upon the Good*. Facing an increasingly
secular and seemingly decadent Boston—full of rapid economic expansion,
alcohol, gambling, and brothels—Mather set forth in *Bonifacius* an assortment of recommendations to the godly for restoring piety and social and
personal morality. Within its time, *Bonifacius* represented an expansion to
include ethics in the increasingly popular spiritual guide, a flourishing genre
of religious manuals that burst with aphoristic prescriptions for, and sum-
mations of, the spiritual life (Hambrick-Stowe 276). While many critics,
including Perry Miller, have seen this work as indicative of a decline of the
Puritan moral vision into legalism and nosiness, it is equally plausible, as
David Levin has suggested, to see it as a latter-day "natural extension of
the kind of impulse that led Puritans to establish the New England colonies
in the first place," that is, the expansion of "God's work in the world"
("Introduction" xv). Along the lines of the Weberian critique of Mather,
Virginia Bernhard has seen in *Bonifacius* a "Puritan Gospel of Wealth"
because Mather argues that the doing of good for one's fellow creatures
will reap divine blessing in the form of material prosperity. In urging the
practice of charity, Mather played on worldly "hopes of temporal advantage" (235). Riches became the "enticing bait" that would spur people to
benevolence, thus "turning self-interest into a social force directed to the
betterment of community life" (238–39). Irony lay in Mather's formula,
argues Bernhard, because his "instructions for getting on in the world
contributed to the very fragmentation it was designed to combat. Instead
of producing a revised version of Winthrop's holy community, it justified
economic individualism and inspired Puritanism's most famous dropout,

Benjamin Franklin" (239–40). In short, according to Bernhard, Mather inadvertently fostered the very individualism and acquisitiveness that he wished to impede (241).

A close reading of Bernhard's assertion calls her conclusions into question. Bernhard's line of argument would have more weight if the sort of calculating charity that she detects amounted to more than even a minor note in either *Bonifacius* or Mather's preaching and were it not far overshadowed by Mather's refrain on extravagant, disinterested charity. While it is impossible to determine what within Mather's message readers might have fixed on, they would have had to have been remarkably selective if Bernhard's interpretation constituted the message they took away from their reading of *Bonifacius.* Mather's discussion of possible divine recompense for the giving of money to the church and poor covers but two pages in a 160-page work and is surrounded by passionate moral and religious arguments for charity. Mather's intention in *Bonifacius* is straightforwardly and unambiguously stated and is often and variously repeated. It begins with the traditional Calvinistic insistence on gratitude for the love of God as conveyed in divine grace, whose recognition is the end and beginning of life. For Mather, as for the Puritans generally, all were to live with "the strains of gratitude . . . since God has brought you into His marvelous light!" (Mather 22). Insofar as that light is simultaneously a restorative love, a true and full apprehension of it quite naturally entails

engaging as many others as we can, to join with us in this our blessedness; thereby promoting His Kingdom . . . and in studying to do good unto all about us; to be blessings in our several relations; to heal the disorder, and help the distressed of a miserable world, as far as ever we can extend our influences.

Indeed, the very inmost character of the love describes the essence of Christian wisdom and "the main purpose and pleasure of . . . life" (6). The moral and experiential desirability of this goal elicits some of Mather's notable verbal histrionics: all "must embrace it with rapture, as enabling him directly to answer the great END of his being. He must manage it with rapturous delight, as a most suitable business, as a most precious privilege. He must sing in those ways of the Lord, wherein he cannot but find himself, while he is doing of good" (19).

Such hyperbolic urgency results, in part, from Mather's characteristic manner of rhetorical inflation when writing on favorite topics of importance. In addition, however, as the whole of *Bonifacius* implies, Mather addresses his work as an admonitory sermon to an increasingly secular audience that, however churchly and pious they might continue to be, are nonetheless sagging in their pursuit of an earnest social holiness. More and more energy and ingenuity seem to pour into money-making and, once gotten, its flamboyant display. Mather seemed to sense, perhaps even more than understand, the increasing vibrations in a gradual seismic change in the religious consciousness and social texture of New England. As prosperity mounted, what psychic energy was before directed to personal meditation and community welfare was usurped in "devising many little things, to be done for ourselves! We apply our thoughts, with a mighty assiduity, unto the old question, What shall I eat and drink, and wherewithal shall I be clothed" (23). While writing *Bonifacius* Mather frequently preached emphatic denunciations of lavish living and wealth and indicted business corruption and ruthlessness. The culprit was clear enough. Instead of satisfaction, economic expansion seemed only to fuel avarice and with that a corresponding decline in community welfare. In the place of the old communalistic ethos of the forebears came widespread material display that competed and blended with, and even sometimes supplanted, usual definitions of respectability.

The predicament is not an easy one for Mather. By 1700 enough structural change had transpired in New England to force clergy to find new ways of conveying their social ideals. As always, they had recourse to the tract and sermon, of which *Bonifacius* is a prime example. By the turn of the century, however, such works necessarily bore more argumentive weight. For one, the traditional status of the clergy had declined, due, in part, to their own wrangling over theology and status and to their role in the witchcraft trials. Moreover, in 1691 the crown had revoked the old Massachusetts Bay Charter and since installed its own governors, none of whom were necessarily sympathetic to the ideals or personnel of the Puritan establishment. Thus, the clergy could not rely on the apparatus of the old church–state alliance that had dominated New England for over fifty years. A last challenge for the old-line clergy was the new rationalistic flavor in orthodoxy that softened the old rigors by insisting upon reasonableness in thought and behavior. Thus, in an increasingly voluntaristic religious environment clergy necessarily improvised what means they could to sustain bygone levels of Christian influence. *Bonifacius* itself is an expression of the problem that attempts to deal with the problem, that is, how best to retrieve the diverted attention of the prosperous saints to the primary work at hand: "WHAT IS THERE THAT I MAY DO, FOR THE SERVICE OF THE GLORIOUS LORD, AND FOR THE WELFARE OF THOSE, FOR WHOM I OUGHT TO BE CONCERNED?" (32).

Very simply, Mather urges a refocusing of attention, concern, and energy. All should meditate, as did their forebears, on their own religious state, inspecting the soul for its affections, its true loves and hopes. Further, the devout should not accept even inadvertent leisure or idleness but turn such minutes to active goodness. Rained-out farmers and unbusy shopkeepers should "[b]e not fools, but redeem this time . . . to the best advantage" (39). With such idleness, "if men would set themselves to devise good, a world of good might be done" (17). One need not look far: "Be glad of opportunities to do good in your neighborhood: yea, look out for them, lay hold on them, with a rapturous assiduity. Be sorry for all the bad circumstances of any neighbor," especially those "who have done hurt unto you" (59, 61). There, as in all domains of life, Christians must comfort and relieve affliction, reconcile conflict, and seek justice (66). Community leaders of all sorts—teachers, doctors, lawyers, magistrates—bear special responsibility by example for the ethos of the society. Ministers, in particular, should be "grave, discreet, humble, generous" and "engines to do good," taking "a particular notice of the widow, the orphan, the afflicted" (71, 73–74). Clergy "ought to be shining examples of liberality to the poor, and pour down their alms like the showers of Heaven upon them. Yet all should endeavor to do what they can this way" (79). Of such are doctors, who, like ministers, "are even overstocked with opportunities, to help the poor, and heal them for nothing" and become for them living angels (101). Above all, the rich must know the divine source and holy purpose of their wealth so they might lavish wealth upon the poor as God has given to them and Christ has bid them (113). These fortunate should go far beyond the tithe in support "for schools, and for colleges, and for hospitals . . . for a general good" (116). Such advice hardly seems counsel for wealth-getting.

Throughout these proposals Mather laments, implores, and cajoles, strategies that indicate the clergy's changed rhetorical predicament. The most concrete and controversial indication of his circumstance's changed political alignments and cultural shape comes in his proposal for "reforming societies," organizations of volunteers that, on one hand, would guard public morality by reporting drunkenness, sloth, swearing, and church absenteeism and, on the other, provide charity and education to the needy (133–34). Later critics, including Perry Miller, would see in the impetus for such organizations concerned about public virtue the nadir of Puritan morality, the angry, nosy repressiveness of the Puritan goblin, and the decay of spiritual fire into a cold and legalistic moralism. In these societies for doing good, other historians see the origins for Franklin's well-known Junta and other public welfare schemes. Given these harsh judgments, it is necessary to put Mather's hopes within their historical context. For one, as discussed before, Boston and New England society seemed to be in a state of decay with conspicuous increases in drunkenness, harlotry, violence, disease, and commercial self-seeking. The social texture of New England seemed to turn wasteful and mean, and such voluntary associations promised one route to at least slowing the erosion. Social needs were clear, and Mather's groups were to reach where church and government would or could not go and there assume responsibility for the relational obligations that government and private social agencies would gradually take on later in American history. The concern for the welfare of the larger society here persists as a remnant of the vanishing New England communalism. As David Levin specifies, "specific needs in the society, needs unmet by government or other established organizations, encouraged the new techniques for organized benevolence and that in the absence of better preventive methods religious writers naturally encouraged Christians to set an individual example" and by organizing set "free men for the practice of virtue in this world" ("Introduction" xxi). The strategy itself comes less from Mather as an expression of his own complex psyche than from either or both of two other sources: the reforming societies of pietist German count Zinzendorf (the Slaves of Virtue) and Enlightenment notions of consensual civic organizations of the sort that Ben Franklin would advocate for Philadelphia (the Society for the Free and Easy).

Mather's case for such organizations appeals to traditional Puritan emphases, and he seemingly goes out of his way to convince a critical and cautious audience that God will note and prosper such grand human ventures. He reminds his readers of biblical encouragements of the active pursuit and expression of love. Foremost is the fullness of wisdom and satisfaction found in active service to God and others, as opposed to the mere avoidance of evil, which is a lesser form of wisdom and virtue. Further, the doing of good offers "a sure way, a sweet way, effectually to bespeak the blessings of God on ourselves," a strategy that harks back to, and insists upon, the older Puritan emphasis on gratitude. Mather then directly invokes divine gratitude: "Who [are] so likely to find blessings, as the men that are blessings?" (150). The appeal here is clearly not to material blessing but more to divine intercession in behalf of the do-gooder. Each good act is both an expression of gratitude and a petition for mercy:

Every action we do for the Kingdom of God, is in the efficacy of it, a prayer for the kindness of God. While we are at work for God, certainly, He will be at work for us, and ours: He will do for us, more than ever we have done for Him; far more than we can ask or think!

The goodness done, if done as a form of prayer, partakes of Christ's repeated promise that God answers in love and mercy all prayer. In pursuing the wisdom of love, the self is also made wise, and thus a reciprocal momentum is established. There is in closing the promise of prosperity, although Mather means the term not in a material, but in a spiritual, sense. Taken out of their pious context, some of Mather's statements can, indeed, be misconstrued, but to do so is to commit a "serious error," cautions David Levin, that misrepresents writers and the time in which they lived ("Introduction" xii). To be sure, Mather struggles throughout to convince his readers that God not only approves but encourages an active goodness (150). Mather implicitly accuses his audience of a step toward quietism, an emphasis upon the private devotional life as the fullness of the Christian life to the exclusion of active social engagement.

Mather does set forth the ideal of an intentioned, disciplined, and ordered individual and social responsibility, seemingly applying to ethics the careful analysis and calculation of modern business planning. The usual notions of "being good," passive and inoffensive, are no longer sufficient, given the social and moral crisis under way. Mather again urges vocational responsibility but emphatically does not urge a heedless pursuit of wealth. Moreover, his concern is to impede the self-centered neglect of societal well-being. He finds greed and business trickery to be "abominations" in the sight of God. A like degree of passion and inventiveness should be put to the service of the community and the God whose love bids that service. Mather attempted to imbue all human activity with a rigorous and ordered focus—grateful devotion to God and eager labor for community well-being. For the New World Puritans, Mather among them, the wellspring and hallmark of work were the divine love conveyed in Grace. In receipt and gratitude of this gift came the impulse to work. Puritan religious psychology postulated that the convert would "rejoice in love, and . . . celebrate . . . with godly works," and in such, "the real motive to work develops" (Charles Cohen 119). "Society is the ground on which the Saints parade their obedience, and the force that energizes their performance is godly love engendered by the apprehension of agape redeeming and regenerating them" (130). Indeed, David Levin points out, "What we need to remember, then, is the firmness with which Mather's good-doing is tied to the praise of God, the certainty with which his exhortations to be diligent rely on traditional ethics. *Bonifacius* is addressed to Christians" ("Introduction" xxi). Mather's vision would long linger in American culture to sustain a deep ambivalence about the purposes of individual labor for the self and riches.

To understand the path of modern culture, and America within it, and self-help within America, it is important to recognize, as Donald H. Meyer has emphasized, that Benjamin Franklin, in his popular and formal writing, "represents a frame of mind that is fundamentally different from that of former ages, one that, in some ways, has more in common with what we call the modern secular consciousness than it does with all the centuries that preceded him. . . . We are, in other words, witnessing an important episode in the shaping of the modern sensibility" ("Religion" 147). Indeed, it is difficult to underestimate the momentous nature of Franklin's thought and public cultural impact. Franklin aptly summarizes this change himself in his account in the *Autobiography* of the summoning of lightning in the discovery of electricity. Wonder lay in the man-made miracle that "electricity could be brought to earth and bottled by the device of a key on the string of a kite." As such Franklin in good scientific fashion recorded "observed fact" that well signified, first, the shape of "the modern period—the appropriation of divine virtues by the earthbound secular self"—and second, in the West as a whole, an "alteration in imaginative perception" (Breitweiser 211; Meyer, "Religion" 165). Franklin's exclusive focus on the efficacy of empirical method in science carried over to religion and ethics, which he believed to be equally orderly, rational, and straightforward and thus readily susceptible to human understanding and use (Meyer, "Religion" 151). Clearly, the cultural shift in the West, with Franklin as the popular American herald, "added to our understanding of the world and our comfort in it" but did so "at the price of transcendence, a sense of cosmic comfort, a magic lamp of enchantment and spirituality" (149). In the wake of this gradual, but enormous, change toward empirical and pragmatic biases, "modern people developed the habit of equating the real with the material, and of regarding what is beyond the sense or immaterial as unreal" (163).

HISTORIOGRAPHICAL DISCUSSION OF FRANKLIN AND HIS LEGACY

Lasting and significant historical ambivalence surrounds the figure of Benjamin Franklin. Whether as a significant participant in American history or in subsequent American culture as one of its shaping myths, Franklin's influence has been enormous. After Washington and Lincoln, probably no American has been better known, and it can be argued that Franklin's actual influence surpasses theirs. Franklin's historical and cultural prominence has elicited widely varying—very often fully opposed—evaluative judgments. After two centuries of interpretive comment, biographers, historians, and literary critics still regularly lament the difficulty of getting a fix on the "real" Franklin.

No small part of this historical quest results from the widespread adulation Franklin enjoyed at the time of his death. Between 1760 and 1790, Franklin's *The Way to Wealth* had been reprinted twenty-one times and for a few years brought Franklin £10,000 annually. In the first decade following Franklin's death, parts of the *Autobiography* appeared with other writings at least fourteen times (Miles 121). The influence of Franklin's writing through *Poor Richard's Almanac, The Way to Wealth*, and the *Autobiography* melded with his fame as inventor, scientist, philosopher, and diplomat to make Franklin a likely candidate for cultural hero. In 1830 Noah Webster included Franklin along with Abraham, Moses, the Mathers, and others in his *Biography for the Use of Schools*. Other schoolbooks added to Franklin's renown. Webster's work followed upon the myth constructed by Franklin's greatest advocate, the Reverend Mason L. Weems, a biographical popularizer who had also written on George Washington (and given us the apocryphal cherry-tree story). Weems's *The Life of Benjamin Franklin* (1816) perhaps did more than any other work on Franklin to establish an enduring reputation and provided a self-help image that persisted throughout the Gilded Age (Buxbaum, *Critical* 5). This rags-to-riches theme exaggerated the drama of Franklin's life to provide grist for Weems's sermonizing mill. In the same way, wanting to provide a Christian culture hero, Weems shined up Franklin's deism to look like old-line orthodoxy. High in entertainment value and moralizing, Weems's *Life* went through eleven editions in thirty years (White 204).

In 1840 popular historian and Harvard College president Jared Sparks added more favorable comment in his edition of *The Works of Benjamin Franklin*. Sparks suggested that in addition to being a wise and cunning businessman and diplomat, Franklin was a kind and honorable man in his public service (Miles 130). Later historians more or less made Franklin into what they wished. The anti-Puritan James Parton's *Life of Benjamin Franklin* (1864) cast Franklin in the mold of a late nineteenth-century social reformer with abolitionist tendencies (White 220). Cultural historian Paul Elmer More saw in Franklin's life a healthy humanistic balance that steered a middle course between religious fanaticism and materialism (White 241). Similarly, Progressive historian Vernon Louis Parrington exalted Franklin's liberation from a regressive Puritanism, as represented by Cotton Mather, into deism and political liberalism (P. Franklin 11–12). The large omnibus biography by Carl Van Doren, *Benjamin Franklin*, is still the widest and fullest of Franklin biographies. Throughout, Van Doren sought to make a coherent whole, "a harmonious human multitude," out of a figure often seen as a welter of inconsistency and contradiction.

While historians were struggling to learn more of, and better understand, Franklin, his popular reputation grew rapidly, especially in the late nineteenth century in that era known, because of its thirst for wealth, as the Gilded Age. Industrialists Jay Gould and Daniel Drew quote Poor Richard, as one chronicler of Franklin's reputation puts it, "with the dexterity of a minister quoting Scripture" (White 287). *The Way to Wealth* became a prototype, frequently plagiarized, for a deluge of handbooks on habits necessary for wealth-getting (Louis Wright, "Legacy" 273; White 288). More than one critic has wondered if Poor Richard was the prototype for the Ragged-Dick figure recurring in Horatio Alger's immensely popular success novels for adolescent boys. For Louis Wright, Franklin and his imitators provided the link that "honed the industrial and commercial spirit" of the Gilded Age to "ideas of the distant past when English commerce began its modern expansion" ("Legacy" 269). In the early twentieth century, the enormously popular periodical *The Saturday Evening Post* took Franklin for its patron spirit and regularly, under the editorship of George Horace Lorimer between 1898 and 1936, extolled his character and many virtues (White 323). Even such groups as the Women's Christian Temperance Union, citing Franklin's insistence on moderation, were eager to appropriate Franklin for their cause (White 335–36). As cultural historian Norman Fiering has noted, the notion of the acquisition of virtue and success by habit, which lies at the core of Franklin's optimistic counsel, has slowly "captured the Western imagination as a means of progress" (207). That disposition to place faith in habit lies at the heart of the self-help tradition, whether it be in the doggedness of the work ethic or the spiritual automatism of positive thinking.

While Franklin has enjoyed much general popularity among the broad public, some historians, a handful of business leaders, and a small, but notable, group of writers have rigorously criticized Franklin's cultural legacy. Nathaniel Hawthorne pointedly indicted Franklin for his prudential ethic. His friend and contemporary Herman Melville, in such novels as *Israel Potter* (1855), attacked Franklin's ruthless moralism and glib providential equations (Gilmore 122–24). Henry David Thoreau in *Walden* (1854) complained of the stifling of the human spirit by the commercial ethos. In the late century Mark Twain proclaimed Franklin's preachings on disciplined money-making to be the enemy of the high times of games and leisure to which all Huck Finns and Tom Sawyers were entitled. Like his predecessors, American novelist Sinclair Lewis steadily leveled a frontal assault on Franklin's model for humanity, which he dramatized in the naive civic boosterism of a Babbitt, in his classic novel by that name (1922). English novelist D. H. Lawrence joined this retinue of critics in his essays on American writers, deeming Franklin the worst of everything repressive and spiritless in American culture (Sanford v). And the debate goes on.

This long and controversial history of Franklin's popular cultural, historical, and literary reputations was first examined by Richard Miles in a very useful 1957 *American Quarterly* article on "The American Image of Benjamin Franklin." Miles summarizes the grounds for Franklin's disfavor among historians and then traces the origins and development of that view. Recent scholarship is then cited to modify or dispel the notion that Franklin dissembled, manipulated, self-promoted, and in general lacked "true ethical sensibilities" (118). Miles's survey concludes that recent scholarship has yielded a "nobler, more heroic Franklin," which, in his estimate, approaches the "authentic" man. A more skeptical view of Franklin and the efforts to dispel distaste for the man and his ethics is Charles W. White's published 1967 Harvard Ph.D. dissertation, *Benjamin Franklin: A Study in Self-Mythology.* In addition to analyzing the considerable evidence of Franklin's self-mythologizing in business, diplomacy, and science, White analyzes the changing popular and scholarly attitudes toward Franklin in American history and thought. The work is notable for its thoroughness and lucidity. In spite of all of Franklin's accomplishments, White concludes, with some distaste, that perhaps "it is more correct to say that Franklin's self-mythologizing has proven to be his greatest achievement" (340).

The most recent and incisive historiographic account of work on Franklin comes in Melvin Buxbaum's "Introduction" to a collection of essays on Benjamin Franklin (*Critical Essays* 1987). The multitude of American and European images make locating the whole or real Franklin difficult, due, in part at least, to Franklin's "having donned many different masks in his public and private lives" (1). Consequently, Franklin has elicited extremes of response from partisans and opponents, endlessly suspended between glorifiers and debunkers. The matter of Franklin's actual religious beliefs provides ample illustration of the interpretive extremes:

Franklin's detractors are once again as guilty of simplism, inaccuracy, prejudice, and distortion as are his friends. If his supporters ignore unpleasant realities, his opponents find serious faults where there were none. To a number of them, Franklin is a man devoid of religious or moral principles or even a hint of spirituality. (5)

Buxbaum argues that the same might be said of Franklin's economic views, in which he was neither reformer nor protocapitalist (8).

Within the changing attitudes toward Franklin, one relatively constant focus of interest for historians and literary critics has been the exact nature of Franklin's religious philosophy and belief. From the beginnings of Franklin's reputation, popularizers offered very different views of Franklin's beliefs. Debate has usually centered on the extent to which Franklin was either agnostic (although the term was not used in his own time), deistic, or traditionally Christian. As discussed earlier, Weems made him into a Christian saint, while Parton and Parrington found in him a bracing alternative to Puritanism. Into this confusion a number of scholars have ventured. Most recently Donald H. Meyer has examined "Franklin's Religion" to conclude that Franklin "represents a frame of mind that is fundamentally different from that of former ages, one that, in some ways, has more in common with what we call the modern secular consciousness than it does with all the centuries that preceded him" (147). For all his belief in God and in divine Providence, Franklin was "untroubled by real spiritual yearnings, indifferent to the supernatural, and unmoved by the Christian message of sin, atonement, and redemption." Meyer argues that, personally and philosophically, Franklin "represents not just secularity but the secularization of religious thought" (149). Like many others then and since, Franklin believed that traditional religious belief of some form continued to be necessary for the great mass of people "as a backstay for morality," without which "the entire social order" might collapse (152).

A full, lucid, and sympathetic treatment of Franklin's religious beliefs comes in Alfred Owen Aldridge's *Benjamin Franklin and Nature's God* (1967). Aldridge argues that in an experimental age Franklin "applied the experimental method to his attempt to unravel the secrets of divinity and morality" and that no "other subject occupied more of his time and reflection." For the most part, Franklin was a deist who discarded supernatural revelation for the belief "that nature communicates directly to all men in all periods of time everything that is necessary to be known about God" (6). While liking Christian ritual and fellowship, intellectually Franklin "had little more faith in orthodox doctrine than in witchcraft or astrology." A central problem for students of Franklin's religious views is "to distinguish between those notions about which he was merely curious or to which he gave only temporary or perfunctory assent, and those which he postulated as firm articles of belief" (8). Efforts to Christianize Franklin, as many of his defenders have, depends entirely on how far the proponent will stretch the term "Christian." Aldridge surveys Franklin's beliefs and the significance of his various associations with different religious groups.

Seemingly frustrated with the persistent reference to Franklin as a Puritan, Aldridge has recently written two essays that take pains to show the complete inappropriateness of the label. In "The Alleged Puritanism of Benjamin Franklin" (1993), Aldridge vigorously attacks the notion that Franklin was, in any sensible way, a Puritan. Theologically, Franklin forthrightly rejected every major point of the Reformed creeds and did not regard the Bible as inspired. Morally, his utilitarian ethics were the complete reverse of Puritan notions of God's moral authority. Franklin insistently argued that the standard for moral truth lay in its practical usefulness or utility for humankind and not in divine decree. Likewise, the notion of sin is discounted. This view derives not from Puritanism but from English deist Shaftesbury. In his economic views, as well as in his theology and morality, Franklin seemed to have far more in common with French satirist Voltaire, whose taste for capitalism and wealth far exceeded Franklin's. Temperamentally, citing Norman Fiering's views, Aldridge asserts Franklin had no use for introspective or "guilt-oriented religion" (365). Rather, Franklin's own tastes and practices suggest that he eagerly pursued "wine, women, and song," being one of the first in the colonies to demonstrate a relish for erotic literature.

In another recent essay on "Enlightenment and Awakening in Edwards and Franklin" (1993), Aldridge reiterates many of the preceding points. While Edwards and Franklin were both theistic and believed in some version of Providence, they parted ways in their sources for authority, Edwards accepting the Bible while followers of the Enlightenment "followed reason, experiment, and history" (29). While Edwards allowed for an intuitive grasp of God so long as it accorded with the wisdom of Scripture, he was still, to a large extent, a child of his century insofar as he was a rationalist within his theology, reasoning insistently and adroitly from the premises of Scripture and contemporary science. Franklin seems to have preferred, to the vagaries of philosophical reason, a kind of commonsense reason or instinct, although this, too, could prove unreliable (34). Edwards gestured in the direction of Franklin's deism in endorsing the centrality of works as opposed to words in fulfilling God's intentions for the world. Franklin, on the other hand, seemed not to reconsider at all the Puritanism that he abandoned in his youth.

A narrower book-length study of one of Franklin's institutional religious embroilments is Melvin Buxbaum's *Benjamin Franklin and the Zealous Presbyterians* (1975). Buxbaum traces Franklin's conduct through a feud with local Presbyterians who laid heresy charges on one of their young clergy. In the course of his history of the event, Buxbaum examines Franklin's carefully cultivated public persona and the history and substance of his changing religious beliefs (82–90). By and large his view accords with Meyer's. The book is especially valuable for its contrast of Franklin's "defensive myth of Franklin" in the *Autobiography* with the historical record (27). In this instance, as in many others, Franklin's autobiographical image "of the respected, useful, and beneficent founder trustee . . . does not correspond with the facts" (23).

One of the most important and carefully wrought essays on Franklin's general philosophical stance is Norman Fiering's "Benjamin Franklin and the Way to Virtue" (1978). Fiering seeks to identify, at the title implies, the origins of Franklin's famous scheme for the attainment of virtue, as found in the *Autobiography*. While Franklin's experiment in virtue has often been described as a secularized version of the Puritan moral legacy, Fiering asserts that Puritanism "has almost nothing to do with Franklin's work in ethics" and seeks to lay to rest the shibboleth that it does (200). Instead, Fiering describes a Franklin influenced by a neopagan, Greco-Roman, Aristotelian understanding of virtue as mediated by Locke (206). This stands in radical contrast to the Puritan anthropology that envisions the infusion of true virtue into the converted heart (201, 205). Franklin deems righteousness a minor chore susceptible to individual intelligence and will and fully in one's own self-interest.

While most historians no longer consider Franklin to be, in any sensible way, a Puritan, the distance of Franklin from Puritanism is emphasized in Elizabeth E. Dunn's " 'A Wall between Them Up to Heaven': Jonathan Edward and Benjamin Franklin" (1993). Dunn argues that while Franklin and Edwards lived in the same society and confronted the same unique challenges it presented, an insurmountable "wall" stood between "Edwards' theocentrism and Franklin's humanism." Nonetheless, while remaining fully opposite each other in their views, each adapted his perspectives to sustain his core beliefs, regardless of how divergent they might be. On science, for example, Edwards "pursued theoretical physics precisely because he wanted to achieve a clearer understanding of God and to give Calvinist religious philosophy a sound scientific basis" (63). In contrast, Franklin's utilitarianism pushed him to understand nature so he might better grasp its potential for use and manipulation. In religion, what Edwards valued in the Great Awakening is what bothered Franklin, and while Edwards embraced orthodoxy because it was true, Franklin opposed it privately but publicly "emphasized the need for religious values to encourage a virtuous citizenry" (67). In general, both "Franklin and Edwards returned again and again to strategies that preserved their value orientations, and those that allowed them to construct a world harmonious with their assumptions" (69). "As an essentialist, Edwards viewed revivalism, science, and reason as means to an inherently valuable end, the glorification of God. For Franklin, means had become ends in themselves, and he applied his usual standard of utility to every case" (70).

In general, scholars explain much of Franklin's religious cast by his steadfastly empiricist frame of mind, a strain in his life that provides much the impetus and strategy for his self-help orientation. I. Bernard Cohen has defined "The Empirical Temper of Benjamin Franklin" as "a respect for the data of experience and application of reason to them" (62). In practice, Franklin "considered an experiential test more important in evaluating the worth of concepts than their logical consistency or their mutual relatedness in a system," as in abstract philosophies and theologies (63). For Cohen, this was the product of both the Enlightenment and a frontier social setting that demanded practicality for survival, which account, in turn, for that "blend of idealism and practicality that he displayed" (60). David Levin explores the same theme in his essay on "The *Autobiography of Benjamin Franklin*: The Puritan Experimenter in Life and Art." Levin urges the reader of the *Autobiography* to keep Franklin's intention and audience clearly in mind, for Franklin wished very much to convey the "picture of a relatively innocent, unsophisticated young man who confounds or at least survives more sophisticated rivals" (53). Franklin lived in "an age of experiments, an age of empirical enlightenment, when every freeman might, if wary and lucky, learn by experience and test for himself" the truth of different "theories and assumptions" (49). For Levin, Franklin remains a Puritan insofar as many of those traits he most esteemed—thrift, conscientiousness, and hard work—derived from Puritanism, even though Franklin would supply a decidedly un-Puritan rationale for their validity. The stance and pattern of Franklin's life were intended to be a philosophic and practical exemplar to its many admirers.

Donald H. Meyer finds the same experimental empiricist sensibility, what he aptly calls an "intelligent handiness," informing the core of Franklin's religion (153). In science and invention, Franklin demonstrated "more than a concern for economy or comfort" but "a mode of attention, a way of seeing and studying the material world, of treating 'things' as phenomena, and analyzing the phenomena into their basic properties to be 'understood' through 'Experiments' " (148). Given an essentially "straightforward and rational" universe, like the one described by Newton, it was reasonable for Franklin to assume "that the same kind of thinking that explains the physical universe would explain, equally well, the spiritual universe" (151). Religion and worship, then, were simple and obvious truths and practicalities. In so doing, Franklin made humankind the judge of the appropriateness of religion rather than the subject of supernatural command or authority.

A last example of this practical empiricism is treated by David Larson in "Franklin on the Nature of Man and the Possibility of Virtue" (1975). Larson concludes that Franklin, as with his theology and epistemology, "tests his theories of virtue by examining their effects upon men's lives because he values experience more than theory" (114). Virtue itself is assessed by actions, motivations being shadowy, and in the end, irrelevant. Only through general consensual agreement about which acts constitute goodness or virtue can all people be expected to do good. Virtue, then, is evident and obvious, and given that, Franklin's chief concern "becomes how to convince men that they should practice these self-evident virtues" (115). The key to his strategy was to suggest that it was in everyone's self-interest and happiness and society's well-being to choose virtue over vice. Knowing benefits and costs of good and evil, each person must choose a right course. "Franklin insisted that moral behavior is profitable as well as intrinsically virtuous because he wanted to make good use of men's selfish as well as their selfless impulses" (120).

A more recent essay contrasts Franklin's understanding of human nature with Jonathan Edwards's views on the same. In "Franklin, Edwards, and the Problem of Human Nature," Daniel Walker Howe describes the way in which both Franklin and Edwards utilized eighteenth-century faculty psychology in their understanding of human nature. Throughout his life, Franklin valued religion for its benefits to self and society, and this "insistence upon discussing the issue entirely in terms of practical consequences became more and more typical" as he grew older (79). Similarly, his discussions of morality featured the "tangible temporal rewards" of virtue, choosing to see virtue as "a good bargain" (80). To Franklin's eyes, people knew well enough what constituted the good, but the self faced terrible obstacles in actually doing it because of its own bad habits and unruly passions. To combat this perennial failure of reason to act, Franklin put forth his scheme for inculcating "the art of virtue," as it is described in famous detail in the *Autobiography*. While Franklin never produced the book he promised on the topic, the *Autobiography* itself is "his own life story . . . related as a sequence of parables, each with its moral lesson" (82). In contrast to Franklin's hopes for habit in sustaining virtue, Edwards simply rejected the authority of prudential self-interest, although he admitted its usefulness in taming some of the excesses of immorality. This sort of motivation did little to alter the profound "self-preoccupation that corrupted the human heart," and for Edwards the only way to address that malady was through the transformation of the heart that was the essence of Christian conversion, resulting in the self-forgetful altruism that Edwards called true virtue, " 'benevolence to Being in general' " (85, 89). The legacy of Edwards was particularly apparent in the "great Evangelical Movement of the nineteenth century, "a major culture-shaping force for its age . . . international and ecumenical in scope, active in both political and private sectors, innovative in its use of the media of communication" (91). At the same time, however, the movement "came to accept the importance of many of Franklin's concerns for temporal human welfare and incorporated them into their own version of the Edwardsian model of faith" (92).

The sort of virtue Franklin's understanding of human allows is explored in Edwin S. Gaustad's "The Nature of True—and Useful—Virtue: From Edwards to Franklin." As the title suggests, Gaustad contrasts the two but finds some common ground in what they wished for virtue. To be sure, "the underpinnings of Edwards' moral philosophy are unarguably theological," while Franklin's sense of the world "begins more with anthropology than with theology, more with works than with faith, more with consequences that with presuppositions" (46). Indeed, the approaches to life and meaning place them in "sharply different cosmologies and theologies," but they did share common expectations for the character of virtue. First, it should be spontaneous and natural, although they parted on how this would be achieved. For Edwards, "true virtue came through a redemptive act that gave men and women a new sense of the heart and a new will"; for Franklin, a habit of virtue resulted from choice and volition (49). Both insisted that genuine virtue resulted in or comprised action, meaning good behavior; mere words or good intentions were not sufficient. Lastly, both respected that prudential virtue of "ordinary morality" that arose from self-concern, although Edwards contended it was greatly inferior to the God-imparted "true virtue" of love for being in general (51).

Franklin never developed a comprehensive or even consistent economic philosophy or theory. His comments on economic matters, such as agriculture, money supply, or trade come incidentally within the consideration of larger issues or in short tracts on specific subjects. Thus, scholars must piece together from random parts whatever can be concluded about his economic views. Here, as also seems to be the case with just about every facet of Franklin's life and thought, controversy reigns. Basing their views on *The Way to Wealth* and the *Autobiography*, popularizers have often adopted Franklin as the godfather of laissez-faire capitalism, a view that is also shared by some conservative scholars. Others see in Franklin the makings of a New Deal economic interventionist. Two recent essays serve as good primers on the issues surrounding the debate. In "Benjamin Franklin's Vision of a Republican Political Economy for America" Drew McCoy argues that Franklin's economic perspective resulted from his desire for a republican society and social fabric. A reciprocal interdependence between government, national economy, and moral social fabric was necessary to have any single element in the mix succeed. This larger vision of cultural function places the admonitions and self-mythologizing of *The Way to Wealth* and the *Autobiography* within a markedly larger context than individual economic calculation and self-aggrandizement. The conditions of early America—economic, political, moral, and geographic—dictated that citizens, if they were to remain free, must practice frugality and persistence. Conversely, "a healthy republican society presented the proper framework for a free government that would in turn sustain the integrity of a republican economy and society" (617). Franklin's vision "had a great and lasting appeal to his countrymen and a significant influence on American public policy for decades to come" (608). The study of the practical applications of that policy is the focus of Tracy Mott's and George Zinke's "Benjamin Franklin's Economic Thought: A Twentieth Century Appraisal." The authors look at Franklin's thought and public advocacy to determine his general attitude toward governmental intrusion into free domestic commerce and trade.

Discussions of the important interpretive problems in reading those works vital for the history of self-help—the *Autobiography, Poor Richard's Almanac*, and *The Way to Wealth*—occur in most works that substantively analyze Franklin. A good, brief, descriptive historical and cultural overview, emphasizing context and eschewing judgment, is J. A. Leo Lemay's "Benjamin Franklin" (1972). Kenneth Silverman's "Introduction" to the Penguin edition of the *Autobiography* is a kindly, but critical, evaluation of the man and the work (1986). Silverman situates Franklin amid colonial historical and cultural shifts in "From Cotton Mather to Benjamin Franklin" in *The Columbia Literary History of the United States* (1988). David Levin's oft-reprinted "The Autobiography of Benjamin Franklin: The Puritan Experimenter in Life and Art" offers a persuasive interpretation of the way in which Franklin's religious and social philosophy shaped the telling of Franklin's own story ([1963] 1970). An indispensable guide to modern scholarship on the *Autobiography* is J. A. Leo Lemay's "Franklin and the Autobiography: An Essay on Recent Scholarship" (1967). John Ross's "The Character of Poor Richard" looks at changes in the nature of Richard's counsel, suggesting that Franklin became more concerned with wealth as a chief concern after approximately the first eight years of the *Almanac*.

The persistent, nettling question of Franklin's relation to Puritanism, first forcefully argued by Max Weber in his classic early sociological study of *The Protestant Ethic and the Spirit of Capitalism*, has received extensive literary and historical scrutiny. Briefly stated, Weber argued that the ordered product- and profit-oriented shape and texture of modern society received a major impetus from the forms of work-world discipline forged by anxious Puritans trying to prove God's favor and salvation by the visible evidences of earthly success. The thesis has fueled controversy ever since, a debate that continues to polarize and sharpen. For the most part, the essential truth of Weber's thesis—that Puritan religiousness somehow played a decisive role in giving birth to habits and values of modernity and has thus contributed to the withering of the human spirit—has been widely accepted, almost a cliché, in academe, the media, and the arts. Scholars in sociology and early American culture divide over the accuracy and continued usefulness of Weber's speculation, especially over the emblematic touchstones for his thesis, Cotton Mather and Benjamin Franklin. Weber argued that the sort of piety designed by English Puritan Richard Baxter provided impetus and shape for Franklin's preoccupation with business utility and efficiency. Later Franklin made specific mention of his indebtedness to American Cotton Mather's

Essays to Do Good. Another way of asking much the same question, without specific focus on Mather, is to wonder how much of a Puritan Franklin remained in spite of his theological and moral deism. Testing out these supposed connections, the intellectual and psychological similarities and differences between Puritan Mather and deist Franklin have become major interests for historians.

Anyone interested in pursuing this important, intriguing, and complex set of historical and cultural questions should start with Weber's *The Protestant Ethic and the Spirit of Capitalism*, which was first published in 1902 and translated into English in 1930. The Puritan was faced with the difficulty of proving his salvation "in a specific type of conduct unmistakably different from the way of life of the natural man" (153). This desperate effort to validate one's salvation by means of asceticism and worldly success led to the "rationalization of conduct with this world," which was a hallmark of Franklin's ethical pattern. When Puritan spirituality depleted, and its original communal, ethical thrust was lost, the behavioral pattern persisted, profoundly influencing Franklin and American "national character" (155). The result was the development of the psychic "iron cage" of "a rational bourgeois economic life" that warred against "the spontaneous enjoyment of life and all it had to offer" (181, 174, 166). Critics of Weber's speculative portrait of Puritanism (which is what Weber himself saw it to be) have doubted, first, the adequacy of Weber's research in Puritanism and, second, in part due to the first, his understanding the psychospiritual dynamic of Puritanism. This debate has recently been revived in a national conference on Weber, essays which are collected in *Weber's Protestant Ethic: Origins, Evidence, Contexts* (1993), edited by Hartmut Lehmann and Guenther Roth.

The first book to compare Franklin and Mather at length is Phyllis Franklin's *Show Thyself a Man: A Comparison of Benjamin Franklin and Cotton Mather* (1969). In a brief and efficient manner, critic Franklin surveys the various intellectual, psychological, and ethical similarities between the two, and the list becomes quite lengthy. The study is limited by her unquestioning acceptance of Perry Miller's harsh judgment of Mather as the nadir of Puritan decline, and that view predisposes Franklin to see Mather as closer to Ben Franklin than he was, even to the point of finding a marked theological kinship between Mather and Franklin. M. R. Breitweiser's *Cotton Mather and Benjamin Franklin: The Price of Representative Personality* (1984) considers the intention and manner with which Mather and Franklin set about shaping their own lives. In Mather he sees a marked tension between subjugation to the traditional ideal and rebellious, individualistic impulses that sought an alternative path from that designed by his illustrious paternity. Somewhat simplistically, Breitweiser sees Franklin accomplishing what Mather wished he had the freedom to do, that is, to shape a new version of the self and find a form, largely the *Autobiography*, to make that inviting and prescriptive for others. While it keeps at the center questions of identity and fate, Breitweiser's psychobiographical approach offers a monochromatic picture of rich and diverse personalities.

If Mather's attempt at adapting the old Puritanism to a pluralistic and increasingly secular setting constituted a step away from the Puritan founders' vision, Kenneth Silverman sees Franklin taking a step further still, arriving at a midplace between Puritanism and Romanticism and modern America ("From Mather to Franklin" 106). Franklin was the child of a different age, "of the new un-Puritan sensibility disinclined to melancholy"; personally, he was "in Puritan terms unable to feel the content of religion." Intellectually, his beliefs "took in rationalistic notions, left out the drama of Fall and Redemption, and made little room for Christ, whose divinity he doubted" (107). In Franklin's ethical literature, such as *The Way to Wealth*, Franklin sometimes argued that "economic well-being can depend on inverting religious values," and the *Autobiography* "reverses the Puritan ethos" and remains "the classic statement of the American dream of material success" (110, 111).

In "The Puritan Ethic and Benjamin Franklin" (1976), Karl Weintraub rehearses Weber's critique of Puritan religious psychology by reference to John Bunyan. Beyond reference to Bunyan, his excursus depends on psychological extrapolation of theological distinctions between Roman Catholicism, Luther, Calvin, and Puritanism; virtually no reference is made to American Puritan literature, and an examination of that literature might have tempered his syllogistic psychologism. He argues, like Weber, that the search for certainty of faith "was best served by a workaday ethic of disciplined labor in one's calling" (230). From this Puritan world, although he gutted its religious content, Franklin "the tepid deist" got his love of discipline, utility, and efficiency: "He is the Puritan personality without the Puritan motivation and the Puritan objective" (231). The free, un-Puritan self followed a moral scheme not because it was metaphysically valid or ordained but because it was personally or morally useful (233). Upon reading Weintraub and others, and after looking over their ahistorical surmises, the critic must wonder, so total is the contribution of Puritanism, what role the Enlightenment played, if any, in Franklin's ethical pragmatism.

Chapter 5

Revivalism, Religious Experience, and the Birth of Mental Healing

Popular images of nineteenth-century America generally recall the era as a pastoral interlude between the storms of revolution and the perils of modernity. Except for the Civil War, seen in popular nostalgia as a bloody, but principled, aberration from bucolic tranquillity, popular notions derived from poetry, fiction, and the graphic arts have celebrated a rural, pious, harmonious, and gentle-mannered people—Puritans without the brimstone and intolerance. Emphasizing small-town social accord and the sway of a more moderate religious teaching, this Norman Rockwell-ish "village smithy" portraiture has almost fully obscured a very different reality—that of a deeply unsettled, even chaotic America, a nation that, on one hand, was largely indifferent to religious matters and, on the other, searched desperately, in the aftermath of the Revolution, for political and religious certainty. In fact, as historians have recently begun to argue, America throughout the nineteenth century was a remarkably diverse, unpredictable, and often discordant patchwork of people, practices, ideas, and attitudes in just about every sphere of its life—whether social, political, economic, religious, or medical.

Through most of the Atlantic colonies, religion seemed of little importance, and even in New England the founders' zeal seemed to deplete steadily. Historians still vigorously debate the cultural or religious significance of church membership, but the fact that by 1683 only seventeen percent of Boston's taxpayers claimed church membership suffices to give serious pause to widespread nostalgia for a pristine Christian America (Butler 60) Very often and much to the discomfort of Puritan clergy, belief in the supernatural was heavily flavored by ample quantities of magic and the occult. Whether the citizenry simply grew irreligious, became in the Revolution hostile to any sort of institutional authority, or no longer felt the persuasive power of traditional ideas and symbols remains hard to discern. When Christianity did reassert itself, it was in the ungainly disorder of the Second Great Awakening, an evangelical venture that brought startling innovations not only in religious salesmanship and piety but also in philosophy, theology, and epistemology. To make matters worse, this great diversity of attitude was beset and aggravated by increasing rates of change in politics, industry, finance, and demography. Indeed, obvious, profound shifts were everywhere afoot, most conspicuously in the incessant movement westward. Other, less spectacular segments of the culture also saw similar degrees of unrest and disturbance. Traditional family and religious life, to name but two central, vital engines of cultural formation, increasingly fell into disarray and uncertainty, thereby enormously exacerbating the stress resulting from the turmoil of widespread societal change.

By any measure of cultural stability, the nineteenth century as a whole—both early and late, and not just the Gilded Age of industrialism and robber barons—was neither calm, homogeneous, stable, nor harmonious. Demographic data alone give some sense of the radical shift in the physical conditions of American cultural life. Between 1800 and the Civil War, the population so mushroomed—from 5 million to 30 million, largely due to high birthrates—that even though urban centers burgeoned, the nation was still able to fill the expanse of the western frontier, which now flourished well beyond the Mississippi River (Noll et al., *Handbook* 172). During the last four decades of the century, thanks to immigration and the size of the continent, the rate of expansion in the number of people and territory inhabited by Europeans would only accelerate. By the end of the nineteenth century, the number of urban centers had increased sixfold, and the frontier had reached its western terminus at the Pacific. With such broad and profound changes, the inner core of American culture inexorably shifted from a rural and agrarian ethos to one that was urban, industrial, varied, and, one might add, very troubled. In these radically changed circumstances, the old social and religious compass points no longer provided either direction or meaning. From the early half of the century to its end, the collective American psyche grew, as cultural historian Robert Fuller has put it, increasingly "adrift from its traditional moorings" (*Mesmerism* xi).

A change of similar magnitude occurred in American religious life, both in mainstream denominations and in popular or nonmainline religious expression, and this proved momentous for the course of American religious history. It has become increasingly clear that changes in the religious ethos of America were no less extreme or fundamental than those in demography and geography. Indeed, the best and only word to characterize the course of American religion in the nineteenth century is "change": fast, unpredictable, and sometimes drastic. Traditional Protestantism, which was largely Calvinist and still the dominant religious force in post-Revolutionary American culture, assumed remarkably new shapes, especially in the response known as revivalism, and from these dramatic changes arose numerous imported and homegrown "new religions" that traditionalists considered to be, at the very least, exotic or bizarre, if not plainly heretical and dangerous. For the orthodox, revivalist camp meetings and Methodist "circuit riders" altered the content, texture, and appearance of American Christianity, and in addition to these innovations within the household of faith, there appeared throughout the nineteenth century assorted, insurgent alternative "religions"—Mormonism, Spiritualism, Shakerism, numerous Eastern religions, Swedenborgianism, Transcendentalism, Roscrucianism, Free Masonry, and mesmerism, to name just a few. Some of these "transfixed antebellum society for decades," as prizewinning historian of American religion John Butler has summarized their impact in the decades before the Civil War (228). Indeed, so diverse and intense was this religious flowering that Butler has called antebellum America an astonishing "spiritual hothouse" that was unduplicated anywhere else in Western culture (256).

From within this superheated array of unexpected and sometimes peculiar foliage emerged a vastly influential and lastingly vigorous melding of religion and self-help—what the eminent historian of American religious life, Sydney Ahlstrom, has memorably called "harmonial religion," whose origins and growth are the focus of this chapter and the following volume (1019). Well before the Civil War, diverse strands of unconventional religious currents, scientific curiosities, health fads, and philosophical idealism surfaced within a disoriented and disorganized American society, and from this cultural potpourri grew first mesmerism and then an assortment of mental healing strategies, the New Thought movement, and Christian Science—a set of religious outcroppings that scholars have gathered together under the useful heading of "mind-cure," which is the term this study employs to refer to the aggregate of different mental healing movements. From these, in the middle of the twentieth century, came the phenomenal success of positive thinking and a myriad of other faith-and-attitude healing and success strategies, many of which are wholly secular. To a remarkable degree, the fruit of these early nineteenth-century innovations has spilled far beyond lecture halls, church buildings, and camp meetings to pervade a large portion of modern American cultural life.

Of central importance in this great sea change in American religious life was the event known as the Second Great Awakening, which in the first decades of the nineteenth century, roughly between 1800 and 1840, alternately rippled and surged across the American landscape from the Atlantic seaboard to the western frontiers. Its significance for the development of modern self-help lay in the fact that the Awakening played a major, if not decisive, role in first jostling and then dislodging the doctrinal and experiential contours of Calvinist Puritanism and New England's hierarchical localism. Indeed, one recent historian of American evangelicalism makes the remarkable claim that the ascent in the nineteenth century of evangelical Protestantism, as a distinct variety of Protestant Christianity coming to the fore amid the waning of Puritanism, constitutes "one of the most successful penetrations of a culture by religious faith" (Sweet 875). In its simplest terms, the Awakening that initiated this process urged individualistic autonomy and subjectivism in piety and ethics, and this crucial shift opened the floodgates to even broader change, the measure of which would appear in a plethora of new religions and, in the focus here, mind-cure movement. The old Calvinism had derived and sustained its religious authority from the value it placed on the knowledge of doctrine and theology, painstaking spiritual self-examination and development, inquiry and judgment by the "saints," and ample witness to good character, and it trusted these processes and criteria as dependable benchmarks for assessing the authenticity of religious conversion. In the old Puritanism, religious knowledge, thoughtful confession, and the collective judgment and wisdom of the community composed the criteria for assessing the authenticity of individual religious experience. At first gradually and then spectacularly, the Second Great Awakening displaced these traditional marks with an emphasis on the intensity of dramatic personal religious experience, especially as expressed in individual decision and in extreme states of emotion, whether as sorrow or exultation. Except in an indirect and now very secondary fashion, neither doctrine nor neighbors played a role in validating the truth or meaning of personal experience; instead, the first and preeminent assessor of the experience was the self in its capacities to choose and to feel. Briefly put, the locus of religious authority shifted from the Puritans's hierarchical corporateness to individual judgment.

It is almost impossible to underestimate the impact that this diffuse and dramatically innovative religious movement had on what we call the American cultural ethos. This dramatic and pervasive evangelical upsurge, as one historian has put it, had by 1830 broken "the back of Calvinism" (Sweet 876). Moreover, for the history of religion and self-help in America, the Awakening is best seen as that event that imbued Protestantism with a new disposition toward individualism and experimentalism in religious experience, a posture that prepared the way for the still more radical departures of Spiritualism, Theosophy, Mormonism, Shakerism, mesmerism, and Christian Science. From within the well-defined orthodoxy and practice of Protestantism grew new sects, and with them came a new openness to religious experimentation and the supremacy of personal religious judgment, attitudes that rejected the theological and spiritual domination of established denominations. To be sure, nineteenth-century America would remain intensely religious, but, for the most part, the forms and substance of its religious life thereafter differed markedly from those that characterized Protestant religiosity at the turn of the century. Most religious Americans continued to be conventionally religious, joining old and new Protestant denominations, becoming Methodists, Baptists, Presbyterians, and the like, but many among these imbibed diverse religious influences into their belief while maintaining mainstream religious identities and practices. Either by means of this sort of quiet syncretism or by flight to the new religions, the inner core of American religious belief, attitude, expectation, and practice underwent in the first part of the century profound and lasting changes. As a result of this religious variety and flux, just about every domain of its cultural life in nineteenth-century America repeatedly exhibited high levels of restiveness, curiosity, ferment, and expectation, and, as we shall soon see, serving as both an expression and catalyst for much of this cultural tumult was the Second Great Awakening.

After the Civil War, as we discuss in the next volume, other trials beset traditional Protestantism. Ordinary Americans would suffer still further dislocations from the lingering grief of the bloody national conflict and would be challenged by the major intellectual assaults of the "Gilded Age." The vigorous skepticism of Darwinism, biblical criticism, and comparative religion questioned the historicity and epistemological presuppositions of Judeo-Christianity. Under the pressure of these multiple assaults, Americans would ever after think of their religious horizons differently. Large numbers from every social and economic strata would search for, and sometimes find, new ways of conceiving of their spiritual, physical, and social fate in this world. By 1900 a conservative and sober Protestantism would again dominate, as it had at the beginning of the century, but, for the most part, save for ethnic enclaves, traditional denominational identity no longer proved an effective hermetic seal from secularism and from other, often heterodox religious influences that ranged from Spiritualism and Mormonism to faith healing and communalism.

Americans of the late twentieth century tend to regard their own culture, including religion, as unusually turbulent, eclectic, and contingent. The countercultural movement that began in the late 1960s gave rise to unconventional, polymorphous religiosity that sought to break through conventional spirituality to explore unknown regions of psyche and soul through such diverse religious resources as Zen, shamanism, and psychoactive drugs, to name but a few. In the 1990s, that search continues in the "New Age" movement, "New Right" politics, and, most recently, the return of the aging "yuppies" to the new forms of the institutional church known as the "megachurch." However extreme and surprising these present religious lurchings might seem, they appear mild and sporadic when compared to the depth and persistence of ferment in the religious history of the nineteenth century. In fact, many of the deepest currents of the nineteenth century continue to shape the deepest religious currents of our own age. For one, the fervor of revivalism of the Second Great Awakening, especially as innovated in camp meetings and consolidated by Charles Grandison Finney, persists in the conversionist strategies of latter-day preachers and evangelists like Billy Graham and Jimmy Swaggart and in the Promise Keepers men's movement. Of greater note still, however, is the extent to which the mental healing strategies of mesmerism, first introduced in the 1830s, would become, through New Thought, Christian Science, and positive thinking, a major popular current in American religion and culture. A close look at the Second Great Awakening's movement toward radical individualism in judgment and experience clarifies the foundations, genesis, extent, and significance of the cultural shift that not only prepared the way for, but made possible, the emergence of such religious movements as mental healing, Christian Science, and New Thought. It is to the complex development and analysis of the Second Great Awakening and the ferment and change it wrought that this chapter turns.

RELIGIOUS INNOVATION: THE SECOND GREAT AWAKENING

The generative hothouse for the many varieties of nineteenth-century religion, from Spiritualism to Christian Science, lay in that broad expansion of Protestantism known as the Second Great Awakening, a profoundly important religious and political "revival" that would do much to push the nation toward a lasting taste for religious individualism. North America's First Great Awakening had taken place in the 1730s and 1740s, and eventually it provided much of the ideological fervor of the American Revolution. In the four decades following the turn of the nineteenth century, the sporadic, but eventually pervasive, religious and social movement that we now call the Second Great Awakening burst forth at different times and places and in different shapes, each manifestation making its own distinctive mark on the American future. It is clear, too, that each successive surge of revival seemed to go ever further in significantly altering the texture and fabric of Puritanism, and conveniently, these successive periodic outbursts of revivalistic fervor have provided historians with useful benchmarks for marking phases of the large change the Awakening wrought in American religiousness.

The first phase of the Second Great Awakening took place in New England within the confines of traditional Puritanism, although distant and disconnected parts of the Awakening seemed to erupt at roughly the same time. The celebrated beginning and high point came at Yale University in 1801, when President Timothy Dwight (1752–1817) converted fully one-third of his undergraduates, many of whom would thereafter pursue the ministry and carry forward the work of revival in villages and frontier settlements. In this conservative or New England first phase of the Awakening, Dwight sought to banish what seemed an increasing tide of immorality and infidelity among students, trends that Dwight thought were interrelated and derived from the influence of deism (McLoughlin, *Revivals* 108). The Yale College president attributed a tide of somewhat faddish unbelief to a deism whose optimistic and reasonable tenets seemed altogether more appealing than traditional Calvinism's austere supernaturalism. In response, however, Dwight "fought reason to reason," thereby supplying evangelicalism with a strain of common sense that proved one of the hallmarks of the evangelical tradition in America (Henry 801). Without diluting traditional Calvinism's stringent doctrines of God's sovereignty and human incapacity for either good or individual freedom, Dwight argued that the nation's fate depended on the embrace of traditional orthodoxy. While this agenda was nobly civic-minded, Dwight insisted that the accomplishment of these social goals depended on dramatic religious encounter that emphasized individual choice, notes that forecast the emphasis within the broad-scale upheaval to come. While the question of to what extent Dwight's work immediately affected the course of the nation is hard to answer, there is no doubt that his disciples played a major role in shoring up the bulwarks of traditional theology, for they, too, thought the fate of culture hung in the balance, and they responded with due urgency. Unbeknownst to Dwight, however, the greatest peril to New England theology lay not in the external threat of deism but would soon come from within the very household of New England Puritan Christianity.

The culprit here proved to be Dwight's heir apparent, Lyman Beecher (1775–1863), the president of Andover-Newton Seminary and the father of two distinguished figures in American history: novelist Harriet Beecher Stowe (1811–1898), who wrote *Uncle Tom's Cabin* (1852), and minister Henry Ward Beecher (1813–1887), who became the most celebrated preacher of the second half of the century. With the success of frontier revivalism and its controversial emotional extremism, which we will soon discuss, Beecher and his compatriots found themselves in a difficult place, both practically and theologically. In response, Beecher and Nathaniel Taylor (1786–1858) set out to soften the stern cornerstones of old-style Edwardsian Calvinism, which itself had been a modification of an earlier Calvinism that emphasized predestination. Either because Beecher was by nature more pragmatic, or because he foresaw the wholesale abandonment of Reformed orthodoxy in the irrational emotionalism of Baptists and Methodists, he admitted that the seeming conflict between God's control in human affairs and human freedom in conversion constituted a mystery and, as such, was open to divergent interpretations as occasion warranted, especially when fending off the seductive voluntarism of deism. The central task for Beecher and other revisionists was to walk a theological tightrope that asserted, as historian of revivalism William McLoughlin puts it, both "the responsibility of men to choose right or wrong" *and* the sovereignty and "power of God" (*Revivals* 117).

The old Calvinism had insisted that, ultimately, God came to humankind and bestowed the grace of forgiveness and redemption; Beecher and Taylor began to push the current in the opposite direction, contending that humankind by itself was capable of choosing God, of finding the path that ended in God. This transferred the impulse and agency of salvation from God to the human person. In this profound and fundamental shift, a latter-day embrace of the Arminian "free will" position, God became essentially passive, always responsive to human initiation, and in its most extreme form, even dependent on human approach. This dynamic would be carried to that logical evangelical terminus in the work and thought of Charles Grandison Finney, but its particular importance for this examination is that it introduced a new and innovative spiritual dynamic that would inform and shape mind-cure in its multitudinous forms. In effect, autonomy and sovereignty departed from God to find a new home in the magisterial human self. This transfer ultimately deprived God of personality, pushing the divine to a measure of abstraction, whose resources always awaited human initiation. God became a reservoir or power station whose contact with the human much resembled the dynamic that characterized electrical current or a water faucet; the exercise of power depends on human agency to turn them on. From this notion, it is but a short step to formulations of God as a divine "Principle" and "All-Supply" that would inform and shape the religious dynamic of the mind-cure movement.

In another significant departure from traditional Calvinism, Beecher and Taylor conceded to revivalism the existence of a third component in the human psyche, thereby adding to Edwards's bipartite self of understanding and will. This third element, the factor that often moved the sinner to serious intellectual contemplation, was the "heart," an entity that was variously defined as emotion, sensibility, or religious affections. The effect of this further rearticulation of Calvinism was to bestow official theological sanction on the evangelical sensibility and the revival ethos in general. So radical was this shift in the intellectual and experiential core of New England Calvinism that Lyman Beecher would later be tried (although acquitted) for heresy. The foremost expression of this new emphasis would come in the frontier revivalism.

Regardless of profound theological changes and perhaps in deference to the spirit of Dwight, the revivals of this New England phase of the Awakening remained conservative in contrast to the later extremes of frontier and the Awakening's most famous evangelist, Charles Grandison Finney. For one, they were parish-based and were not characterized by the hysteria or frenzy of the frontier manifestations of the Awakening. In addition, itinerant, full-time evangelists were discouraged, and the revivals remained under the control of settled clergy who visited different parishes to provide that fresh voice that was often needed to instigate revival. Still, changes had taken place. The Reformed preacher-revivalist had come to see conversion as a practical matter of affectional-rational persuasion toward which people could employ certain useful and proven approaches and arguments. In moving toward an instrumentalist embrace of strategy as a sure means of instigating revival, the preachers diluted Edwards's emphasis on the mysterious, miraculous, and arbitrary action of God in prompting conversion. This progressive shift in understanding religious psychology and the role of Providence betokened the acceptance in New England of the Arminian free self that came to dominate the Second Great Awakening as a whole. Within the history of American religion and as a portent of things to come, the individual's religious fate had been pushed toward the realm of free human agency—to romp as it would with the spirit of God.

Of an importance equal to the theological inclinations of the New England revival was the New England theology's exaltation of ethical Christian life. For Dwight and his many disciples, conversion was far more than just a spiritual matter. In keeping with sober, spiritual persuasion and moral seriousness, the Awakening in New England stressed individual moral choice by accentuating a portrait of conversion that entailed a Christian life of lasting practical fruit in service to church and society. Part and parcel of Puritan notions of spiritual conversion, this activist component would soon appear conspicuously in the formation of assorted, independent, voluntary associations for mission work and social reform. State after state formed missionary societies for domestic and foreign ventures. In 1826 these individual state organizations combined to form the American Home Missionary Society. Its desire was to evangelize and civilize the ever-expanding American frontier, and decades of vigorous effort would, indeed, have a profound effect on frontier life. The impetus for foreign missions emerged from the "Haystack Prayer Meeting" at Williams College in 1806, and its converts ventured forth to evangelize, this time covering and, to some extent, colonizing the globe. Similar impulses and movements founded the American Bible Society in 1816 and the American Tract Society a few years later; together their distribution of Bibles and pamphlets amply supported and expanded the work of evangelists and missionaries. From this first phase, then, with its emphasis on dramatic spiritual and moral choice came a new urgency in the task of making America a Christian nation.

The full measure of the vitality of this evangelical movement appears in the fact that it did not confine itself solely to the ill health of American spiritual life. This early brand of evangelical activism understood the moral fruit of conversion to entail far more than the spiritual renewal or even the personal rectitude of the convert, and in this it recalled the old Puritan "compulsion to transform the world" in its totality, as historian of American religion Sydney Ahlstrom has memorably put it (427). Evangelical zeal fostered a moral activism that embraced a broad range of social concerns. Fearing that the country's considerable appetite for drink would impair its capacity for self-governance, theologian and evangelist Lyman Beecher spearheaded a decades-long temperance crusade. This concern for national well-being also appeared in organizations laboring in behalf of the poor, the disabled, the insane, and the criminal. Nowhere would the effects of the revival be more directly felt than in the abolitionist movement (Lyman Beecher's daughter, Harriet, authored *Uncle Tom's Cabin*, the 1852 antislavery novel that Abraham Lincoln credited with starting the Civil War). While none of these reformist movements were the sole inspiration or property of revival-bred evangelicals, their roots in the New England revival did provide a deep, lasting, and energetic catalyst for a wide range of reform. When its practical and organizational achievements of this early zeal combined with later millennial and perfectionistic contributions of the Awakening, the horizons of social reform stretched even further toward radical experimentation in social organization, human rights, science, medical practice, and theology. In any case, historians of both revivalism and reform agree that the assorted strands of social reform initiated by Protestant evangelicals generated, as William McLoughlin has summarized, "the most powerful reform era in American history" (*Revivals* 130).

New England theology eventually faced the strong competition of the more sensationalistic frontier theology. Almost simultaneous with the revival in long-settled and strongly Calvinistic New England was one of a very different flavor along the western frontier in Kentucky and Tennessee, and this constituted the second distinct phase of the Second Great Awakening. Not only was the location for the revival far distant from New England, but so were its sponsors, theology, methods, history, and fruit. By 1800 the three prominent denominations in America—Presbyterians, Methodists, and Baptists—had established a foothold in the sparsely populated regions of the West. In the 1790s, one Presbyterian minister, James McGready (1758?–1817), had improvised what he called a "camp meeting," an occasion for dispersed believers to gather for several days for religious education and fellowship. A follower of McGready, Barton Warren Stone (1772–1844), took the occasion a step further to use the gathering for revival. Stone advertised a large meeting for August 1801, at Cane Ridge in Bourbon County, Kentucky. Somewhere between 10,000 and 25,000 people showed up, and under the sway of powerful revivalist preaching great numbers of people underwent religious conversion and, more than that, experienced extreme degrees of religious enthusiasm: besides spontaneous singing, dancing, and laughing, some new believers exhibited more sensational agitation in "jerking" and "barking," to name but a few of the manifestations that campers thought to be inspired by the Holy Spirit.

Theologically, the frontier revivals were the legacy of the Arminian "free will" theology that stemmed from the English influence of John Wesley. This was a still more diluted version of the new voluntarist New England theology of Beecher and Taylor that had shaped the New England portion of the revival. While not diminishing Calvinistic emphases on the transcendence of God and the depravity of humankind, the frontier revivals uniformly emphasized individual choice in religious decision making, a feature that exalted, potentially at least, individual freedom to establish one's own criteria for belief. Specifically, throughout the western revival, the reflex was to elevate intense, subjective experience, usually marked by great emotion, as a valid test for authentic religious revelation, and this was usually at the expense of traditional Calvinistic caution about the perils of individual religious autonomy and subjectivity. In this second phase of the Awakening, the eternal seesaw in religion between reason and nonrational knowing tipped decisively toward subjectivity. For example, traditional Calvinism had "frowned on emotional displays and expected conversion to take place over a long, slow period of spiritual regeneration" that involved soul-searching, the careful study of the Scriptures and creeds, and the guidance of a theologically trained clergyman (McLoughlin, *Revivals* 115). In revivalism, however, through the aegis of God's chosen agent, in this case the evangelist, the weight of dramatic, intense, and decisive personal experience in immediate, powerful, and direct encounter with God worked to discount the value of the rational preparation and knowledge imparted by the ecclesiastical "hierarchies, seminary professors, dry learning . . . and 'cold' formalism" that seemed to characterize regular denominational practice (Ahlstrom, 475). One sociologist has described revivalists as valuing

subjective religious experience and direct revelation as sources of wisdom and knowledge more than systematic church instruction. They relied more on the personal leading of the Spirit than they did on certified theologies and doctrine. . . . They deemphasized the importance of doctrine and focused on the emotional and ethical responses of individuals. (Thomas 69)

Instead of the Puritan insistence on educated clergy and doctrinal precision, the revival promoted the usually unlearned itinerant evangelist's homiletical simplicity and passion because these stimulated direct, soul-shaking encounters with God. With this came "an expansion of religious feeling unknown in American history" and a new set of distinctive criteria for assessing true religion (Mathews 199).

For most Americans, then, supporters and opponents alike, revivalism fostered, in McLoughlin's words, a "new morphology of conversion," a radically new conception of how God might be encountered and experienced and, in addition, of the fruits of conversion (*Revivals* 115). In this departure, revivalism radically altered, according to Leland Jamison, "the ideas, attitudes, feelings, dreams and hopes" that had thus far largely comprised the American religious sensibility (quoted in Ahlstrom 475). In short, the substance and style of the frontier revival came to direct much of the disposition or temperament of American religion away from hierarchy and tradition and toward individual experience and authority, a shift that would have enormous consequences insofar as it shifted the locus of religious authority to endow individual subjectivity with far greater credibility. No longer was the "authenticity of conversions . . . judged by doctrine as was insisted upon the eighteenth-century, but by the intensity and quality of the experience" (Thomas 70). In other words, the Awakening as a movement recognized the validity and value of the individual spiritual self and thus, as historian Nathan Hatch has put it, "empowered ordinary people by taking their deepest spiritual impulses at face value rather than subjecting them to the scrutiny of orthodox doctrine and the frowns of respectable clergymen" (10). Once again and from a different source, this new high regard for the solitary individual's epistemic capacity would have great importance for what followed. For one, it prepared for, and gave immediate credibility to, the proliferation of the unconventional religious, social, and scientific views that were soon to break upon the American scene. More than that, it created a cultural climate that would ever after be readily disposed to the ethos of popular authority and individual notions of self-help. The fact that the individual believers could alone, individually, by themselves, better fathom the mysteries of grace than creeds, doctrines, traditions, denominations, seminaries, or congregations denoted a major shift in the sensibility of popular religion in America—"a quantum jump" that produced "a radically different religion" and, for that matter, culture (Thomas 68).

The third and last phase of the revival came some years later and occupied a middle ground, both geographically and religiously, between the New England and frontier revivals. To a great extent, it was also a summation of the whole of the revival, reiterating and consolidating the startling alterations in religious experience and practice that frontier revivalism had initiated and extending the Arminian theology of voluntarism. With heavy migration from New England into the Old Northwest, an area stretching from western New York into Indiana, came Presbyterian and Congregational home missionaries who saw the new regions as fertile ground for denominational expansion. Many of those students earlier converted by Dwight and his followers now did the work of planting churches in the first two decades of the nineteenth century, but actual revival among these Yankee settlers did not begin until the emergence of evangelist Charles Grandison Finney (1792–1875), who is generally recognized as the father of modern revivalism (Henry 802). In 1821, the twenty-nine-year-old lawyer was dramatically converted and soon after set forth to proselytize in the Erie Canal towns of upstate New York. The results were, as Sydney Ahlstrom comments, "spectacular," and Finney soon became famous not only for his successes but for his controversial "new measures," a set of persuasive methods that caused great alarm among his conservative Presbyterian brethren (460). In fact, Finney's new measures were not all that new or original, for Finney had simply gathered and regularized random "techniques that had earlier appeared singly and sporadically" (Henry 803). For traditionalists, Finney's oratory was too blunt, too forceful, and too vernacular. Moreover, in the midst of his addresses he often mentioned by name conspicuous sinners and opponents, thereby at least guaranteeing audience curiosity. The institution of the "anxious bench" for those in spiritual struggle also worked to increase audience involvement. Again violating decorum, Finney allowed women to speak in meetings, and his revival series met every night, instead of only on Sundays, until he got the results he wanted. He advertised upcoming "crusades," as they were now called. When attacked, Finney defended his means by referring to their efficacy in winning large numbers of converts.

Despite opposition from Beecher and others, Finney prospered remarkably. In methodology and theology, he departed from old-style Calvinism and codified in practice and writing the remarkable innovations that would come to constitute modern revivalism. By 1831 he had moved to New York City, where his devoted patrons rented halls and constructed churches for his preaching, culminating with the building of the Broadway Tabernacle. In 1835, when ill health curtailed his activity, he accepted a professorship at Oberlin College in Ohio, where his next thirty-one years of teaching and service as president made Oberlin a center for revivalist thought and activity. In hindsight, there is little difficulty in discerning the lasting imprint that Finney's practice and theology stamped on American religious life.

As troubling as Finney's successful methods were to even Progressive Presbyterians, who were Finney's chief sponsors, of greater concern still were the theological suppositions that lay behind those practices. So alarmed was evangelist Lyman Beecher that he threatened to meet Finney at the Massachusetts state line to prevent him from entering, although four years later Beecher's opposition relented, and he invited Finney to preach in Boston (Henry 803). Finney's innovations would, as time would tell, have great consequences not only for Calvinist theology but for the "religiousness" of later America. Like the "free will" Wesleyan revivalists of the Awakening's second phase, Finney's understanding of conversion emphasized individual autonomy rather than divine intervention in effecting conversion. Given this understanding of divine–human interaction, Finney concluded that revivals did not depend on miracle but could be designed in such a way as to ensure success. Assuming a rational and mechanistic universe and mind, as described by Enlightenment science, the preacher's task was to persuade audiences of the necessity of personal religious choice. The logic of the head and the heart would then inexorably reorient the prospective convert toward salvation. Paradoxically, in Finney's revivalism, emotion became both the catalytic agent for, and validating fruit of, the decisive use of persuasion and reason. On one hand, emotional urgency, as evident in passionate, plain-spoken preaching and in "special measures," was necessary to prod benumbed sinners to exercise reason in apprehending their woeful spiritual and moral condition. If truly grasped, the would-be converts necessarily responded with considerable emotional alarm to their metaphysical peril, as in finding oneself tied to a railroad track and awaiting the arrival of a fast-approaching express train. So, too, emotional relief, if not ecstasy, would follow upon liberation from sure death by the engine of sin and hell. Here, given the rationally inured self, emotion instigated rational perception and followed upon it, but for Finney the crucial transaction in the process was rational analysis and free choice. The burden of persuasion, both emotional and rational, lay upon the revivalist and the wise use of instrumental means with which to elicit repentance and conversion. The burden of choice, free and voluntary, lay upon the auditor. With this emphasis, the self became empowered before God and could, in effect, seek its own salvation and, as we shall see in the development of mind-cure, its own health. For health, as for salvation, the believer could choose and procure. Moreover, the act of belief brought immediate results and rewards; all devolved upon the free agency of human choice.

A wholly voluntaristic theology of conversion was not Finney's only conspicuous revision of Calvinist theology. Also receiving Finney's reappraisal, arising, in part, from his high regard for human freedom, was Puritanism's pessimistic estimate of the convert's capacity for virtue and purity. Puritanism's sober realism about human nature held that spiritual and moral improvement, even after conversion, was slow and demanded hard spiritual and moral labor in concert with the grace of God. That pilgrimage toward holiness, what the Puritans called sanctification, was lifelong and, despite the best of intentions, susceptible to detours and self-deceptions. For the Puritan, conversion was, indeed, decisive, a crucial and indispensable reversal of one's direction in life, but given that, it was still only a first step on a very long journey toward human wholeness, a fullness of being and love that would very likely come only in the afterlife. American Puritanism, then, envisioned the Christian life as fostering and increasing intimacy with God that produced growth in wisdom, love, and righteousness. Like Puritanism, most phases of the Second Great Awakening entertained similar activistic conceptions of conversion that featured moral action as one prominent mark of conversion. Beginning with the western revivals, however, and finding its full articulation in Finney, many revivalists embraced the notion of human perfection or "entire sanctification" in which redeemed sinners could forthwith achieve a condition of "holiness" in which they would no longer sin. For Finney, this perfectionism "developed logically out of his belief in free will," the logic for both notions coming, in large measure, from evangelist John Wesley, Methodism's founder, who had come to America during the First Great Awakening some eighty years before (McLoughlin, *Revivals* 128).

Historian of revivalism William McLoughlin summarized the logic of Finney's perfectionism as an admixture of human capacity and radical divine love:

if immediate conversion is available through an act of human will, then, through God's miraculous grace, all things are possible: human nature is open to total renovation in the twinkling of an eye and so, then, is the nature of society. The world is unfettered from tradition, custom, institutions, is unconditioned by history of environment. Society is totally malleable to the power that works in harmony with God's will. (*Revivals* 114)

Finney believed that conversion could return the believer to "where Adam was before the fall"—a condition of "perfect holiness" wherein one lives in a moral and spiritual condition "commensurate" to God's own being (quoted in McLoughlin, *Modern* 103, 104).

Finney's perfectionist views became more extreme as he grew older and brought him to separate completely from even the Presbyterian sympathizers who had supported his revivalistic innovations. Finney's views were not, however, uncharacteristic of his time, and his perfectionistic hopes would replay in countless forms throughout the century. Indeed, perfectionistic hopes flourished, and Finney was merely the most conspicuous and respectable proponent of an optimistic attitude toward self, spiritual potential, and goodness that flourished in great varieties in mid-nineteenth-century religion and politics. Among the well-known Shakers, famous still for their simple furniture and delicate hymns ("Simple Gifts"), the quest for moral perfection was central and led to such practices as celibacy and communalism. Even though this lifestyle was stringent, as indicated by their ban on sex and childbearing, Shaker communities attracted over 6,000 members in the two decades following 1830 (Marty, *Pilgrims* 192). A still more extreme perfectionism was voiced by John Humphrey Noyes (1811–1886), the controversial leader of the communalistic Oneida experiment, who in 1834 declared that he no longer sinned. So great was Noyes's confidence in his spiritual and moral purity that the social practices of his various perfectionist communities ignored conventional Christian mores to practice complex marriage, male continence, divine healing, eugenic experimentation, and theocratic democracy (Noll et al., *Handbook* 204).

A last example, occupying the extreme end of the continuum and the most enduring of these expressions, appears in the metaphysical and spiritual idealism of Christian Science and the New Thought movements, theologies that denied the reality and confinement of the material world. Here Finney forges a notion of human potentiality and well-being that is but a small step from the sort of perfectionism with regard to health that mind-cure advocates would envision and espouse. The belief in the capacity of the self to attain a state of perfection, in this case spiritual and moral, would decades later figure prominently, with the promise of physical health added, in the religious vision of Mary Baker Eddy. New Thought also conceived of the self as a part of the Divine Mind and therefore in its inmost center as good. While most Americans looked askance at these radical perfectionistic experiments, the frequency, variety, and notoriety of such groups give some indication of the extent the average citizen imbibed this newfound and sometimes euphoric confidence in the spiritual and moral capacities of the self.

The Second Great Awakening spurred one other powerful ideological engine of cultural ferment, and that was the doctrine of millennialism, which "constituted the social equivalent of . . . perfection" and grew quite naturally from it (McLoughlin, *Modern* 105; Thomas 75). Based on biblical historical schemes, millennialism held that "Christ was to come to earth, eradicate all social ills, and reign for a thousand years before the final judgment" (Banner 226). While some Protestants debated whether this thousand-year era of global peace and well-being would precede or follow the Second Coming of Jesus Christ, future-gazing became a favorite topic. While most conservative Protestants were, in fact, postmillennial, embracing the hope that Christ would return after a golden era toward which Christian America was leading the way, a few sects were premillennial, believing that Christ's return would initiate a new day and that that day was not far off, some followers even predicting a specific date for the Second Coming. In any case, amid the metaphysical fires of revival, questions about history, its meanings, and its directions received widespread public attention. That such curiosity took place in America is not surprising, given a heritage of Puritan notions of special historical destiny, the much vaunted ideal of "a city upon a hill." Added to this was the lingering, but still fervent, egalitarian optimism, both secular and religious, set off by widespread revolutionary democratization of Europe and America. Indeed, the world seemed to be getting better, and by and large Jacksonian America had no difficulty believing that America played a special role in realizing a remarkable future for the creation. Even evangelical political conservatives, generally from privileged classes and suspicious of societal leveling, took heart in the revival since it seemed to enhance virtue and morality in the land. Predictably, then, for Christian America, whatever its political or religious leanings, the coming of the revival seemed still another decisive indication that God was fast initiating a dramatic turn in human history. So pervasive was millennial expectation that when it combined with revivalism's other main features—religious enthusiasm, human freedom, and moral perfectibility—the Awakening at once comprised, as historian Gordon S. Wood has put it, "the time of greatest religious chaos and originality in American history" and generated in the years after 1830 "the most fervent and diverse outburst of reform energy in American history" (quoted in Hatch 220; Walters ix).

INTERPRETING REVIVALISM: HISTORIANS SEEK UNDERSTANDING

While historians largely concur in this portrait of the narrative history and religious effects of the Second Great Awakening, they vigorously disagree on what caused the revival and the value of its social and cultural fruit. On this matter, as on others, different paradigms of historical causation and expectation yield different conclusions, and the Second Great Awakening in particular poses significant interpretive challenges that pertain directly to understanding the emergence of mind-cure in America.

The Awakening ranged geographically from settled New England to frontier Kentucky and religiously from the intellectualism of old-style Calvinism to the emotion-driven brimstone of the camp meeting. Indeed, in its length, size, and diversity, the Second Awakening remains relatively uncharted, especially in relation to the quantity of historical attention given to Revolutionary and Jacksonian events and contexts. Moreover, the Awakening suffers, perhaps as a result of the lack of investigation, from a dearth of theoretical attention (Hatch 221). In short, as numerous historians have complained, the Second Awakening constitutes "a movement whose complexity eludes precision" in definition and, even more so, in explanation (Mathews 199; Hatch 221). Further, adequate understanding of the Awakening has been constrained by the historical profession's tendency to deal with elite groups within broad social movements because these groups possess an articulate verbosity that, first, leaves an accessible "paper trail" and, second, appeals to historians' own class-grounded intellectual and political biases (Hatch 222–24). Nonetheless, despite its difficulties, the Awakening has received notable attention, however limited, and has begun to entice ever greater historical examination and reflection. Thus far, historians' search for satisfactory explanation of the origins, history, and effects of the Awakening has, by and large, generated three distinct points of view. Here, as with other eras in American religious history, we can readily trace the course of two distinct and competing approaches; each in its own way has been singular and reductive in its vision. Within approximately the last decade, however, more expansive and complex syncretistic models of explanation have emerged, and these have allowed for more satisfying and less tendentious renderings of the Awakening.

Understandably, given the subject matter, the oldest and most persistent strain of explanation for the revival has been religious and apologetic in impulse and focus. Evangelical Christian historians, most recently, Richard Lovelace, see the revival as God's direct response to prayer for renewal (46–48). Among those church historians less openly apologetic, the focus of historical examination has been upon the theological, methodological, and organizational dimensions of the Awakening. By and large, these historians have provided useful accounts of denominational development and change. The interests of these "church" historians have too often been limited, as Donald Mathews has complained, to either the permutations of New England theology or the surfeit of emotionalism in its frontier phases (202). Considerable attention has been devoted, then, to revisions of New England theology, as in the ideas of the New Lights or Lyman Beecher or the wrangling over Finney's "new measures." Implicitly at least, by the intensity and duration of this focus, a good deal of the historical writing on the Awakening has ascribed revival to changes in theology or methods of proselytization. These traditional narratives have contributed greatly to constructing a record of the religious, intellectual, and, to some extent, social events and changes within the Awakening, and thanks to these accounts and religious histories, we now have a relatively complete and factually accurate historical chronicle of the Awakening.

On quite the other extreme from religious causation have been the arguments of socioeconomic historians who have, in recent decades, dominated American religious historiography. In brief, these historians have seen social and economic motives, even though wholly subconscious in participants, as creating in various ways the widespread susceptibility to, and expressions of, revival, including the social reform movements that sprang out of the revival. A standard work in this mode is Paul E. Johnson's *A Shopkeeper's Millennium: Society and Revivals in Rochester, New York, 1815–37* (1978), a study of Rochester's changing social and economic structures surrounding Charles Finney's revivals in Rochester in 1830. Johnson argues that the revival served as a means for the economic leaders of Rochester to regain control of a chaotic civil climate and increasingly unruly working class. This crisis arose from Rochester's rapid economic expansion as a manufacturing center, a development that abruptly severed traditional workplace bonds between masters and craftsmen and segmented personal life and work life. The impersonality of the protoindustrial workplace wrought a workforce—"normless men on the make"—displaced, autonomous, rowdy, and largely devoid of moral-social nurture (33).

Located on the Erie Canal and, as such, both a boomtown and fleshpot, Rochester was soon beset by a series of social crises over moral issues, and its respectable citizens launched temperance and Sabbatarian crusades that met with little success. Eventually, disagreements among the economic elite over Masonry and strategies of social control became so extreme that leaders and churches fractionalized and diminished the town's ability to govern itself. Chaos within and between classes bred a crisis of authority; in short, as Johnson summarizes, "society was coming apart" (72). Into this situation came Finney, whose six-month visit "laid the foundation for moral community among persons who had been strangers or enemies" and gave the strife-ridden churches "a militance and unity that had been unthinkable only months before" (101, 95). Conversions ran apace, and the churches and community found a new harmony and purpose that effectively subdued the forces of chaos by quelling liquor sales and worker perfidy.

For Johnson, economic motives underlay and pervaded the revival. On one hand, its appeal for workers was simple. While kinship or spiritual motives might have had some role, "with all of this said, the most powerful source of the workingman's revival was the simple, coercive fact that wage earners worked for men who insisted on seeing them in church," and as a result the ambitious laborer, whether consciously or not, adopted "the religion of the middle class, thus internalizing beliefs and modes of comportment that suited the needs of their employers" (121, 138). This, of course, according to Johnson, was exactly what the middle-class manufacturers wished would happen: "Revivals provided entrepreneurs with a means of imposing new standards of work and discipline and personal comportment upon themselves and the men who worked for them, and thus they functioned as powerful social controls." This religion of "rich evangelicals" was "order-inducing, repressive, and quintessentially bourgeoisie," thus supplying "a middle-class solution to problems of class, legitimacy, and order generated in the early states of manufacturing." Moreover, the individualistic free-will religion of evangelicalism was ideally suited for the management needs of the middle class insofar as it "enabled masters to present a relationship that denied human interdependence as the realization of Christian ideals" (138). A new "pious enclave within the working class" worked to provide "masters with more than willing workers and votes for Whig repression. Sober, hardworking, and obedient, they won the friendship and patronage of the middle class, and a startling number of them seized opportunities to becomes masters themselves." The old paternalistic controls of master and apprentice were outmoded but, by means of revival, "could indeed be replaced by piety and voluntary self-restraint: free labor could generate a well-regulated, orderly, just, and happy society" (141). The willing subscription of bourgeois mores and religion through the aegis of revivals furnished "the most total and effective social control of all" (138).

Paul Johnson's account of the radical social changes wrought by manufacturing and commercial expansion offers a provocative and complex account of the interplay of setting, economics, and religion. The introduction of socioeconomic factors into the causative debate over the Awakening added a vital, if not exactly crucial, dimension to understanding the sorts of ferment that contribute to extreme religious reorientation. Still, like others who share his historical paradigm, Johnson has been roundly criticized for the ultimately reductive interpretation of revivalism: all mysteries clarify when seen through the prism of social control, class, and economics. Lately, however, this approach has undergone vigorous critique by historians who, first, wish to stress a broader set of motive factors (not excluding Marxist insights) and, second, give greater credit to the influence of innovative religious and political ideology and means.

The first note of protest against the socioeconomic reductionism was sounded by Lois Banner in her 1973 study of evangelical social reform movements, "Religious Benevolence as Social Control: A Critique of an Interpretation." Marshaling considerable evidence and logic for her case, Banner faulted liberal or Progressive historians for portraying the "post-Revolutionary generation of religious humanitarians as conservative and self-serving" in using revival and reform "to gain power over society for their own conservative, if not reactionary, ends" (218), in other words, "for 'social control,' not social improvement" (219). In explaining the entirety of the Awakening from such a perspective, the Progressive historians' "social control" theories not only ignored "some significant factors about the genesis and goals of religious humanitarianism" but fell into their habitual error of believing "that reality is always mean, hidden, and sordid and that men normally act not out of generosity but from fear and from considerations of status and gain" (219). Against this reductionism, Banner accounted for the rise of reformism by pointing to the well-entrenched tradition of benevolence in New England, the relative security of the clergy, the universality of Christian benevolence, patterns of denominational development, the reformers' evangelical zeal, and, lastly, the pervasiveness and power of the millennial expectation that shaped Christian Republicanism.

A thoroughgoing, closely analytic critique of economic explanations comes in Curtis Johnson's study of New York's Courtland County, *Islands of Holiness: Rural Religion in Upstate New York, 1790–1860* (1989) and in George M. Thomas's *Revivalism and Cultural Change* (1989). While these scholars argue for two different explanatory rationales, together their analyses of past assumptions about the origins and nature of revival raise serious questions about the common view, as Curtis Johnson summarizes it, "that early nineteenth century revivals were attempts by the rising industrial bourgeoisie to discipline the unruly laboring classes" (77). To the contrary, Curtis Johnson found that many of the central assumptions of widely accepted Marxist analysis of the Awakening have little, if any, foundation. For one, classic Marxist analysis of class structure simply does not apply to rural early nineteenth-century America, where, simply put, there was no landless proletariat for exploitation, except for a brief time in Rochester (Thomas 85–86). Second, looking at the revival as a means of social control, Johnson discounted the assertion that "wealthy persons joined the evangelical churches and then used religious authority to curtail the personal liberties of society's less wealthy and unchurched members" (Johnson 79). Not only had the samplings of previous studies focused narrowly on urban, upper-crust churches, such as Presbyterians and Episcopalians, where such tendencies might appear, but in Courtland County, a representative rural district, wealthy commercial interests had opposed revival because vigorous churchly presence tended to scrutinize and then to curtail business morality. According to Johnson, a third class-oriented theory suggests that revival flourished among subsistence farmers whose experience predisposed them to accept a theology that emphasized personal independence and choice. Actually, the revival grew as subsistence declined, and a market economy gained strength in Courtland County, a view that is supported as well by George Thomas in *Revivalism and Cultural Change*. Thomas's close examination of patterns of market expansion and revival in rural areas also concludes the direct opposite from the preceding: those most affected by the market's demands of "effectual individuation . . . would be more likely to subscribe to revivalistic pietism" (83).

Against religiously or politically reductive models of historical explanation, the last two decades of scholarship have seen the rise of a more expansive model of explanation that does not reject political or religious approaches but incorporates them as important elements in a much fuller explanatory portrait. For example, William McLoughlin, the foremost proponent of this syncretistic explanatory perspective, argues that with revivals there "can be no single cause for such wide-ranging transformations in thought and behavior upon which millions are ready to stake their lives." Rather, satisfactory explanation must ever strive to encompass "more complex social and intellectual relationships" (*Revivals* 9). In short, he wishes to cast the explanatory net farther to include as full a list of motive forces as possible. Like many social and economic historians, McLoughlin believes that revivals arise as a compensatory movements aiming to remedy different kinds of deficits or disappointments among participants. As a representative of what one historian calls "the crisis theory perspective," McLoughlin takes his inspiration from contemporary anthropology, especially the work of Anthony F. C. Wallace and Clifford Geertz (Thomas 84). For McLoughlin, America's series of awakenings—five in all, including the English Puritan revolution—are really revitalization movements that work to reinvigorate confused and demoralized social groups, whether backwoods farmers or National Aeronautics and Space Administration (NASA) scientists. In an American setting, revivals have, amid various kinds of social strain, regularly renewed national commitment to a well-defined and lasting set of core beliefs that have been in place since the first days of English settlement—specifically, ideas and feelings having to do with national destiny, democracy, and individualism. Typically, when individual or social attitudes or behavior have departed too far from national core beliefs, personal anxiety, social discord, and anomie increase, and Americans must reorient their core beliefs in order to account for changed religious, intellectual, and social realities. As a result, religious practice in America "has been progressive or syncretic, offering new definitions for old truths," which enables people to again live in harmony with themselves and others (McLoughlin, *Revivals* 18). This transaction lies at the heart of the revitalization process that awakenings represent.

McLoughlin's interpretive approach supposes that awakenings result from disequilibrium, stresses, or shifts in a significant part of cultural system (Thomas 84). Another to push markedly away from Progressive socioeconomic explanation toward the causes and significance of the Second Great Awakening is Donald Mathews, who has argued that awakenings should be seen as a cultural organizing event. Like historians before him, Mathews conceded that religious factors, like the erosion of Calvinism, and economic causes, such as those suggested by the social control theorists, contributed to the Awakening. Mathews went on to observe, however, that "too many unsettling things" remained to make either or both sufficient explanations for the length, breadth, and vitality of the revival (200). In contrasting the First and Second Awakenings, it became clear that each had a different social function—namely, that in the Second Awakening theology and even revivalism itself did not loom so large as the fact that the revival "was an organizing process that helped to give meaning and direction to people suffering in various degrees from the social strains of a nation on the move into new political, economic, and geographical areas" (202–3). Beset by "rapid economic change, the reshaping of social relationships, uncertainty about the direction and lasting quality of political institutions, and geographical mobility," America suffered "a general social malaise" (206, 213). To this the revival provided as antidote "a general social movement that organized thousands of people into small groups," specifically, churches and reform societies, that effectively supplied a new "common world of experience for Americans" (215). Countless displaced or disoriented people found surcease from anxiety in the social and religious world of revival and, in doing so, united with other Americans in the reformulation of a deep core culture of belief and mores that, on a daily basis, quelled fear and renewed personal and social cohesion, meaning, purpose, and hopefulness.

Running directly counter to the economic analysis of Paul Johnson in *Shopkeeper's Millennium* is Leonard I. Sweet's summary analysis of "Community vs. Individualism" in his essay on "Nineteenth-Century Evangelicalism" in 1988. Contrary to the divisive coercion that Johnson claims characterized the revival in Rochester, Sweet contends that, in general, revivalism "was a primary agent for creating a new sense of community based more on shared faith and feeling than on inherited social status." Indeed, revivalism "cut across social, class, and educational lines, creating unity and community out of diverse and sometimes antagonistic social groups." Evangelicalism's communal democratic character engendered "intimate fellowships" that go a long way in "explaining the social interaction and close spiritual ties that often developed between blacks and whites, especially in the old South." For its first couple of decades, the Second Great Awakening was wholly biracial, inculcating and demonstrating "modes of social organization with standards of self-worth based not on deferential patterns or establishment definitions but on new distinctions that revolved around religious and communal values validated by the group itself." Moreover, in an increasingly individualistic America, revivalism worked to soften social isolation and conflict: converts stepped from "a cold, chaotic world into the warmth of a caring, intimate, disciplined, and orderly environment." Admittedly, conversion was a "profoundly individual experience, but because of the structures of revivalism it took place within the connectedness of community" (887). People were no longer alone but part of a wide national network consisting of churches, groups, and periodicals that all accentuated a collective identity as participants in a markedly new personal and social identity. Unfortunately, this sense of community within the evangelical movement sometimes displaced other sorts of community identity based on geography, clan, or authority. Ultimately, by the time of the Civil War much of the original social cohesion of revivalism eroded as middle-class values and secular individualization pushed community-based belief toward privatization (888).

The large contours of Sweet's view find ample support in Nathan O. Hatch's prizewinning *The Democratization of American Christianity* (1989), which also emphasizes the unsettled political, social, and cultural aftermath of the American Revolution. Hatch argues that Americans had taken the Revolutionary rhetoric of liberty at face value and that after the Revolution the new nation struggled to find a way to fulfill the promise of the rhetoric in new social forms. Given this setting, Hatch contends that a good part of the Awakening was fueled and characterized by the enormous ideological allure of a radical egalitarianism that "offered to common people, especially the poor, compelling visions of individual self-respect and collective self-confidence," imparting to them a new measure of personal dignity, importance, autonomy, and hopefulness (4). The impulse and rhetoric for this religious populism, which would become a lasting major strain in American religious life, lay in the populist political language of liberty in the Revolution, an event that

dramatically expanded the circle of people who considered themselves capable of thinking for themselves about issues of freedom, equality, sovereignty, and representation. . . . Ordinary people moved toward the new horizon aided by a powerful new vocabulary . . . of liberty that would not have occurred to them were it not for the Revolution. (6)

In many ways, argues Hatch, the Awakening represents the "incarnation of the church into popular culture" and is, as such, "the story of the success of common people in shaping the culture after their own priorities rather than the priorities outlined by gentlemen" (9).

Hatch argues that after the Revolution, in "cultural crisis as severe as any in American history," most Americans suffered "acute uncertainty" about the displacement of traditional authority that the Revolution had expressed and achieved. The Revolution had successfully subverted traditional medieval, hierarchical ideal of cooperation, and the new democracy, however appealing, was yet to prove lastingly reliable. Within this widespread distress, most people were confused about the daily practical meanings of their new nationhood (23, 6). No country had quite gone this route before. The result was, understandably, widespread and "intense social strain and dislocation" in all levels of society but especially among the previously powerless, for the Revolution had engaged their very souls with the contention that their in-

dividual lives, choices, and rights were inviolable and worth dying for. Socially and politically, the single largest cause for this anxiety appeared in
questions among the lower classes about the rightness of a "hierarchical,
ordered society" in which all defer to their social betters, a practice that had
been a mainstay of human culture (23). In taking the rhetoric of liberty
seriously, countless numbers of people pushed its applications beyond England and the king to any sort of claim to social superiority based on lineage,
class, education, or wealth. "Respect for authority, tradition, station, and
education eroded," and esteem for politics declined, as might be expected,
but so did regard for law, medicine, and religion (6). Religiously, the rejec-
tion of elitism led to discounting the authority of the past and to a "violent
anti-clericalism, a flaunting of conventional religious deportment, a disdain
for the wrangling of theologians, an assault on tradition, and an assertion
that common people were more sensitive than elites to the ways of the
divine" (14, 22).

This new sense of personal authority and empowerment led to waves of
religious experimentation that fell quite outside the bounds of traditional
religious thought, practice, and expression. Great numbers of ordinary people felt "empowered . . . by taking their deepest spiritual impulses at face
value rather than subjecting them to the scrutiny of orthodox doctrine and
the frowns of respectable clergymen" (10). The consequences were a passion
for equality and a personal and national optimism in the possibilities of
individualism, the truth and value of the individual spiritual and political
self. Alienated from gentry culture and its churches, many common folk
struck out on their own, exhilarated by their encounter with the supernatural
and their new vocabularies of popular sovereignty. The religious and political
conjoined to create a new kind of religious populism that has "remained a
creative, if unsettling, force at the fringes of major Protestant denominations" (16). In the discarding of professional monopoly and authority of
the educated elite over law, medicine, and the church, there emerges a new
democratic self-confidence in the autonomy, enterprise, and potential of the
self, especially when it is infused with, as revivalism abundantly provided,
the immediacy and inspiration of the divine. It is fair to say that from this
context of radical ferment about the role of the common self and the meaning of democratic society is a new, while Hatch does not employ the term,
"do-it-yourself" ethos, at least part of which prepares the way, amid this
new confidence in the power and insight of individual vision, for the appeal
of radical medical-religious improvisations like mesmerism, the progenitor
of mind-cure, and, for that matter, modern psychotherapy.

AMERICAN ROMANTICISM: NATURE, HARMONY, AND HEALING THE SELF

The Second Great Awakening forged a new style of religiousness in American culture marked by greatly increased individualism and privatization in

religious experience and its legitimation. Whether in Calvinist New England, frontier camp meetings, or the urban revivals of Charles Finney, the new evangelical religion, as Catherine Albanese couches its effect, "put its premium on the direct experience of individuals as the test of true religion." The old Calvinism had stressed epistemological caution and corporate checks in assessing what the self could claim in religious knowledge. In the First Great Awakening in the 1740s, pro-revival "New Light" theologian Jonathan Edwards had argued for a balance of rationality and the "affections," as he called them, in evaluating the authenticity of conversion. In the Second Great Awakening, however, evangelicalism altered the criteria for validating the truth of one's religious experience, and that was distinctly toward the personal and subjective: "one had to know the truth by feeling and by doing" (*Nature* 117). The knowledge of creeds or the assurance of ministers and consistories no longer sufficed to authenticate the reality of one's belief; what became known as "heart knowledge"—and only such knowledge, a dramatic psychoemotional encounter with the love of God that reoriented the inmost depths of the self, its basic leanings and dispositions, what Edwards called the "affections"—constituted a trustworthy foundation for belief. This sort of knowledge, an essentially nonrational knowing, a seemingly oxymoronic epistemological mode, mystified many traditional theologians and philosophers. Calvinists like Jonathan Edwards had always stressed the necessity of some measure of affectional experience of God, but at the same time these theologians and ministers amply warned of the susceptibility, even likelihood, of self-deception if one inordinately or exclusively trusts the "spiritual" alone. Excessive trust in feelings, how one felt at any given movement, seemed to give epistemological warrant to the caprices of rampant subjectivity. If portions of the old Calvinism, Unitarianism in particular, had constricted knowledge solely to the rational and propositional, then the new evangelicalism swung the pendulum to the opposite extreme, trusting primarily in the intensity of extreme emotional states as "proof" of God's action in the self. Implicit within this profound shift in Christian understanding and experience were not only a different definition of the knowledge of God but also a new "style" of arriving at such knowledge that exalted the subjective domains of the self.

American revivalism transferred the locus of spiritual authority from external repositories in clergy or church to the individual and within the individual self to the spiritual or wholly affective. Regard for rationality persisted, to be sure, especially within the commonsense philosophical appeals of evangelists from Dwight to Finney, but in the end rationality was no longer prized above, or even on the same plane as, subjectivity as a preeminent means of apprehending religious truth. In this regard revivalism, a vastly popular religious movement, participated in, and echoed, the currents of the intellectual movement known as Romanticism that came to flourish in Europe and America in the early decades of the nineteenth century. In fact, a strong case can be made that what became known as Romanticism was, in fact, no more than a more "dressed-up" intellectual's version of the "heart religion" of continental pietism and British evangelicalism. After all, both revivalism and Romanticism were but two of the "many instances of the widespread religious ferment which took place in America during the first half of the nineteenth century" (Buell 4). Seen from this perspective, revivalism comes to look less like an aberrant, "fanatical" religious impulse confined to the churchly or to untutored rubes on the frontier than simply the most intellectually energetic and sophisticated portion of an expansive cultural movement that profoundly affected the mood and foundations of the whole of Western culture.

The impact of Romanticism in America is not easy to gauge, but it is safe to say that some aspect of the movement, and it was a very diverse movement, touched virtually every area of Western cultural life. Because of an enormous diversity in themes, locations, and people, scholars have approached the challenges of definition with considerable caution. In this regard, it is best to speak of Romanticism as expressing far more than one emphasis or insight but as consisting of a constellation of themes and subjects within a distinctly new and pervasive cultural mood. This range and variety are apparent in the very general definition offered by one scholar:

Romanticism revolted from reason and preferred emotion and nature to science; it stressed individual accomplishment and a liberation of the unconscious; it revived pantheism, idealism, and Catholicism; and it reveled in things medieval and exotic. No one definition is satisfactory, for too many human traits and a unique mood defy a simplistic approach.

Indeed, genuine Romantics were "overwhelmed with the abundance of life and no one member of the movement can be palmed off as representing the whole" (Shriver 1103).

Romanticism bears mention in this account because certain currents within it, by and large, provided much of the intellectual framework and inspiration for what is variously called mind-cure, metaphysical religion, or "harmonial religion." If revivalism provided a new epistemological "style"—one emphasizing the autonomy of the self and the primacy of feeling in knowing—then American Romanticism, especially the important sliver of it known as Transcendentalism, supplied the central ideas and predominant metaphors for the shape, substance, and texture of the mind-cure and positive-thinking movements that would follow. Like the larger Romantic movement of which it was the foremost American expression, Transcendentalism was by no means "an organized school of thought with fixed doctrines," for "Transcendentalists had no specific program or common cause, and their beliefs were often in a state of flux" (Buell 3). Even with the advantage of considerable hindsight, historians have had a difficult time in pinning down a set of common beliefs for this very small group of well-educated seekers; indeed, efforts at definition "have generated much heat and little final resolution" (Albanese, "Transcendentalism" 1117). In September 1836, a small group met, calling itself the Transcendental Club, and their purpose was not so much a meeting of minds in doctrinal consensus but a gathering "of temperaments, of yearnings, of aspirations, and of rejections, what . . . emerged was not so much a philosophy as an atmosphere and a state of sensibility" (Warren, Brooks, and Lewis 12).

In briefest terms, Transcendentalism was in its founding stage a tiny and loose intellectual movement peopled by some of the most famous literary and intellectual figures of the early nineteenth century: Ralph Waldo Emerson, Henry David Thoreau, Orestes Brownson, Bronson Alcott (father of Louisa May, author of the classic *Little Women*), and Margaret Fuller, who was America's first prominent feminist. Philosophical, literary, and social, Transcendentalism emerged "among New England intellectuals, mainly in the environs of Boston in the 1830's," and while it enjoyed celebrated literary and social notoriety, its "root impulse" was theological (Warren, Brooks, and Lewis 10). In specific terms, the movement "served as an expression of radical discontent with American Unitarianism (which, in turn, was a liberal movement within Congregationalism), arising from objections to Unitarian epistemology and the Lockean psychology upon which it was based" (Buell 4). Locke's epistemology was "sensationalist," thoroughly rooted in the exigencies of rationalism and materialist perception, and Romantics generally wanted a warmer and more expansive and intuitive epistemological model that would give warrant and status to the claims of subjectivity. For them, the claims of imagination, of emotion, and, in their deepest hopes, of intuition seemed to offer surer and more satisfying paths to truth. In this regard, these sophisticated philosophical and religious radicals shared in elaborate form the same starting point as frontier Baptists and Methodists; Catherine Albanese suggests that for Transcendentalists, "the primacy of inward experience and intuition was key, and an impatience with inherited external forms provided strong accompaniment" ("Transcendentalism" 1118). As three legendary interpreters of American literature have put it, in language that sounds strikingly similar to the voluntarist religious epistemology of revivalism,

the transcendentalist found in the mind itself intuitions that need no proofs, intimations that were guaranteed to be right by the very fact of their appearance in the mind. The moment when an intuition appeared might indeed be very thrilling, and the thrill itself might be taken as a proof of the 'truth' received. (Warren, Brooks, and Lewis 17)

Beyond this shared taste for nonrational routes to truth, there were other points of contact: "Methodism and the more general evangelical movement had been marked by themes found in romantic circles later . . . emphasis on the individual, challenges to old religion, and humanitarian impulses" (Shriver 1105).

Transcendentalists drew their intellectual support and fire from a host of ancient and modern European and British thinkers and writers, the most prominent being Plato, Kant, Rousseau, Schleiermacher, Hegel, Fichte, and Coleridge. While Romantics and Transcendentalists both were deeply indebted to these figures, American Transcendentalism, especially in the person of its intellectual leader, Ralph Waldo Emerson, who in 1838 published the Transcendentalist's manifesto *Nature*, owed much to the thought of a relatively obscure eighteenth-century Swedish physicist, mystic, and theologian, Emanuel Swedenborg (1688–1771), one of the "new spiritual heroes" of whom the young Romantics made much. In Swedenborg, Emerson found the "doctrine of correspondences," a visionary formulation of the way in which the human relates to the divine (Albanese, "Transcendentalism" 1120). Swedenborg postulated, or dreamed, a metaphysical structure consisting of an interpenetrating macrocosm and many microcosms; specifically, within the larger divine sphere were individual human microcosms, all of which were enveloped within the transcendent divine macrocosm of spirit and nature. Of great importance for Swedenborg and for his Romantic disciples was the supposition that the human was like the divine in kind and substance, albeit a pale reflection thereof; the two did indeed correspond but differed in degree. In fact, in this perspective the whole world in its seemingly disparate parts actually "fitted," each meshing with a corresponding part in ascending purer spheres of reality that culminated in the divine. Like idealists of various sorts, Emerson and his followers held that reality was first and foremost spirit, and the physical world of nature was a direct, expansive, and superior manifestation of divine.

As such, it was entirely appropriate and important for the religious seeker to turn to nature, first, for the clues of divine reality that it offered and, second, to imbibe its glory, for nature in all aspects clarified and witnessed to the reality of the divine. The more people were able, by whatever means, to penetrate or absorb the divine, the fuller and more meaningful their lives became. For the Transcendentalist, this goal was not a difficult quest. Since the macrocosm of the divine already incorporated the many lesser microcosms, and there were many levels and routes of approach, and everything essentially partook of the same spiritual ether, there was not a radical disjuncture, as there had been in Puritanism, between the human and the divine. One great, clear repository of the divine was nature, both as law and as beauty, and consequently American Romantics of all kinds fervently pursued, as Thoreau had at Walden Pond, the presence and wisdom of the divine; God was all about, teaching and inspiring the humble questing pilgrim. Within this equation, natural facts were also spiritual symbols, replicating divine truth through the immediacy of the physical world. Properly seen and understood, nature was a telling revelatory vessel or fount of divine reality, as were other parts of human reality. Consequently, one large dimension of each person's religious task was to discern, since the divine was everywhere available to everyone, the means and meaning of divine speech in nature, the religions of the world, and personal intuition. Catherine Albanese concisely summarizes this radically hopeful religious posture:

Real religion meant living in tune with the divinity within oneself, listening for the answering divinity in nature and spirit. It meant openness to intuitive knowledge, awareness that intuition corresponded to reality outside the self. In short, living in harmony with the cosmic law meant cultivating the ground for mysticism. ("Transcendentalism" 1121–22)

Three emphases within Swedenborgian Transcendentalism later played a crucial role in the development of the theology of the mind-curists' metaphysical religion. The first of these was the conception of God as an abstract principle whose essence was distilled in the correspondence of the laws of nature and of human nature. This notion of the godhead constituted a significant departure from traditional Christian theology insofar as it imbued orthodoxy's personal God with a good deal more impersonality and accessibility, pushing the traditional character of God to assume the complexion of an ever-present force of cosmic law, the circumambient macrocosm, that shaped and sustained all that was. God came to perform much like the law of gravity; one simply had to see its reality in order to understand and employ its forces. Following from this notion of the godhead was a drastically different understanding of the shape and goal of the religious life, and this, too, became a central concept for those in the nascent mind-cure movement. Instead of the reconciliation with God as the end of the religious life, as it had been in Christian orthodoxy, the mind-cure movement set the goal of achieving an inner harmony with the benign character of the universe. It worked like this. Swedenborg's hierarchical universe consisted of ascending spheres—physical, mental, spiritual, angelic, and divine. Because each dimension connected with every other, individual personal fulfillment depended on achieving, as Robert Fuller has put it, "rapport with other levels on the cosmic scale," from which issues all true progress. Besides spiritual well-being, physical health became possible when the body achieved "inner harmony by first becoming attuned with the soul, the soul through contact with superior angelic beings, and so on up the spiritual ladder" (*Mesmerism* 90).

If the individual person could but clarify and live with the divine in harmony, an important New Thought term, as revealed in readily discernible laws and spiritual realities, then the soul invariably came to participate more fully in the divine macrocosm and became more divine, enjoying and absorbing in almost limitless measure the love and power of the divine. It is clear, then, that much more was at stake in Swedenborg's elaborate metaphysical theory of correspondences than idle speculative fancy. This was a metaphysical scheme that allowed for immediate access to the profounder spiritual currents of ultimate reality, currents that potentially had enormous benefit for the self in its spiritual, psychological, and, as we shall see, physical dimensions. Again, Robert Fuller compactly catches the dynamic of enrichment at work within the doctrine of correspondences: "When inner harmony or resonance between realms is established, energy and guiding wisdom from the higher plane can flow into and causally influence the lower plane," and in this new relationship or understanding, the recipient received what Swedenborgians called " 'psychic influx' from the higher planes of reality" (*Alternative* 51). In short, the product of insight and intuition was harmony, and the result of harmony was an inrush of delight and power, as befitted the divine itself. This motion of divine "flow" into the self, "influx," as Swedenborgians called it, became the explanatory concept for the mechanism by which the self could attain spiritual felicity and personal wholeness: in finding the divine, the divine flowed into the self, restoring the diminished, disjointed, or distorted, a possibility that potentially included the physical. For example, most American Transcendentalists generally identified nature as the most immediate repository of spiritual reality, seeing it as a kind of halfway house to God. For them, the natural world, immediate and irrepressible, contained the plenitude and power of God. Lovers of nature saw it in aesthetic and spiritual terms as an immediately accessible redemptive force that might restore the ragged and dispirited human psyche.

The consequences of this formulation were enormous. Suddenly, to an extreme that not even the most radical Finneyite perfectionists would have dreamed possible, the self and its capacity to absorb, or even become, divine, since it already was, in part, divine, became virtually limitless. Perception led to harmony, which led to wholeness. Notably absent from this new spiritual economy were orthodox Christian notions of moral and spiritual contrition and repentance as prerequisites for genuine encounter with the divine. The sort of union with the divine later envisioned by New Thought proponents would have been anathema to the Puritans and even to the most hopeful revivalists. As a number of cultural historians have pointed out, this ease and nature of access to the divine constituted a major shift in American religious life, compared to which even pietism and revivalism set forth a comparatively rigorous route to the holy life. This drastic elision of a central Christian notion and the substitution of it by a corresponding trust in "harmony" composed the central premise of "harmonial religion" as defined by Sydney Ahlstrom: "those forms of piety and belief in which spiritual composure, physical health, and even economic well-being are understood to flow from a person's rapport with the cosmos" (1019). Robert Fuller writes of a "form of piety in which 'harmony,' rather than contrition or repentance is the sine qua non of the regenerated life" (*Alternative* 51).

From general Romantic exaltation of nature as a reflection of God, as ambiguously containing and, in the best of moments, revealing God, it was but a short step to a general veneration for all things natural. Romantic enthusiasm for nature partook of, and to some extent encouraged, a broader cultural reevaluation of the meaning of the term "natural." Many different currents contributed to this increased esteem for the natural world, deism and urbanization in particular, but oddly so did revivalism in its populism and in its desire to recapture pure and "primitive" religious experience. Within the pervasive antiecclesiasticalism was this logic: if one could but set aside the encumbrances of theology, doctrine, and church, all of which cloaked and distanced God, and meet God simply and purely, well, then, so much the better. If somehow God was in nature, or if nature was naturally good, as seemed implicit in much Enlightenment thought, then one should simply turn to nature for its natural redemptive forces. Clearly, this optimism about the character and resources of the natural world challenged Christian orthodoxy, which had always conceived of a radical disjuncture between the divine and the human that resulted from the primal event known as the Fall. Following that moral cataclysm, all of the natural world, including humanity, had descended to a lesser or inferior state and lived in need of divine forgiveness as a first step in the restoration and renewal of the original lost harmony that pervaded Eden, a realm that signified intimacy and trust between the Creator, nature, and humanity. Alienation, enmity, disease, and death followed upon the rupture brought on by the Fall. Christian orthodoxy had contended for centuries that it took a special initiative on the part of God to heal the breach between the divine and humankind.

However, in a dramatic turn in Western cultural history, in the early nineteenth century, nature itself suddenly became redemptive, as great numbers of people sought to get "back to nature." Large portions of the culture concluded that people suffered because they had broken the original natural concord with nature, moved too far from its benign wisdom. To find healing for spirit, mind, and body, all must return to its generative healing forces. Religion was not the only place where this impulse came to flourish, for the same appeared in multiple efforts at health reform. The most conspicuous of these was dietary reform, such as undertaken by Sylvester Graham and his famous cracker and the rise of grain cereals in general. Indeed, there came to be a widespread, fervid search for "natural remedies" that did not afflict the body with the harsh strategies practiced by heroic medicine, which was the standard health care for the times. Heroic medicine was so named "because it so challenged a body that it stimulated all of the patient's recuperative powers to get well" (Albanese, *Nature* 121). Indeed, doctors blistered, bled, and purged to an extent that often made the cure worse than the disease and that usually worsened the patient's condition and chances for recovery. The purpose of the new innovative therapies, then, was to escape conventional medical torture by bringing physical systems back in line with nature, from which "civilized" people had wandered. A host of remedies with "natural" intent came and went, such as hydropathy and homeopathy, but of these passing ones several remained, most notably, osteopathy and chiropractic.

Central to these and to mental healing was the supposition that the surest route to health was the restoration of harmony between the self and the natural world, a return to the foodstuffs and rhythms of pristine nature. Such claims and hopes derived both from revivalism but, more especially, from Swedenborg-inspired Romantic dreams of harmony and immediately accessible spiritual power that inhered in nature itself and that might readily flow into the self, medicating the assorted ills of spirit and body. Apparently, this notion was greatly appealing to Americans, and it prepared the imaginative soil of mid-nineteenth-century America for the full-scale development of what we now call spiritual healing. As Catherine Albanese comments, it is not remarkable that Americans sought new and different ways to get better but that so very many looked "to what were essentially methods of religious healing" (*Nature* 121). Without metaphors of harmony, "influx" or spiritual flow, and natural potentiality provided by Romanticism, the progress of many health reform movements would have been ever so much more difficult. Romanticism supplied an appealing and potent "poetics of sympathy" that "provided the perceptual frame, the focusing lens, through which the centrality of mind could be experienced and practiced," and Romanticism's predominant images contrasted markedly with images of spiritual conflict that characterized Calvinism and with images of battle that informed and shaped orthodox heroic medicine (Sizer 413–14). How much this would prove to be the case is made clear in the development in America of "mind-curist" spiritual healing, first in the form of mesmerism and then in the histories of the Church of Christ, Scientist and the New Thought movements.

THE COMING OF MESMERISM AND MIND-CURE

Into this period of diverse ferment in American religion and culture came one of the more peculiar—and undoubtedly the most significant—European importations in America—a new medical and mental theory called animal magnetism or mesmerism, the later term identifying the discovery with its founder, Anton Mesmer (1734–1815). The significant part of what Mesmer discovered is what the twentieth century has called hypnosis. Even when this bold new theory is put in context of the "spiritual hothouse" that was early nineteenth-century America, a soil that attracted and supported much curious medical and religious fruit, animal magnetism stands out in its time as one of those innovations that exerted in their heyday a peculiar appeal and power. More than that, the ideas about body and soul that emerged from mesmerism initially flourished, went through assorted permutations, and ultimately provided a major new and, as time would show, lasting strain within religious experience and self-understanding of Americans (it was also a major stepping-stone on the way to modern psychoanalytic theory and practice). Indeed, the arrival of mesmerism on North American shores initiated an unforeseeable turning or pivot in American cultural history that first infiltrated and then spilled far beyond the boundaries of traditional religious belief, piety, and ecclesiastical life.

The premier accomplishment of this transatlantic interloper was to inject into an already optimistic nation still another potent dose of hopefulness. If the regnant optimism rested upon Puritan eschatology, democratic hopes, and economic opportunity, fired as well by revivalism and Romanticism, this one pushed religious possibility still further in that it advocated a deep belief in the almost infinite potential, first, of the human mind and, second, of religious belief itself to overcome just about all the ills of the human condition. Its first dramatic focus was upon healing, as we will see in the careers of healers Phineas Parkhurst Quimby, Mary Baker Eddy, and Warren Felt Evans. The irrepressible hopefulness of mesmerism's many descendants, religious leaders such as Charles Fillmore, Emmet Fox, and Norman Vincent Peale, promulgated the belief that mind and belief might together conquer all of life's woes, whether physical illness, emotional distress, or plain bad luck. Indeed, the religious orientation that devolved out of mesmerism seemed remarkably suited to speak to whatever ills beset the time in which it found itself, whether America in the early nineteenth century or America in the mid-twentieth century. At the beginning, though, the chief appeal of the many therapeutic and philosophical variations on mesmerism lay in the great practical possibility of medical help in an era in which the practices of conventional medicine were more likely to kill one than bring about improvement or cure.

All of this began in France in the late eighteenth century. As many historians of medicine and psychiatry have recounted, Viennese physician Franz Anton Mesmer claimed to have discovered, with much sensation accompanying his promotion of the final idea, a previously undetected and vital element within human physiology, namely, the presence of what he called animal magnetism. Mesmer identified this as an invisible fluid that permeated the body and provided it with its dynamic force. Good health depended on the even distribution of this fluid throughout the body. When this balance was upset for one reason or another, ill health resulted. This mysterious inner system was apparently susceptible to different kinds of influences, and its easy flow throughout the body could be disrupted or impeded by obstructions. Passing magnets over the head or body improved flow and balance and returned this mysterious system to better function. With this discovery, Mesmer claimed to have exposed a single unitary cause for all sickness and from that, a sure means to cure. Within the European Enlightenment of the late eighteenth century, anxious as it was to uncover and embrace a material foundation for all of life, Mesmer's theory made good sense, meshing very nicely with other Enlightenment notions of a simple mechanical material universe. In addition, Mesmer was a good publicist, arranging for a healing competition with a well-known Roman Catholic priest-exorcist. The contest was a draw, but the immediate effect was to discount orthodox Christian suppositions about disease and exalt Mesmer's claims of a physical foundation for life, health, and disease. In the long run, conventional religion lost because it did not win. If science could do as well as religion in effecting cure, what good or truth lie in the latter? Following the competition and the publication in 1779 of his popular treatise, *Reflections on the Discovery of Animal Magnetism*, Mesmer rode a wave of popularity. Royal commissions in France, one including Benjamin Franklin in its membership, examined Mesmer's claims of cure, found them real enough, and then fudged on the truth of Mesmer's explanation for the healings. They found no empirical evidence for the existence of animal magnetism and attributed the cures to the patients' imaginations.

Meanwhile Mesmer's notoriety and ego grew with the measure of his success. He attracted a large following, started his own Society of Harmony, and charged big fees for curing and for teaching others his healing secrets. He embellished his healing practices as well, imbuing them with a cultic flavor and flamboyant ritual by often wearing a purple cape and utilizing a wand. The ambiguous findings of the royal commissions gave many adherents second thoughts, and Mesmer's personal obnoxiousness lost him favor with many followers. Eventually, he abandoned Paris and died in seclusion in 1815 at age eighty-one. However obscure his personal fate or questionable his contributions, some of his ideas flourished because his notion of unitary mechanical causation supplied, on one hand, the hope for a clear, immediate, and desperately needed solution of human illness and, on the other, almost paradoxically, testimony to the reality of "a depth to human experience which defied reduction into the mechanistic categories of Enlightenment (and Mesmer's own) rationality" (Fuller, *Mesmerism* 10). Oddly, then, Mesmer's ideas simultaneously supported both Enlightenment rationalism and Romantic claims of a mysterious and protean hidden self.

What Mesmer himself did not achieve in realizing the nature of his discovery emerged from the work of a long train of disciples. The marquis de Puysegur applied the name mesmerism to what Mesmer had called animal magnetism, and he delved into the strange mental state that has since become known as hypnosis, the condition with which mesmerism was to be identified when it arrived on American shores. De Puysegur had stumbled upon the human unconscious, which he and others thought to be in several ways superior to normal waking consciousness. He continued to believe in the reality of an invisible magnetic fluid but thought it to be the medium by which thought influenced the body. As such its chief agency was not physical but psychological. In an insight that would prove indispensable to later generations of mind-curists, de Puysegur concluded that thought was the decisive agent upon the body, not physical apparatuses like magnets or water. Like Mesmer before him, de Puysegur did not recognize the full ramifications, especially the religious ones, of what he had stumbled across. Those applications would arise after mesmerism made its journey across the Atlantic.

Mesmerism did not find its way to America until 1836, nearly a half century after the height of its popularity in Paris. Frenchman Charles Poyen, who called himself a professor of animal magnetism, found Americans virtually ignorant of animal magnetism and undertook a lecture tour throughout New England, and very soon his presentations of the magnetic state or hypnosis became a popular curiosity and entertainment. Poyen characteristically used paid subjects who traveled with him as well as volunteers from the audience. Most people came for Poyen's sideshow displays of uncanny physical states and evidence of clairvoyant, extrasensory perception. Of those who attended Poyen's lecture demonstrations, many came looking for cures, and many got what they came for. Much to Poyen's surprise, as Robert Fuller observes, the habitually religious Americans quickly sought to derive religious meaning from mesmeric phenomena (*Mesmerism* 22–26). To Poyen, all of mesmerism's curious manifestations were entirely naturalistic, lacking in supernatural or metaphysical significance. Poyen returned to France in 1839 but was followed in New England by English phrenological proselytizer Robert Collyer, who was more inclined to ponder the extraordinariness of mesmerism's accomplishments. Finding himself the nearest thing to an expert on mesmerism in America, Collyer ventured a three-month series of lecture-demonstrations in Boston that roused such attention and curiosity that the city council appointed a twenty-four-member commission to investigate the legitimacy of Collyer's claims. Their conclusions affirmed the reality of a mesmeric state and assured the public that no deception was involved in Collyer's feats.

The success of mesmerism as a phenomenon was so great that one contemporary estimated that by 1843 there were between twenty and thirty traveling mesmerists in New England and over 200 resident mesmerists in Boston alone (Fuller, *Mesmerism* 30). Within this craze and with the later fad of Spiritualism, sensation and chicanery characterized at least some of the stage performance, but the general public clearly responded enthusiastically to these displays. Some few voices of concern were raised, first, about the extent to which the sensationalization of mesmerism diverted scientific attention away from serious attention to hypnosis and, second, about the potential for mesmerism to become a sort of mind control, especially in the symbiotic bond created between mesmerist and subject. In the latter instance, novelist Nathaniel Hawthorne regularly warned of this danger, and short story writer Edgar Allan Poe satirized the gullibility of supporters. A third danger lay in the potential for telepathic mental influence, a kind of malicious thought transference. Through the last half of her life, the founder of Christian Science, Mary Baker Eddy, dreaded the incursion of damaging mental influences exerted by her enemies, of which she contended there were many.

Despite these warnings, great numbers of Americans remained curious about mesmerism's spiritual significance, its psychological meaning, and its medicinal powers. This interest was, in part, sustained by the flock of traveling mesmerists and also by an abundance of pamphlets and books explaining its significance and how to induce the mesmeric state of consciousness. As might be expected, the medical establishment stridently opposed any suggestion that mesmerism was capable of curing any physical condition, but mountains of personal testimony, a very convincing sort of evidence for the general public, suggested otherwise. Great numbers of ordinary people claimed to have been cured by mesmeric healers of just about every malady under the sun. Questions about the effectiveness of mesmeric therapies raged in the mid-nineteenth century and, for that matter, continue to this day in legal contests over the reality of faith cures and the reliance of doctrinaire Christian Scientists upon belief alone to effect healing. At times, as is now to some extent the case, no one on the scene really understood what happened within the varieties of mesmeric therapy or by what means consciousness acted upon itself or upon the body to accomplish whatever healing occurred, and an array of views of these matters filled the landscape of debate on animal magnetism. But, as mesmerism's foremost historian, Robert Fuller, concludes, "what is certain is the fact that literally thousands believed animal magnetism to be the sole agent responsible for their recovery from heart disease, epilepsy, inflamed joints," and a host of other afflictions (*Mesmerism* 43).

This diversity of opinion on the what and how of mesmerism might have eventually depleted the movement if it were not for mesmerism's conspicuous religious and curative powers. When conjoined, these two elements— the spiritual and physical, perennial concerns of the human species—constituted a formidable appeal, especially as they argued for the interdependence of traditionally separate and even contrary aspects of personhood, the spiritual or mental and the physical. Moreover, the hope of mesmerism suggested that there might, in fact, be a way for the spiritual and physical to harmonize, bringing physical and emotional health and a new fullness of being of the sort for which humanity has always yearned. As historian Catherine Albanese has suggested, the promise of righting a lost innate balance or harmony within the human self, one that obtained in the original creation, has been a powerful and persistent current in the American religious ethos (*Nature* 106–16). Making that ideal seem plausible was no small accomplishment. Within the widespread religious tumult and high expectations of the early nineteenth century—romanticism, revivalism, millennialism, perfectionism, and Spiritualism—that dream did not seem in the least far-fetched, just as it continues to this day to attract countless followers.

PHINEAS PARKHURST QUIMBY

Histories of mesmerism, Romantic possibility, American religion, modern psychiatry, and much of contemporary American culture assumed a wholly new dimension with the career of one of the least known, but more important, physicians in American history. By almost any standard a truly original thinker, Phineas Parkhurst Quimby (1802–1866) was not very likely the first to understand clearly the psychosomatic interrelations of the mind, spirit, and body. Many others experimented with mesmerism and mental healing, but Quimby's historical legacy has been fortunate in two regards: first, he left a sizable mound of private papers on his thought and work, and he thereby concretized his achievements for later historical scrutiny, and second, he happened to treat a number of people who later became leaders in different segments of the diverse American mind-cure movement, most notably, Mary Baker Eddy, the founder of Christian Science. As such, Quimby is usually credited with being the father of mental healing in America, although prominent Christian Science historian Stephen Gottschalk has recently proposed Warren Felt Evans, another patient of Quimby and a popular New Thought writer, as the real founder of mental healing in America. Quite apart from these considerations, however, it is clear that Quimby was the first to utilize mesmerist insights to develop a thriving medical practice, healing thousands of sick people in his decades of practice in Portland, Maine. There is simply no record of any early or late mind-cure healer who enjoyed such success. Moreover, Quimby searched in fresh and innovative ways to understand the means by which his numerous healings took place, and his strategies and ideas continually evolved as he struggled to improve his work and to understand more fully the curative mystery he had ventured into.

Quimby's background was not of the kind that seemed likely to produce a medical pioneer. The son of a blacksmith with very little formal schooling, Quimby as a young man was apprenticed to a clock maker, a trade he took up with success. Restless and inquisitive, he also became a daguerrotypist, which was a forerunner to modern photography, and a talented amateur inventor, devising a steering mechanism for boats and a version of the band saw. In both his vocation and his sidelines, Quimby seemed the embodiment of Yankee ingenuity, possessing a relentless curiosity and a practical bent for fixing just about anything, as we shall see in his encounter with mesmerism and mental healing. Like many other early inquirers into mesmerism, Quimby was primarily interested in the new phenomenon for its very immediate and practical healing capacities, and the theory that undergirded the idea of mesmerism was in itself that sort that would apply to the natural-born tinkerer. Most mesmerists, like Mesmer himself, theorized that individual well-being was affected by an invisible, fluid energy that permeated all of reality and conducted electrical energy within the body and from one person to another. With clairvoyant capacities, mesmeric seer-healers believed they could detect the condition of the flow of this pervasive invisible fluid in the patient's body, and if the flow was impeded, they thought they could prescribe cure or transfer by different means their own healing electrical energy. For Quimby, this made eminent good sense and suggested a hopeful and quite specific route to healing.

With this physicalist understanding of mesmerism as his starting point, Quimby soon abandoned his trade as clock maker and inventor to undertake his own healing practice, a career that would last twenty-eight years and treat over 12,000 patients, including the daughters of Supreme Court justice Ashur Ware (Fuller, *Mesmerism* 121). Quimby's mesmeric suppositions worked in practice, and cures abounded, as did notoriety. Before long, Quimby became the most prominent and successful of those healers who took their initial interest and methodology in mental healing from itinerant mesmerists. A few others, most notably, Warren Felt Evans, approached the same conclusions as Quimby did, but Evans came to them through his study of Emanuel Swedenborg. Not an intellectual but an eager theorist, Quimby published during his career as a healer only a few articles, and those hardly begin to account for his vital role in shaping modern American popular culture. Moreover, exactly what Quimby thought, did, or wrote at any one time in his medical practice continues to be a matter of some debate. Rather, much of Quimby's importance lies, first, in the innovative therapeutic strides he made in his Portland, Maine, office; second, in his sporadic development of theories about why and how his patients got better; and last, in whom he treated, most notably, Warren Felt Evans, Julius Dresser, and Mary Baker Paterson Eddy. These three would prove almost single-handedly responsible for carrying Quimby's insights into the mainstream of American religious experience and cultural life, although two of the three would distance themselves from Quimby. Without Quimby, however, a modest and comparatively obscure physician of the mind from Maine, the texture of much popular modern self-understanding would be notably different. His influence is readily and daily observable in a myriad of current quasi-Christian, intention-shaping, and attitude-inspiring books and assorted electronic media. In the overwhelmingly secular realm of modern psychology, Quimby's influence is no less prominent in preparing a receptive ground for the theories about the existence of the unconscious and the acceptance of the methods of modern psychotherapeutic practice.

An adequate appreciation of Quimby's life and findings and his mostly unrecognized influence is necessary to understand fully most modern self-help philosophies. His life, in particular, bears notice because, in many ways, it anticipates the character of his audience and influence. Quimby's first encounter with the curious relationship between mind and body came as a young man when Quimby himself was diagnosed with consumption, what we now call tuberculosis. It is even possible to argue that Quimby's career as a healer began with an accidental self-cure. Dismally plagued by ill health in his early thirties, Quimby attempted to repeat the experience of a friend for whom horseback riding had been curative. Unable to ride because of his weak state—his condition had been notably weakened by regular doses of calomel prescribed by his doctor of "heroic" medicine—Quimby instead opted for carriage trips. On one such excursion, Quimby's horse balked, and the invalid was forced to run it up a long hill. Strangely invigorated by this effort, he drove the beast furiously homeward, arriving there in possession, at least temporarily, of his old vigor (Braden, *Spirits* 48). The incident planted an intellectual seed in Quimby that would begin to blossom some years later, specifically, in 1838, when he attended a lecture-demonstration on mesmerism by Charles Poyen, the Frenchman who had introduced mesmerism to America two years before. Quimby was transfixed with what he saw and took to following Poyen around, trying to learn as much as he could. Nor was Quimby unusual in the measure of his curiosity, for mesmerism ignited great public enthusiasm and curiosity, and soon there arose great hordes of mesmerists traveling the countryside to cash in on the national craze. In addition to seeing and talking with Poyen, Quimby attended the demonstrations of another prominent traveling mesmerist, Englishman Robert Collyer, who promulgated mesmerism with a kind of evangelistic zeal. Some historians identify Robert Collyer as the mesmerist Quimby encountered; this divergence, in fact, has not been satisfactorily resolved, although he apparently did later also encounter Collyer. Over these years Quimby's interest deepened, and he absorbed all he could about mesmerism's intriguing phenomena. To his surprise and delight, Quimby discovered that he himself possessed considerable mesmeric powers, and he soon gave private demonstrations to family, friends, and neighbors. Such was his success that he "went public" with his abilities, and by 1843 he had given up making clocks to become a touring mesmerist.

In his early success as a mesmerist, Quimby was lucky to find a particularly sensitive hypnotic subject, Lucius Burkmar, and for several years the two traveled around New England giving mesmeric demonstrations. Burkmar exhibited unusual clairvoyant and telepathic powers but was also adept in the diagnosis of disease and the prescription of remedies, and many cures were effected, so many that Quimby was soon being touted in the press as the world's leading mesmerist (Fuller, *Mesmerism* 120). With time, however, Quimby became convinced that Burkmar's diagnoses and the remedies prescribed were of little actual use in assessing and treating the physical maladies of his patients; they were not in themselves accurate diagnoses or prescriptions. Often the medicines Burkmar prescribed were patently silly and clearly had little causal significance in accomplishing cure. On one occasion

Quimby substituted a cheap medicine for the costly one Burkmar prescribed (Burkmar had apparently struck a kickback deal with the local druggist), and the patient recovered just the same. To Quimby's mind, then, Burkmar's diagnoses only mirrored what the patients themselves thought were the causes of their sicknesses. Burkmar's remarkable clairvoyant capacities simply revealed what patients already thought about their own diseases. They recovered because Burkmar's revelations so startled them that they subsequently placed full confidence in Burkmar and whatever he prescribed. Gradually, Quimby came to conclude that the curative agent was not Burkmar's diagnostic expertise in assessing the cause of disease, for he was simply revealing with his clairvoyant powers what the patient already thought. Nor did it lie in his therapeutic recommendations since these depended on Burkmar's impressions of the patient's impressions.

Indeed, Burkmar's remedies were, in effect, placebos in which the patients had nonetheless trusted—and efficaciously so. Healing was accomplished by the patient's faith in the medicine, not by the medicine itself. From this recognition, it was for Quimby but a step to the conclusion that the operative and effectual principle was the suggestion of healing at a subconscious level and the confidence of the patient in the remedy prescribed. The disease, then, could be judged to be—in origin at least, whatever the patient's physical symptoms, mental or psychological—the product somehow of the patient's mistaken perceptions of self and reality. Supposing this to be the case, the route to cure became simply a matter of changing what in the patient's mind—usually mistaken ideas about the self, God, or the body—caused the symptoms. Quimby concluded that the patient's wrong beliefs and, usually following therefrom, the patient's disturbed mental condition caused the bad health, and he set about correcting these mistaken beliefs by reshaping the attitudes and the faith of the ill. The catalyst in healing, then, was what patients thought about themselves, the illness, and the healer—in short, whether the patient placed confidence in the prescriptions handed down by Burkmar in his clairvoyant state. For Quimby insight into this patient-healer dynamic amounted to a decisive turn in his conceptualization of disease. In the mind or psyche—two terms whose exact definitions and parameters remain in dispute—lay the origins of disease. While many mesmeric healers had concluded that patients' expectations were at least partly responsible for their cures, Quimby's "more radical conclusion" held that "their illnesses were caused by their ideas or beliefs in the first place" (Fuller, *Alternative* 59).

Despite his insights into the psychological origins of much disease, Quimby found them readily compatible, at least in the early part of his career as a healer, with his belief in the sort of physiological system propounded by mesmerism's theorists, namely, that of an invisible fluid whose free flow throughout the body determined good health. Robert Fuller summarizes Quimby's understanding of the relation of animal magnetism to physical health: "[T]he real source of human health was the magnetic fluid, or vital force, flowing into the human nervous system from some deeper level of the mind." Mind and fluid were thus interconnected. Within this vision of the physical-mental interplay, Quimby contended that "beliefs functioned like control valves or floodgates" and were capable of impeding or distorting the free flow of magnetic forces necessary for personal health (*Mesmerism* 122). It was the physician's task to free or to redirect this invisible fluid by some means or another, and for Quimby this means changed significantly over the years of his practice as he became more convinced of the primacy of what we now call psychological factors. Whether he ever fully discarded the mesmeric theory he imbibed upon coming across mesmerism remains, as suggested earlier, an open question. However, clear modifications in Quimby's therapeutic approach reveal much about the trajectory of his thought, specifically, his drift away from the mesmeric toward the psychological.

The task of understanding whatever movement took place in Quimby's thought is complicated by the fact that Quimby's written descriptions of his ideas and practices were relatively few and unsystematic and were sometimes opaque and contradictory, and they still elicit considerable debate about their authenticity. The question of Quimby's ideas is complicated by the fact, as Robert Fuller suggests, that Quimby and just about everyone else in his day "lacked a vocabulary with which to communicate the paranormal features of mesmeric cure" (*Mesmerism* 125). What Quimby encountered, after all, did not fit with prevailing understandings of physiology, mind, common sense, or religious experience, although it perhaps most closely approximated the sort of psychic turmoil and transformation instigated in the throes of revivalism. Like the revivalists of the Second Great Awakening, Quimby had in his healing practice encountered the power of the subjective domains of the self to alter radically the individual's perception and experience of God, the self, the world, and personal well-being. Then as now, large portions and potentialities of the self remained uncharted and fundamentally mysterious, lying quite beyond science's rational explanations of material causality.

It is not entirely clear if Quimby ever finally resolved by exactly what means this mental disturbance came to manifest itself physically as disease. On this, as in other aspects of his thought, Quimby himself, always a doer more than a systematic researcher or thinker, may well have remained unclear. On the basis of his 2,100 pages of manuscript writings, Charles Braden suggests that Quimby eventually gave up all dependence on mesmeric theory as an explanatory model (*Spirits* 54). On the other hand, Quimby's most recent commentator, Robert Fuller, contends that Quimby continued to tie disease and healing to mesmeric theories about the body's system of magnetic fluids; wrong beliefs blocked the free flow of the magnetic fluid that sustained the body's vital force (*Alternative* 59). Christian Science historian

Stephen Gottschalk contends as well that Quimby essentially remained a mesmerist and that Horatio Dresser, the editor of Quimby's papers, significantly exaggerated Quimby's religious leanings ("Harmonialism" 910). Quite apart from this question of to what extent Quimby retained mesmeric ideas and practices, Quimby's important conclusion was that regardless of how disease manifested itself in the body, disease itself clearly emanated from the mind's own thoughts and, conversely, that changed ideas or attitudes in the mind brought healing. Ultimately, disease was the product of what the mind thought and felt; the decisive factors in illness lay in what the patients believed about their illness, and the crucial element in returning health was the confidence placed in the curative abilities of the healer. With remarkable insight and prescience, an uneducated New England clock maker detected and understood the substantive psychosomatic interconnections and disturbances that generate much illness. To be sure, this complex of ideas did not come to Quimby all in a flash or as a great revelatory avalanche, but their clarity and strength slowly grew during his twenty-eight years as healer.

The immediate result of Quimby's first hints about the hidden relationship between the mind and the body was the conclusion that a clairvoyant intermediary was very likely unnecessary in changing patients' beliefs about sickness and health. After several years together, Quimby dispensed with the help of Lucius Burkmar. With considerable mesmeric abilities of his own, Quimby induced in himself, quite at will, a quasi-hypnotic state of hypersensitivity that, as Robert Fuller put it, "put him into instant rapport with a stratum of [his patients'] mental life about which they were largely unaware" (*Mesmerism* 123). Just as Quimby had relied on Burkmar as a vital element in his diagnostic and therapeutic armory, he also employed in his early days several other mesmerism-based strategies to increase his therapeutic effectiveness, techniques that he later would gradually discard or, depending on the patient, use selectively. In addition, in a unique aspect of early mental healing theories, Quimby believed throughout his career that the healer could transfer some of his own vital magnetic energy to the ailing patient. In the early days, he accepted this notion in a narrowly literal or material sense, and that led Quimby to try different means to enhance movement of his energy to his patients. To induce this more efficient transfer Quimby often laid his hands on the head of his patients, and sometimes before doing so, he wet his hands with water to improve conduction of magnetic energy. It is not certain whether Quimby ever thought, or thought for very long, that these methods accelerated healing, but he perhaps sensed that he did, at the very least, have in them potent means of imparting ritualistic weight to his healing therapy (Braden, *Spirits* 65). For almost all of Quimby's patients, the laying on of hands and the use of water carried enormous symbolic power in their resonance with traditional Christian images of healing, baptism, and spiritual rebirth. These techniques soon became hallmarks of mesmeric healing, but for Christian Scientists these same devices became an indication that a healer merely practiced mesmerism as opposed to what they deemed an authentically Christian approach to healing. How much the use of hands or water helped effect Quimby's remarkable healing record or when Quimby left off believing in their efficacy is not known; it is certain, however, that these means did little to hinder his success.

While Quimby did largely dispense with the use of water and hands in his therapy, he did apparently retain belief in the telepathic powers of mesmerism. Throughout his career, Quimby seemed to believe in a sort of telepathic transfer of vital energy or images of health from himself to his patients. Whether he embraced this with equal conviction throughout his career or slowly phased it out of his repertoire of healing strategies is again not certain and is subject to some debate. Regardless, until virtually the end of his career, Quimby frequently promised to treat patients even when they were physically removed from him by means of what came to be called "absent treatment." For Quimby and for others who followed in his wake, the power of hypnotic telepathy was such that one could employ solely mental means or conduits to transfer to another one's own impressions, desires, or energy—again, exactly what was transferred remained murky— and in this transfer the physical distance of the healer from the patient was apparently of little importance. Quimby believed that he could surely effect this sort of transfer with the patient in his own office merely by focusing his mental energy and even his own physical vitality on his patient, and, given the theory, there seemed no logical reason that the same could not be accomplished over great distances. Patient Mary Baker Paterson, the founder of Christian Science who was for two years a devoted client and student of Quimby, petitioned Quimby for his therapeutic intervention by this means, and throughout her long life she fervently embraced the belief that one person's mind had the power to affect, either positively or negatively, the well-being of others. Indeed, one of Eddy's most controversial beliefs, one that repeatedly won her much unpleasant notoriety, posited the reality of what she called "malicious animal magnetism" or, in its acronym form, MAM. On numerous occasions Eddy accused her opponents, of whom there were many, of "mental malpractice," the use of the telepathic power in MAM to damage others physically or spiritually. Her most sensational charge was that her enemies had conspired to murder her third husband, Gilbert Eddy, whose deteriorating health and death resulted, according to an autopsy, from heart disease.

What is clear is that, over the years, Quimby began to introduce additional alternative routes to healing, relying more fully on the benefits of understanding, sympathy, and persuasion. Relatively early in his career, Quimby began to doubt the adequacy of some mesmeric healing practices. For Quimby, experience seemed a good teacher. He observed, for example, that after his mesmeric treatments of patients, their symptoms often reappeared. The often merely temporary abatement of ailments that followed upon Quimby's mesmeric remedies suggested that the origins of disease required more prolonged or intense adjustment of patients' expectations about illness and cure. This approach was confirmed by Quimby's increasing facility in assessing the psychoemotional moods or conditions that might cause or aggravate physical sickness. Together, the temporariness of some of his cures and his recognition of depth and persistence of underlying emotional conditions prompted Quimby to shift his treatment further in the direction of "talk," an effort to persuade his clients that their illness resulted from mistaken notions of themselves, illness, God, medicine, and the like. In short, Quimby moved to counsel his patients to reorient their attitudes. Robert Fuller goes so far as to contend that Quimby virtually browbeat some of his patients into changing their ideas and attitudes about fundamental aspects of their lives. In this regard Quimby anticipated the "talking cure" of modern psychotherapeutic practice, and his contribution in initiating a process that would prepare American culture for the emergence of modern psychotherapeutic understanding simply cannot be underestimated (*Mesmerism* 134).

A second alteration in Quimby's thinking would have similarly great consequence for American culture, specifically, its religious life in the history of New Thought movement and Christian Science. Quimby's early experiments with hypnosis and healing arose from a wholly practical and personal incentive—specifically, the matter of getting well. As in the reigning medical practice of the day, Quimby was justly concerned with mundane matters of cause and effect. To an uncertain extent and for obscure reasons—mysteries that plague historians to this day—Quimby gradually moved to spiritualize at least some of his previously purely mundane mental cure. He came to believe that he had discovered the healing principle in the miracles of Jesus in the New Testament. This insight involved a reenvisioning of the makeup of the human person, especially in recognizing the existence in each individual of an unconscious, which was deemed by Quimby to be a divine element partaking of the very substance of God, a concept that he perhaps borrowed from Romanticism. This agent or portion of the self—a repository of divine receptivity that was much cultivated by Quimby—allowed Quimby to penetrate other minds to treat and diagnose the wrong belief that denies the primacy of spirit in the attainment of health. Quimby would come to identify his remedies with the miracles of Jesus, arguing that he had found the principle by which Jesus accomplished the healing of the faithful. That this radically new method for treating bodily ills was effective was entirely clear to Quimby and many of his contemporaries. It has been estimated that from his Portland office Quimby treated 12,000 patients in seven years, by any standard a staggering number. Most of these sensible, ordinary people came after hearing Quimby's successes among relatives, friends, and neighbors. Moreover, lest Quimby's practice be thought of as lowbrow quackery, it bears repeating that two of Quimby's most devoted followers were the daughters of the highly respected U.S. Supreme Court justice Ashur Ware.

No doubt at least some of Quimby's appeal derived from his condemnation of two prominent American cultural entities that he deemed responsible for much of the ill health with which many of his patients entered his office. With both institutions, Quimby had had his own personal exasperations, but whatever these were, they were amply added to by the toll he suspected these cultural goblins imposed on his patients. Early in his medical career, Quimby had pledged himself, in an oft-quoted statement, "to make war with what comes in contact with health and happiness," and in choosing these two enemies, Quimby arrayed himself against two of the strongest cultural forces in midcentury America. As one might expect, given Quimby's views on healing, the first of these was the medical profession, whose shoddy work and poor understanding he blamed for much sickness in those who visited his office in earnest search of cure. Insofar as Quimby believed that the origins of disease lay in mind or spirit, to that extent he believed that conventional medicine, with its wholly materialist understanding of illness, was mistaken. Its errors were added to by the success the profession enjoyed in duping the public into a kind of mass "mis-think" about disease. Not only did doctors not know what they were doing—they were, in fact, entirely mistaken—but they nonetheless successfully prodded everyone to "mis-think" exactly as they did. In this estimate of contemporary medical practice, Quimby was not far off the mark, given its condition in mid-nineteenth-century America, for medicine in the early nineteenth century was still largely in the hands of "heroic" physicians whose regimen of bleedings, blisterings, and purgings damaged more than they helped patients. The plethora of highly popular alternative healing strategies that sprang up early in the century—hydropathy, the Graham diet, and even some currents of Spiritualism—all bespoke the restlessness of the public in searching for not only cure but less assaultive routes to it.

Some surprise perhaps lies in the fact that Quimby's other archantagonist was the conservative Protestant culture in which he found himself. In this discontent, however, he was by no means alone, as the lives of numerous intellectuals and quite ordinary people like Mary Baker Eddy and Warren Felt Evans clearly show. Quimby might perhaps have expected to find some support within traditional Christianity, a religion that made much of the spirit, for his emphasis on the primacy of the mind or spirit. However, while Quimby exalted Jesus and his healing work, he had little patience for either the institutional church or Christian theology, which in his time and region meant Calvinism. Again, this was not without good reason. In understanding the body and soul, the church was strictly dualistic. To be sure, everyone possessed a soul or spirit, but that ethereal aspect of being was starkly separated from the realm of the physical, that material part of the self that most often served as a source of spiritual subversion and even destruction. In this regard, the church simply reinforced, in effect, the malpractice of the medical profession in its glib dismissal of the role of spirit in physical well-being. Moreover, what the church said about the spirit terribly misconstrued the nature of spiritual well-being. Specifically, Quimby identified Congregationalism's heavy insistence on darkness and evil as the wellspring for much of the illness he encountered in his patients during his decades of practice. The matter is neatly put by Charles Braden: Quimby observed that "many of his patients' fears, beliefs, and feelings . . . were bound up with the religious creeds and experiences" (*Spirits* 69). While the dire assessment of the human predicament in old-style Calvinism depressed people, its morality constricted their lives and bestowed on them large burdens of debilitating, disease-producing guilt. Very often, many of Quimby's views on the subject echo the anticlericalism of the Enlightenment that indicted a "priestcraft" that uses religious superstition to hold frightened believers in sway (77). Part and parcel of this was the clergy's misuse of the Bible, which occasioned much false belief and, from that, disease (78–79). While Quimby himself was not, by any means, irreligious, he flailed away at those cultural institutions, the church and medicine alike, that bamboozled their adherents, which was just about everybody. In 1830 in Maine, these two were just about the only games in town, the only choices by which people might define and understand themselves.

Despite this hostile attitude toward the theological misinterpretation and spiritual oppression of traditional Protestantism, Quimby progressively moved to "spiritualize" his healing theory and practice. As the numerous commentators on mental healing observe, it is entirely possible to practice mental healing without any kind of theological or metaphysical framework whatsoever, and many well-known mental-curists and positive thinkers, such as Emile Coue, went on to do so. Nonetheless, Quimby ventured to employ some religious explanations in his own search to understand the mechanisms that resulted in his healings. Quimby himself was often mystified, as he frequently confessed, by exactly what means he accomplished healing. Sufficiently and modestly cognizant of the large domains of mystery in which he walked, namely, the psychological and the metaphysical, he was more than willing to ascribe the recoveries he effected to the variety of miracles practiced by Jesus in his famous feats of healing. When asked, as he regularly was, for the source of his powers, Quimby made ready and frequent reference to having found the healing principle practiced by Jesus. Indeed, for Quimby, as is understandable, healing became the prime focus of his interpretation of religion and the person of Jesus, who was for Quimby simply a human possessed of a greater degree of "Christ" than ordinary humans, a fact that then explains his kinship to the divine. The notion of Christ as a separable commodity in Jesus departs markedly from conventional Christian theology, and for Quimby and for his followers in Christian Science and New Thought, this Christ equates with what he calls "Science." In an essay written in 1863, four months after Mary Baker Paterson became his patient, Quimby actually employs the term "Christian Science," although its exact origin in Quimby's usage is unknown (Braden, *Spirits* 75–78).

Exactly what Quimby embraced theologically is not altogether clear; some scholars claim more than others. Temperamentally, he was not a discursive, philosophical thinker accustomed to writing theological treatises on how his ideas departed from tenets of orthodox Christianity. Charles Braden reiterates the frequent plea that, when it comes to Quimby, "[I]t is extremely difficult to get a thoroughly consistent idea of what he did think, perhaps just because he himself was not clear in his own thoughts" (81). Quimby insisted that Jesus healed by changing the ideas of the sick, just as Quimby himself labored to get his patients to view the world and themselves differently. What is important to note is that through the later part of his career Quimby regularly offered religious explanations for his methods and that those were sufficient to attract the close attention of a host of devoted followers, such people as Warren Felt Evans and Mary Baker Paterson, who read and copied Quimby's disparate manuscript writings on the topic of religion and healing. What is clear in Quimby's approach, as Robert Fuller summarizes, is that Quimby "psychologized" Christian doctrines "so as to better square with the phenomenon of mental cure," in the process postulating that God is a kind of "emanative spirit" to which people must reconcile themselves to achieve "psychological self-adjustment" (*Mesmerism* 129). With a new and proper sense or idea of the Christ within, what Quimby called "Truth," patients find health and happiness.

By 1866 Quimby was ill and worn out, apparently from seeing too many patients and taking too little care of his own health. Very likely, Quimby never anticipated that his ideas, however convinced he might have been of their truth, would have such consequence in the length and breadth of American culture. He died on January 16, 1866. Historians still struggle to characterize his work and to assess his legacy. One long-running dispute focuses on the measure of Quimby's religiousness, especially in regard to the origins of patient Mary Baker Eddy's ideas and the subsequent history of Christian Science. Disciples of New Thought, initially two generations of the Dresser family, contend that Quimby supplied Eddy with major insights that later became central concepts in her theology of healing and for which she gave Quimby no credit, and about this there has been a long-running dispute. Christian Science historian Stephen Gottschalk contends that Quimby had, at best, only slight influence on Mary Baker Eddy but that Quimby was also of little consequence for the history of New Thought, designating in Quimby's place Warren Felt Evans as the vital generative figure in New Thought history. In any case, in Gottschalk's judgment, Quimby's significance has been greatly inflated, and, more than that, Quimby always remained in theory or practice a "mesmerist," a term Eddy used to disparage other proponents of mental and religious healing. Gott-schalk does credit Quimby with expanding "the principle of healing through suggestion. . . . He came to see disease as caused by negative opinions . . . that the patient entertained and healing as the result of the 'explanation' through which the patient was delivered from the effects of this ignorance." In this regard, Quimby did much to establish "an empirically verifiable sci-ence of mental healing" ("Harmonialism" 904). Last, citing Robert Fuller, Gottschalk asserts that Quimby did much to psychologize religious doctrines to make them conform to the realities of his mind-cure practice, although in Gottschalk's view this is a rather negative achievement, especially when contrasted with the rigorous theological approach of Mary Baker Eddy.

For Robert Fuller, the most recent academic historian of mind-cure, Quimby profoundly shifted the focus within American religion from objec-tive empirical standards for well-being to markedly internal ones. As Fuller puts it, Quimby set forth a "psychologized rendering of the Protestant ethic" (*Mesmerism* 131). One became responsible for what one believed, and given the power of belief to affect physical circumstance, those right beliefs accounted for health or success. Moreover, in moving from mesmeric manipulation to "talking" to his patients, a new reliance on what today is called counseling, Quimby anticipated key elements in modern psychother-apy, an achievement for which he has never been given sufficient credit (132). In this shift from manipulation and suggestion to urging his patients to insight and understanding into the psyche and God, Quimby supplied "Americans with completely new assumptions about the ontology of psychic life" (134). Ultimately, Quimby and his disciples introduced into American culture a potent new ideology that soon became a self-help spirituality and popular psychology (136).

Catherine Albanese joins Fuller in acknowledging that Quimby did, in-deed, play a vital role in creating a new self-help ideology. For Albanese, Quimby accomplished this by adapting the often inconsistent language of Transcendentalism into a form of nature religion "for soothing a pervasive national trouble" (*Nature* 106). Albanese relies on Quimby's private jour-nals, not published until 1921, to argue that Quimby, do-it-yourself ama-teur theologian that he was, nonetheless "hammered out a confused—but still commanding—theology of healing, forming a charter document for American metaphysical religion" (108). Beginning as a doctrinaire mesmer-ist, over time Quimby made the vital transitional leap from conceiving of illness as a matter of magnetism to understanding mind as the catalytic force moving the vital fluids of magnetism. From Swedenborg he borrowed for his homespun theology the notion of correspondence, and this idea became key to his healing practice. Strangely, it was Quimby who knit together major currents in the popular mentality, particularly those from Sweden-borg, assorted Romantics, and perhaps even Emerson, to make his healing theory and methodology a vigorous sort of applied Transcendentalism

(114). Importantly, Quimby always emphasized the mind-body connection and, borrowing heavily from Swedenborg's notion of correspondence, the dominance of mind over body, although he was not a thoroughgoing idealist denying the reality of matter. In 1887 different New Thought writers discovered Emerson, whom they soon adopted as their philosophical fount, and Quimby was soon all but forgotten. Perhaps he would have been if it had not been for the work of his most famous patient, Mary Baker Eddy, the one singularly responsible for systematizing and thrusting the possibility of religious healing into the main currents of American religious life.

FIGURES IN THE EMERGENCE OF NEW THOUGHT

Warren Felt Evans

A host of healers and proselytizers followed in the wake of Quimby, many deeply influenced by their contact with the man, his curative powers, and his ideas. The first and perhaps most prominent and prolific of the many New Thought writers to follow in Quimby's wake (selections from Quimby's own manuscripts were not published until 1921) was Warren Felt Evans (1817–1889), whom Charles Braden, one of the early and still best historians of mind-cure, regarded as "one of the most effective of a long line of New Thought writers" (*Spirits* 130). In fact, the measure of Evans's significance has recently become a matter of controversy since a prominent historian of Christian Science, Stephen Gottschalk, has argued that Evans, not Quimby, was the real discoverer of New Thought and that Evans's books had a much greater consequence for the development of mind-cure in America than Quimby's medical practice or the eventual publication of his manuscripts. This dispute, which we shall look at shortly, is only the latest spat in a century-long debate over the measure of Quimby's influence on the mind-cure movement in general and on specific figures like Mary Baker Eddy and her formulation of what she came to call Christian Science. Whatever the case may prove to be, there is no doubt that what came to be known as the New Thought movement would have emerged much later and in different form if it had not been for the early and very popular articulation of its crucial concepts in the many books by Warren Felt Evans.

Born in Vermont in 1817, the sixth of seven children of a farm family, Evans attended both Middlebury and Dartmouth Colleges, although it is unclear whether he, in fact, graduated from the latter. Ordained a Methodist Episcopal minister at just twenty-one years of age in 1838, he seemed ill suited for the conventional pastorate, going through eleven parish appointments in a few short years (Teahan, 64; Fuller, *Mesmerism* 146). Apparently, he also felt considerable discontent with the conventionalities of Methodist theology, for he early embraced, as had many other restless intellectuals, the teachings of Emanuel Swedenborg, the Swedish scientist-philosopher-mystic. Amid this initial enthusiasm for Swedenborg and for reasons that are no longer entirely clear, Evans visited Quimby in 1863, and his encounter with Quimby seemed only to solidify, given what we know of Quimby, Evans's Swedenborgian leanings. In the year after his visit to Quimby, the measure of Evans's commitment to Swedenborg appeared in two very public ways: he joined the Swedenborgian Church of the New Jerusalem, remaining a reader in the church for five years, and he published his first book, an admiring proclamation of Swedenborg and his historical significance, *The New Age and Its Messenger* (1864). Historians have usually assumed, although it has lately been called into question, that Evans went to Quimby in ill health and that Evans was healed by Quimby, in the words of New Thought historian Martin Larson, of a "mysterious malady" (72). Whatever the case, in 1867 Evans opened his own mental healing practice in Boston, which he sustained for twenty years until shortly before his death. In 1869, six years before the appearance of Mary Baker Eddy's *Science and Health*, Evans published the first of his many mind-cure books, *The Mental-Cure, Illustrating the Influence of the Mind upon the Body.*

Evans's career proved important for four reasons. First, according to the most recent historian of mind-cure, Robert Fuller, the course of Evans's own thought changed over the years. At no time was he an unthinking or uncritical disciple of Quimby, which is the impression one receives of many of Quimby's followers, and according to Fuller, Evans set about melding Quimby's ideas, insofar as he absorbed them, with a notably broader philosophical understanding of philosophy and religion. While perhaps himself as restless and inquisitive as Quimby, Evans's preparation and field of inquiry lay in theology and philosophy, and in these he roamed far and wide: Western idealism, Oriental thought, modern science, and Western mysticism, to name but a few (Teahan 64–70). As a result, as Fuller points out, during the course of Evans's many books there was a "progressive attenuation of mesmeric healing into popular philosophy" (*Mesmerism* 146). Through the course of his many books, the prominence of Quimby's pseudomedicinal materialism declined, to be supplanted by ever greater emphasis on the predominance and potentiality of the spirit, a notion that also received emphasis by Quimby but was constrained by the healer's understandings of magnetic physiology.

Second, among all the early New Thought advocates, Evans stood out, for evident in his books was his very wide reading in philosophy, psychology, science, and medicine. These distinctly philosophical elements imparted to the new movement a much-needed measure of intellectual respectability. If mind-cure had seemed quackery, with Evans's many books, all philosophically adept, mind-cure began, at the very least, to assume a measure of intellectual credibility and plausibility. In all of this and perhaps because of it, Evans gave little credit to Quimby, mentioning him in his books only once and then in the company of other mental healers. In the eyes of Quimbyites, this remains a notable omission for, as Martin Larson comments, in Evans's intellectual journey Quimby was very clearly "the catalyst which enabled him to formulate his own philosophy and make the decision to become a therapeutic healer" (73). Skeptics of Quimby and his influence, such as Stephen Gottschalk, might argue that Evans failed to acknowledge Quimby's influence because Quimby had little influence upon him, Evans having already arrived at his own conclusions before he ever met Quimby. Again, whatever the case may be, Evans's own considerable body of work added intellectual dignity to mind-cure, greatly furthering thereby the appeal and popularity of the fledgling New Thought movement.

So intent was Evans's effort to secure for mind-cure greater credibility that he elaborated an extensive intellectual and doctrinal core that has ever since more or less characterized most of the New Thought movement. This third reason that Evans's significance is an especially notable achievement is that it was accomplished within a movement that has historically taken pride in a staunch antidoctrinalism and in an eager theological syncretism. For his two decades as New Thought's chief theologian, Evans did more than any other figure of his time to articulate the nature and substance of this New Thought. Martin Larson goes so far as to pronounce Evans to be "the first and indeed the only important figure . . . who attempted to work out a consistent and philosophically supported system of what may be called mental or metaphysical healing, during the first two decades after the death of P. P. Quimby" (127). As such, Charles Braden explains, his views remain "basic to the understanding of the development of the whole metaphysical movement in America" (*Spirits* 93).

Last, Evans's enthusiasm for the substance of New Thought and his own speculative cast of mind culminated in a series of books that not only articulated his developing ideas about the substance of mind-cure but found a ready audience amid the multifaceted cultural "dis-ease" of the Gilded Age. In short, Evans did much to popularize New Thought. The frequency and success of his numerous books spread the hopefulness of the New Thought vision of health, happiness, and God. More than anything else, this contribution in publicizing and explaining New Thought accounts for his prominence in New Thought and very likely constitutes his foremost achievement within its history. A recent student of Evans, John Teahan, sees him as a "key transitional figure between American romantic idealism, classically expressed in the Transcendentalist movement, and the less intellectual forms of New Thought and positive thinking" (78). As such, Evans's sizable quantity of work offered "a highly articulate response to nineteenth-century religious and psychological discontent" (79). The very popularity of Evans's sizable tomes, comparative best-sellers in their day, clearly prepared the way for the diffuse movement's speedy organizational development in the 1880s. Three years after his first mind-cure book, *Mental-Cure*, came *Mental Medicine: A Theoretical and Practical Treatise on Medical Psychology* (1873), which sold 15,000 copies and went through fifteen editions by 1885 (Larson 75). The fact that much in these many books seemed redundant did little to slow Evans's productivity, and more books followed apace: *Soul and Body: Or the Spiritual Science of Health and Disease* (1876); *The Divine Law of Cure* (1881); *The Primitive Mind-Cure, the Nature and Power of Faith, Elementary Lessons in Christian Philosophy and Transcendental Medicine* (1884); and *Esoteric Christianity and Mental Therapeutics* (1886). In Martin Larson's enthusiastic words, in these many books Evans "blazed a new trail for the religion of science, health, success, happiness, and prosperity" (73). Indeed, probably no one was more responsible for the diffusion of what became known as New Thought than Warren Felt Evans.

The usual understanding of the origin of Warren Felt Evans's career as mental healer, medical philosopher, and author is nicely summarized by Gottschalk: "[H]istorians have generally portrayed Evans as a Quimby disciple whose own work in mental healing was launched after he was supposedly cured by Quimby of a long-standing ailment in 1863" ("Harmonialism" 904). Recently, however, Gottschalk has dissented sharply from this view, suggesting, first, that Evans learned little from Quimby and second, that Evans's early popularization of New Thought in his best-selling books constitutes mind-cure's primary source and disseminator in America. Indeed, a strong case consisting of common sense and chronology can be made for Gottschalk's claims. In terms of breadth of influence, it is an indisputable fact that Evans published a number of best-selling books on mind-cure long before Quimby's manuscripts appeared in print, which waited until Horatio Dresser's 1922 edition. While various patients and students of Quimby had seen and even copied some of his manuscripts, it seems unlikely that enough of Quimby's writing had circulated to account for the influence usually ascribed to him. In any case, Gottschalk blames Horatio Dresser, the well-known son of Julius and Annetta Dresser, for Evans's eclipse and Quimby's unjustified prominence. Dresser's parents had attacked Mary Baker Eddy for stealing from Quimby for her early lessons in Christian Science. So when it came time for Dresser to write his *History of the New Thought Movement* in 1919, he sided with his parents' account of the matter. Moreover, when Dresser edited the Quimby manuscripts in 1921, his editing proved highly selective, and further, in the selections published, Dresser undertook minor changes that "had the effect of giving a religious cast to Quimby's thinking that differs markedly from the impression given by his manuscripts as a whole" ("Harmonialism" 910). Because of family politics, then—specifically, his desire to perpetuate his father's denial of Eddy's uniqueness—Horatio Dresser took the side of the pro-Quimby, anti-Eddy forces. Within this debate, it is important to note Gottschalk's own deep commitment to Christian Science and the theological originality and uniqueness of Mary Baker Eddy. This contention largely shapes Gottschalk's treatment of Quimby, Dresser, Christian Science, and New Thought in his

"Christian Science and Harmonialism" in the recent *Encyclopedia of the American Religious Experience* (1988). There is some support for Gottschalk's view in John Teahan's essay on Evans, in which he supplies some evidence for Gottschalk's claim. Teahan makes reference to early published quotations from Evans's journal, now extinct, that indicate that as early as 1860, Evans had concluded that all disease originated in the mind (64). In any case, if Gottschalk is correct in his claim about Dresser's approach to the debate over the comparative influence of Quimby and Evans, then the consequence has been the serious historical neglect of the real founder of New Thought in America, Warren Felt Evans.

Regardless of the catalytic agent in Evans's career, whether his own thought or the influence of Quimby, what is clear is that he would later imbue his early ideas and practices with esoteric Christianity, an influence that would come to permeate his work as healer and New Thought proselytizer. In moving in this direction, he endowed New Thought with a coherence and intellectual stature it had not previously enjoyed. However, at the time of his first book, *The Mental-Cure, Illustrating the Influence of the Mind upon the Body*, published in 1869, Evans embraced such commonplace mind-cure ideas, again whether Quimby-inspired or personally derived, as physical manipulation, the laying on of hands, absent treatment, the transfer of vital energy from healer to patient, and mesmeric power, concepts that were prominent in Quimby's own teachings to his small band of disciples, of which Evans was one, at least for a time. To these core beliefs, Evans added doses of Spiritualism, Swedenborgian angelology, and theory about the correspondence between the mind and the body. In fact, the greatest distinctive in this first book was Evans's persistent emphasis on the intimate interdependence of the spirit and the body, a closely interlinked metaphysical correspondence, and this emphasis forecast the theological path he would follow in his future books.

By the time of his fourth book, *The Divine Law of Cure*, Evans had become a thoroughgoing philosophical idealist, which was the course taken by many religiously inclined intellectuals in New England, all influenced by Swedenborg and a part of the ethos of Transcendentalism, but at the same time Evans remained close to the mainstream of late-century American Christianity. Like many New Thought figures, while retaining the contours and much of the language of traditional orthodoxy, he often poured notably different meanings and concepts into traditional terminology. Nor does he seem to have reacted as violently or distanced himself so extremely as Martin Larson suggests in *New Thought Religion*, arguing very insistently that Evans repudiated "totally all the dogmas of orthodox Christianity" and, again, as if to emphasize his point, "abolished the creeds of Christendom" (76, 77). Indeed, throughout his analysis of Evans's views, Larson is overeager to distance Evans from any vestige of traditional belief, and one must wonder about the objectivity of Larson's reading of Evans's thought. In contrast, historian John Teahan argues that Evans retained a high regard for Christianity, although he stridently and persistently criticized the ecclesiasticism of the institutional church that had long since forgotten the truths of primitive Christianity, especially the healing power of Jesus (66). Academic historians, such as Charles Braden, Robert Fuller, and Teahan, allow for greater continuity between traditional Christian concepts and Evans's alteration of them than does Larson. It is perhaps more accurate to say that Evans, like others in the New Thought movement, reinterpreted much of Christianity, but that in doing so, they often made prominent again historic minor strains in the broader Christian tradition, such as gnosticism. Or, as Evans did increasingly throughout his career, New Thought advocates interpreted Christian doctrine in light of perspectives gained from the study of other major world religions.

There is no question, however, as in the case of Quimby before him and with peers like Mary Baker Eddy, that Evans's thought constituted a major departure from Christian orthodoxy. On the major points of traditional Christian doctrine, such as the nature and status of the person of Jesus, there is significant theological blurring. As would be characteristic of most theologically inclined mind-curists, Evans drew a sharp distinction between Jesus the person, Christ a divine entity, and the rest of humanity. Although Christological debates have flourished throughout the history of Christianity, most have allowed a dual, simultaneous personhood in the Incarnation; in his inmost nature, Jesus Christ was both/and, human and God, fully. For Evans, though, Jesus the man grew into Christhood, as ordinary humans may grow into what New Thought writers often referred to as "the universal Christ" (Braden, *Spirits* 106). Nor does "the historical Jesus . . . exhaust the Christ Principle, but . . . Jesus, serving as the mediator between man and God, was its greatest instantiation." The Christ dwells in all, and all persons participate in the divine by their very nature (Teahan 69). Here Evans differs little from the views held by Mary Baker Eddy. However, by his last book, *Esoteric Christianity*, Evans had conjoined God and Christ and Spirit, thereby suggesting a kind of pervasive, pantheistic reality, although the divine and the human were not wholly identical, and people could move to closer unity with God (Teahan 69–70). As source, person, and teacher, Jesus was the foremost revealer of this reality. With the notion of correspondence derived from Swedenborg, Evans deemed individual people to be finite manifestations, miniature incarnations of the unlimited reality represented in Jesus, who modeled humanity's path by becoming the Christ. Evans was similarly innovative on other critical points of orthodox Christian theological emphasis. Spiritual reality, if not exactly the only reality, surely predominated and was at best a manifestation of the thought of God. One commentator summarizes Evans's views: "Since God, the Divine Mind and Spirit, comprehended all reality as an ultimate unity, Evans would not deny the reality of the material world, although he followed Bishop Berkeley in his refusal to grant it a separate existence outside the mind" (Judah 164). So also physical bodies seemed but the projections of individual personal thought. Given this idealist monism, it is not surprising that Evans had little to say about evil, which he considered to be, in the words of Charles Braden, "only the negation of good" (*Spirits* 109). Evil was, to be sure, a real force, and Evans did not deny its reality, although he felt it amounted to no more than simple ignorance, misunderstanding, error, or misapprehension of truth.

The questions of exactly where and how far Evans departed from Christian orthodoxy are of more than abstruse theological curiosity, for at least some of these points of departure signal important changes in American religious belief and religiosity, specifically, the manner in which Americans have come to conceive of themselves and of God. A major point of contention in this discussion focuses on the apparent shift in American cultural life from a religious understanding of God to a markedly psychological approach. One way of clarifying the issue is to note Evans's understanding of the notion of conversion. Traditional Christian theology emphasized the necessity of the reorientation of the whole self, especially in its spiritual and moral dimensions. The key stages in this reorientation involved repentance and conversion wherein would-be converts confess to God their evil deeds and inclinations, accept the loving forgiveness of God called grace, and at least begin the process of spiritual and moral renewal that sets them on the path of faithfulness to God. In the short history of American Christianity, often heavily evangelical in its emphasis, this indispensable process of redemption was initiated by a deep, personal sense of the moral and spiritual unworthiness of the self. The question here is to what extent New Thought discarded this accent to make of belief a notably utilitarian attitude that spoke mostly to meeting psychoemotional needs as opposed to spiritual-moral demands. These categories are not readily pulled apart, and this discussion necessarily deals with emphases within the broad range of religious experience. Historian Robert Fuller sees New Thought disposing of the old conversionist demand. Because of mind-cure's understanding of human nature and God, it simply did "away with the necessity of repentance or contrition as a means of reconciling oneself with God's will." Instead, they constructed a "pantheist ontology" and "spiritual abundance" was to be had for the mere thinking of it (*Mesmerism* 152). In contrast, J. Stillson Judah argues that Evans retained much of his revivalist heritage (he had been a Methodist) insofar as he believed that physical health depended on the extent of the individual's "recognition of one's Christ nature" (166). The achievement of "what he later called Christian perfection" depended on "the transformation of man's fear, anxieties, hates, envy, jealousies, etc., to love, sympathy, faith, etc." (166–67). While this change notably entails religious posture of moral reckoning, Judah does concede that Evans increasingly stressed right thinking as the route to personal wholeness and happiness, and this shift necessarily detracted from attention placed on repentance and rectitude.

Whatever changes Evans's ministry and writing wrought in American religious culture, they all began with his stalwart, lifelong attempt to effect healing for himself and countless others, and for Evans full recovery or optimum health could result only from discovering in "this present existence . . . the true nature of the real man . . . the clue to a life of health, happiness, and peace" (Braden, *Spirits* 112). To this end, Evans remained eclectic, willingly referring his patients to conventional medicine or psychologists if he thought these professionals might help particular ailments and patients. From start to finish, although methods and theory changed, Evans thought illness issued from wrong thought. How much the correction of wrong thought also entailed what Braden calls the "restoration" of the soul is often open to debate (Braden, *Spirits* 117). Stephen Gottschalk largely agrees, asserting that from first to last Evans remained at heart a mesmerist in thinking that suggestion and mental influence were decisive mechanisms in changing human belief and effecting well-being ("Harmonialism" 904). John Teahan agrees in part but contends that Evans's use of suggestion was shaped by his lifelong mysticism and was always in behalf of getting patients to realize their participation in the divine so all may "ignite the flame of the Spirit within" (76). There is also debate on how far Evans expanded his quest for health to include other vital dimensions of ordinary human experience, specifically, those elements that would become mainstays in the panoply of New Thought hopefulness, "success, happiness, and prosperity" (Martin Larson 73).

The Dressers: Annetta, Julius, and Horatio

Other disciples of Quimby, friends and acquaintances of Warren Felt Evans and Mary Baker Eddy, would also play a vital role in the promulgation of New Thought in America. Chief among these were Annetta and Julius A. Dresser (1838–1893) and their son Horatio W. Dresser (1866–1954). The parents were healed by Quimby, and they became lifelong advocates of Quimby's methods and what would become New Thought, although they waited almost twenty years after their time with Quimby to assume a public role in the mind-cure movement. In 1883, after a long sojourn in the West, they returned to Boston to start what would become a burgeoning mental healing practice. They began with discussion groups among patients and then offered classes in what they called Mind Cure Science (Fuller, *Mesmerism* 139). In many ways, the Dressers seemed the first family of New Thought, the parents becoming prominent advocates in Boston, especially in opposition to Mary Baker Eddy, and son Horatio writing the first history of New Thought, sustaining the intellectualism of Warren Felt Evans, and editing the *Quimby Manuscripts*.

Julius Dresser was born in Portland, Maine, in 1838. While a preseminary student at Waterville College, he fell sorely ill, and, thinking he was going to die, he made his desperate way to Quimby's office in Portland. Along with his future wife, Annetta Seabury, who was also under Quimby's care at the time, Dresser was healed and became an enthusiastic student of Quimby's theories and even set about trying to explain them to others. Still, unlike some of Quimby's other students and for reasons that remain unclear, Dresser was not inclined to take up Quimby's mantle and begin healing others. Instead of ministry, either in the conventional pastorate or as a Quimbyite mental healer, Dresser took up journalism and soon became a newspaper editor, first in Portland and then in Webster, where he edited the *Webster Times*. In Webster Dresser received in February 1866 a letter from Mary Baker Glover Patterson shortly after her famous fall on the ice in Lynn, Massachusetts. Their mutual healer-teacher, to whom both owed their health, Phineas Parkhurst Quimby, had died but six weeks before, and amid her sorrow and injury, whether real or phantasmal, Mrs. Glover searched for a new healer and mentor who might not only cure her but assume Quimby's mantle as spiritual guide. She clearly saw Dresser in thought and stature as the most likely successor to Quimby, and she implored the editor to take up the leadership of Quimby's healing practice. This he stalwartly refused to do, perhaps because his new son was but weeks old, until at last some sixteen years later, when he and his wife returned from the West and began their own healing practice in Boston.

In 1883, upon the Dressers's return to Boston, Julius took a course in what was by then called Christian Science from Daniel Arens, one of the deserting dissidents from Mary Baker Eddy's movement. Noting the striking similarities between Quimby's teachings and the version of mental healing taught by Arens, who had learned it from Eddy, in February 1883 in the *Boston Post* Dresser publicly charged Eddy with substantial plagiarism from Quimby's unpublished writings, thus igniting a controversy over originality that would rage for generations (Judah 270). Mrs. Eddy responded, and an unfruitful exchange followed in the *Post's* pages. A fuller account of Julius Dresser's charge appeared in 1887 in *The True History of Mental Science*, the movement's first history, which paid considerable attention to Quimby's life and his role as founder of mental healing, a focus that would necessarily conflict with Mrs. Eddy's increasing claims for herself as a distinct and separate wellspring for her Christian Science quite apart from Quimby, whom she termed a mere "mesmerist." Annetta Dresser would add still more fuel to this long-smoldering dispute in 1895, two years after husband Julius's death, with *The Philosophy of P. P. Quimby, with Selections from His Manuscripts and a Sketch of His Life.*

The setting for this conflict over origins lay in Quimby's Portland office between 1859 and 1865, when he had gathered about him patients who would later turn out to be the leaders of metaphysical healing in America:

Warren Felt Evans, Annetta Seabury, Julius Dresser, and Mary Baker Glover Patterson. Apparently, Quimby had in his last years written many pages, more than 2,100 in all, which are now housed in the Library of Congress. In the form of a journal of ruminations, most of the entries explained his healing practice and theories, amid other subjects, and he apparently hoped to publish his medical views in book form sometime in the future, but his death ended the venture (Judah 159). During these years, he allowed some of his patients and students at least partial access to read all or part of these fragments, even allowing some to copy them out in their own hand, either as a service to him or for their own purposes. In any case, Dresser found striking similarities between Quimby's teachings and those of Mrs. Eddy, the rising and very controversial star in metaphysical healing circles who insisted on the uniqueness and originality of her vision of Christianity and healing. As thoroughgoing Quimbyites and recalling Eddy's early public expressions of deep indebtedness to Quimby, the Dressers were duly provoked by Eddy's claims. The controversy was not an easy one to sort out, and even though an edition of *The Quimby Manuscripts* was published by son Horatio Dresser in 1922, the dispute still has ardent proponents on both sides. In the last decade it has been reignited by the charge of historian of Christian Science Stephen Gottschalk that the real father of New Thought was Warren Felt Evans and that Quimby's contributions were minimal ("Harmonialism" 909).

Neither Julius or Annetta would add new or different ideas to Quimby's thought, for they regarded him as the master. For the time being, their foremost proponent was Warren Felt Evans, but their spat with Mary Baker Eddy over origins served to emphasize a very public distinction between New Thought and Christian Science, one that only became more conspicuous over the years as Mrs. Eddy became more radical in her claims of distinctiveness. Because they had never fallen within Eddy's orbit of influence and upon their return to Boston appeared as autonomous outsiders within the sometimes dubious circle of Boston healers, they managed to increase both visibility and credibility for the notion of mental healing. Their stalwart integrity appeared in other ways as well. Stillson Judah casts Julius and Annetta Dresser, as well as son Horatio, as conscientious New Thought critics, even though they as a family dwelt as close to the center of the burgeoning movement as any few people in the country. Judah contends that they together regularly opposed and decried many developing currents among assorted New Thought leaders and popularizers. For example, Annetta Dresser attacked the use of affirmations, the practice of positive verbal repetition, rather like chanting a mantra, that many recommended as a healing method. These, she contended, departed from Quimby's habit of participatory sympathy and diagnostics on the part of the healer. In the 1890s son Horatio criticized the exultation of "thought" as an instrument of power by writers like Ralph Waldo Trine and Henry Wood. The emphasis on power shifted focus away from the spiritual to the mental, away from spiritual cure to mental manipulation, from love to selfishness, from worship to egoism. As Judah summarizes, for the Dressers, "the change of will was more important than the secondary power of mind; disinterested love was rated higher than affirmations. He was especially critical of those who believed that the mere recitation of an affirmation magically brought corresponding change in the body, or prosperity without work" (190). According to Braden, none of the Dressers were enthused about some New Thought emphases on "supply" and material prosperity, which they thought risked a terrible confusion of ends and means: one might use the spiritual to obtain material wealth.

The influence of the senior Dressers would pale beside the accomplishments of son Horatio Willis Dresser (1866–1954), who would become, in the assessment of Martin Larson, "one of the most prolific and popular New Thought writers" and an "outstanding spokesman for the movement in general" (189). Neither an organizer nor an original scholar or thinker, Dresser nonetheless did much to promulgate and dignify New Thought as a religious and intellectual movement. He was by no means content to ride his popularity within the movement, for soon after becoming a noted New Thought writer, he severed all formal ties with New Thought organizations, later did doctoral work at Harvard University with William James and Josiah Royce, and ended his career as a Unitarian and writer of academic histories of philosophy. For these reasons he seems a figure of unusual interest who has been almost entirely neglected by scholars of American intellectual history. Unfortunately, Gail Parker's look, in her *Mind Cure in New England*, at Dresser's thought, displayed as it is in more than thirty books, is no more than a glimpse and, at that, a very impressionistic one that adds little to understanding or appreciation.

Born in the year Quimby died, 1866, Horatio was quite literally born and bred within the birth years of metaphysical healing in North America. Given his background, it is not surprising that son Horatio himself had begun to practice mental healing by the time he reached age eighteen. He twice traveled to Europe before entering Harvard College at age twenty-five in 1891. His education was disrupted following his father's death two years later, but he did eventually finish his undergraduate degree. He published his first essay, "The Immanent God," in 1894, and a year later appeared his immensely popular first book, *The Power of Silence*, which by 1903 went through fifteen editions. *The Perfect Whole* soon followed. So popular were these first two books, which were intended to be popular expositions of Quimby-Swedenborgianism, that a brief compilation of the two, called *The Heart of It*, was soon offered, and this, too, did very well. His purpose and emphasis as a New Thought writer appear rather plainly in the list of the books that soon followed: *In Search of a Soul* (1897), *Voices of Hope* (1898), *Voices of Freedom* (1899), *Methods and Problems of Spiritual Healing* (1899),

Living by the Spirit (1900), *The Christian Ideal* (1901), and *A Book of Secrets* (1902). In addition to this regimen of authorship, Dresser in 1896 started his own monthly magazine, *The Journal of Practical Metaphysics*, which in 1898 merged with the influential New Thought journal, *Arena*, and Dresser became its associate editor. In addition, during these busy years, Dresser served briefly as a leader in various New Thought organizations, both in Boston and nationally.

The year 1902 seems to mark a distinct change in the course of Dresser's thought and career. While Dresser did not forsake his role or interest in the metaphysical healing movement, and while he continued as one of its most conspicuous and esteemed spokesmen, he withdrew from all New Thought organizations. He had accomplished much by his mid-thirties, and he must have wondered what more he would like to do with his life. His course of action through the next decades suggests that he wished to find a wider intellectual and personal horizon. This was, to some extent, forecast by his publication in 1900 of *Education and the Philosophic Ideal*, a book that signals broader interests than mental healing and New Thought religious philosophy. In 1905 Dresser started graduate work at Harvard University, studying under William James and Josiah Royce, and he received his doctorate in 1907 at age forty-one, making him very likely the best educated of all New Thought writers. The effect of his time with James, the founder of the American study of religious psychology, appears in Dresser's next book, *Physician to the Soul* (1908), which "advanced significantly in the direction of religious psychoanalytic therapy," according to New Thought apologist Martin Larson (192). At the same time that Dresser ventured in this somewhat new direction, he sustained his lasting interest in New Thought, editing in 1917 *The Spirit of New Thought*, a collection of twenty-two essays by himself and other leaders in the movement written in the years between 1887 and 1916. In 1919, Dresser was ordained a minister in the Swedenborgian Church of New Jerusalem, although in 1925 he retired from clerical life to write books. He was also invited to write *A History of the New Thought Movement*, which appeared in 1919 and remained the standard history until Charles Braden's *Spirits in Rebellion* appeared in 1963. Perhaps his most lasting service to students and scholars of New Thought was his edition of *The Quimby Manuscripts*, which appeared in 1921.

Throughout this second phase in his career, Dresser seemed intent upon placing New Thought within the larger context of the long history of Western philosophy and also within the then-emerging field of modern psychology. In the 1920s Dresser, for the most part, left behind New Thought publishing and writing and turned to academic historical writing, producing book after book in psychology and philosophy: *Psychology in Theory and Practice* (1924), *Ethics in Theory and Application* (1925), *A History of Ancient and Medieval Philosophy* (1926), *A History of Modern Philosophy* (1928), and *Outlines of a Psychology of Religion* (1929). His last book,

Knowing and Helping People, appeared in 1933 and was distinctly Unitarian in flavor. Dresser spent his last decades teaching and counseling at the Church of Our Savior, a Unitarian Congregational church, in Brooklyn Heights, New York, activities he continued until shortly before his death in 1954 at age eighty-eight.

It is very difficult to derive a fair estimate of Dresser's thought and significance on the basis of secondary sources, and he is one of those figures in American religious history who deserves careful, protracted study, if only for his apparent influence on American philosopher-psychologist William James. While Dresser clearly has significance for intellectual historians, he perhaps retains greater significance for cultural historians insofar as his popular writing, like that of Warren Felt Evans, served as an early and important conduit of New Thought ideas and seminal self-help notions into the religious mainstream of American culture. Both Charles Braden and Martin Larson assert Dresser's significance without really showing it. Larson's brief summary of Dresser credits him with being a forerunner of Freud, which is a sort of inflation characteristic of Larson, although Dresser did become increasingly interested in psychology in his later years, publishing numerous textbook-like studies and teaching both it and philosophy. Nonetheless, throughout *New Thought Religion* Larson seems intent on validating the claims of New Thought religion by showing how much it anticipated the Freudian currents in modern psychiatric theory. At the same time, especially in the case of Dresser, Larson tends to mute his proximity to traditional Christian theology and devotion by selecting those emphases that comport best with subsequent New Thought. Moreover, in his brief analysis of Dresser, Larson persists in using a kind of mentalist vocabulary, although Dresser himself was more comfortable with conventional religious terminology and, like all New Thought writers, poured his own meanings into those terms (190). Larson's interpretation contrasts sharply with Braden's judgment that regardless of how psychological Dresser became in his emphases, "he never lost the central emphasis upon the spiritual" (163). Moreover, Larson seems to have little regard for Dresser, perhaps because Dresser disputed the idea that mental powers could or should be used to gain economic prosperity, although Dresser's dissent fits well with what Braden interprets to be a persistent, primary concern for spiritual growth and wholeness.

Gail Thain Parker's treatment of Horatio Dresser in her *Mind Cure in New England* is impressionistic in the extreme. She spends fifteen loosely constructed pages characterizing a career that spanned fifty years and thirty-two books on a wide range of demanding topics. After a brief bit of entirely speculative psychobiography that suggests Horatio was embarrassed by his parents' ready supernaturalism, she characterizes his career as a war on religious experience in behalf of a rationality that would ensure his respectability and elevate him above the ordinary credulous New Thought believer:

"[H]e became a man dedicated to preserving his own sense of superiority, and as the resident intellectual of mind-cure movement he could look down on the wishful thinking and foolish exotericism of the faithful. . . . Once he got started, Dresser's condescension knew no bounds" (140). Such commentary is, to say the least, unnuanced. As Robert Fuller comments on Parker in *Mesmerism and the American Cure of Souls*, Parker's tactic is to throw "suspicion on the depth or integrity of the mind-curists' interest in the subconscious mind" (211). Besides flimsily supported commentary, Parker's usual habit is to assail the character of those of whom she disapproves.

Horatio Dresser remains one of several New Thought writers who did much to shape the religious ethos of twentieth-century American culture but whose life and work have received scant attention in American cultural studies. He is one of those figures marginalized as a sect leader or fanatic by the scholarly establishment. That peremptory judgment overlooks the breadth and seriousness of his learning and the general common sense with which he approached the capacities of the mind and spirit. In addition, Dresser's importance perhaps looms larger than usually thought, if only, as Stephen Gottschalk suggests, for his apparent influence on William James's portrait of the "once-born" religious mentality in James's classic *Varieties of Religious Experience* (1902). It is important to note as well Dresser's eminent common sense that informed his religious and medical judgments amid the often grandiose claims of other New Thought writers. For example, he recognized the reality of physical disease that required the treatment of regular physicians, but at the same time Dresser recognized that there was "a horde of terrible psychosomatic ailments which are beyond the reach of drugs or medicine, but which often appear as purely physical maladies" (M. Larson 195). Charles Braden's assessment that Dresser made "no significant new contribution to the development of New Thought" may claim too little for Dresser, especially given the wide range of his thought and writing. Still, just as during his life he was a significant "personal link between early New Thought and its later manifestations," his work in retrospect remains a valuable route into the origins and development of the New Thought movement (*Spirits* 163).

Ralph Waldo Trine

The best known of New Thought writers was Ralph Waldo Trine, who was born in the same year as Horatio Dresser, 1866, and outlived Dresser by four years, dying in 1958 at the ripe old age of ninety-two. Most of his success came in his early years, specifically with *In Tune with the Infinite: Fullness of Peace, Power, and Plenty*, probably the best-selling of all New Thought books, which he published in 1897, when he was but thirty years old. Trine went on to publish a number of other books, and while several of those did well—Charles Braden suggests a number sold over a half million each—none began to match the success of *In Tune with the Infinite* (165). Trine's greatest best-seller sold over a million copies in the years immediately following its publication, and it has since been translated into some twenty languages and also into braille. New Thought historian Martin Larson reports that there have been over fifty editions (169). Total sales since publication are now estimated to be over 4 million, and the 1995–1996 *Books in Print* still lists *In Tune with the Infinite*, now published by mainstream publisher Doubleday. In addition, there are eight other Trine titles by various publishers, some in multiple editions.

Not much is known about Trine's life. He was born in Mt. Morris, Illinois, and attended Knox College, graduating at age twenty-five in 1891. He did further study in history and political science at the University of Wisconsin and Johns Hopkins University, and his work in these disciplines apparently made him into something of a socialist, a part of the political spectrum that runs directly counter to the sort of conservative economic individualism that has emerged among the better-known New Thought advocates and latter-day positive thinkers. Moreover, in a further odd twist, he ascribed his socialism directly to his New Thought philosophy, even at one point intending to publish a book of social commentary from a New Thought point of view. While his socialism is a curious turn, so apparently was his embrace of New Thought. Charles Braden confesses that he can find no discernible causative influences in Trine's attraction to New Thought; no precipitating illness or parental influence seems to have brought it about (*Spirits* 167). Similarly, Martin Larson admits that he cannot account for Trine's embrace of Swedenborg and New Thought. In fact, Larson notes that the book Trine published the year before his famous best-seller appeared, *The Eclectic Amalgam: What All the World's A-Seeking* (1896), seems for its day a somewhat typical synthesis of liberal religious and social thought: it is antiecclesiastical, anticlass and anticapitalism, pro-body, pro-Jesus as teacher, and pro-indwelling divinity. As such, *In Tune with the Infinite* constitutes a marked departure insofar as it is, says Martin Larson in somewhat heated prose, a "symphony vibrating with a new vision" (169). In more tempered language, Charles Braden concurs on the singularity and appeal of Trine's accomplishment: "No single writer has expressed its essential message more clearly or more engagingly than he." Trine himself thought the success of *In Tune with the Infinite* lay in its universality, the book's ability to speak to many diverse kinds of readers from all around the world about common human problems and hopes (*Spirits* 166).

One likely explanation for at least part of the book's enormous and lasting popularity lay in the sensitivity with which Trine approaches his American readers. Unlike other New Thought writers whose vocabulary, replete with New Thought terminology, tended to emphasize the distance of New Thought from traditional Christianity, Trine seemed to go out of his way, either by conviction or guile, to articulate his ideas so they seemed compatible with traditional Christian beliefs: as Charles Braden comments, Trine's "vocabulary was one which raised little or no question in the minds of the orthodox, or at least in the minds of the more liberally oriented church-Christians" (168). By changing just the inflection and perhaps at times also the meaning of that traditional language without discarding the language itself, Trine's insistence on traditional Christian concepts and terminology foreshadowed the manner in which later popular writers, such as Norman Vincent Peale, reiterated traditional language while significantly changing connotations and meanings. The popularity of Trine's best-seller also offers a notable indication of a nascent pattern within the contours of American religious life, namely, the phenomenon of members of orthodox churches of different kinds remaining happily and faithfully within their denominational affiliations while seeking and freely partaking of theologies and spiritualities that, in small and large ways, depart from the central tenets of faith and practice of their primary institutional allegiance. For reasons that remain unclear, many Americans firmly situated within established churches and no doubt some firmly committed to no formal religious attachment at all began to "browse" for more satisfying additional or alternative sources for their religious understanding and nurture. To be sure, some of the popularity of books like Trine's very likely results from curiosity that titles and the very fact of their popularity seem to elicit. Still, the enormous and lasting success of *In Tune with the Infinite* suggests that the book struck diffuse and deep religious longing and curiosity that were in considerable measure not being fulfilled by more conventional religion. What is perhaps most striking about this emerging pattern is that it signals the beginning of a habit of "double-dipping" within mainstream American religion. While religious diversity is, by no means, unusual for the United States, as the religious hothouse of the early nineteenth century well shows, in the late nineteenth century Americans begin to reveal a taste for religious syncretism, a posture that keeps the believer within the confines of traditional religion but also readily allows for private inquiry through an array of books and ministries that supplement the believer's primary religious affiliation and nurture.

At least part of the reason regular, "churched" people felt comfortable with Trine's book is Trine's strategy of meeting his orthodox readers halfway. He not only moderated his language, as discussed earlier, but also seemed to mute the significant doctrinal departure by New Thought writers from Christian orthodoxy on the question of the nature of Jesus' Christhood. Most New Thought writers emphasized the distinction between Jesus the person and a "Christ principle," a characterization of the divine that stood apart from Jesus the person and into which Jesus the person grew. In practical daily life the ordinary person could attain this Christ principle either because the Christ already dwelt within the self or because it was a pervasive principle or law to which all have access. While ultimately embracing these

New Thought distinctions, Trine nonetheless significantly blurred the boundaries between Jesus, the self, and the Christ. Last, he readily and frequently made reference to the historical Jesus, a stratagem that greatly personalized the texture and content of New Thought with its insistence on abstract and often very impersonal divine principles. In American Christianity, with its heritage of Calvinist piety and its persistent revivalism, references to a personal, living Jesus did much to allay readers' suspicions of heterodox theologies.

A last dimension of *In Tune with the Infinite* that helps to explain its popularity is Trine's extension of the power of thought to the world of the material, specifically, to the promise of the "plenty," as his subtitle puts it. Until Trine came along, New Thought writers had largely concentrated on the power of belief or thought, categories that soon blurred, to effect healing and physical and emotional-spiritual health. With Trine, however, the limits of these original emphases begin to disappear. Nor was this expanded emphasis to material well-being anything particularly new in the larger culture or specifically confined to New Thought alone. Of course, deep into the Gilded Age, as Mark Twain had called it for its fascination with wealth, a great many people were preoccupied with ways to obtain money and wealth. If the glory of material gain was not the very air of Gilded Age culture, it was very much in the air. Moreover, the use of faith or mind to control the physical world was not new, although it had been confined to distinct strands of the movement. The most conspicuous of these was Mary Baker Eddy's Christian Science, which had always entertained the notion that "thought" could affect the material or physical world. Antagonists could bring affliction to one another's spirit and body by "malicious animal magnetism." It seemed logical, then, admitting mind and material (insofar as Eddy believed in the material world) could be shaped and affected by the use of "thought," to believe that other "material" sectors of reality could be similarly affected. In Christian Science the usual term for this was "supply," which meant the provision by God of the physical necessities and desires of life in response to the petitions of believers. While other New Thought writers had considered and even advocated the possibility of "prosperity" as a logical extension of the promise of health, with Trine and the long train of New Thought counselors that would follow, we see the embrace and popularization of the "health and wealth" school of New Thought (Judah 186–88). Plenty and personal power became major emphases that would notably alter the gist of mind-cure and profoundly affect twentieth-century American culture.

Trine also expanded, perhaps inadvertently, another emphasis within New Thought and did much to popularize it. The gist of this change is contained in the main title of his book—"in tune with the Infinite"—and that phrase denotes a shift in emphasis within New Thought understanding of how and what the believer believes. With Trine we see the seeds for the eventual secularization of New Thought ideas, specifically, as he sees belief as a cause-and-effect mechanism by which the believer might readily attain results that address felt needs, whether for health or wealth. Writers like Warren Felt Evans and Horatio Dresser emphasized New Thought as a religious and spiritual venture whose chief benefits were spiritual. In Evans and Dresser, health often seemed a by-product of a significantly changed perception of the world. Emphasis fell upon one's spiritual apprehension of the nature of reality. However, in a marked departure, Trine and later writers reduced New Thought to will and thought itself, the notion that thinking this or that would invariably achieve particular goals such as health, confidence, and prosperity. Charles Braden's brief summary delineates the metaphysical mechanism at the heart of Trine's approach:

To come into harmony with this will and therefore with all the higher laws and forces available and to work in conjunction with them in order that they can work in conjunction with man is the secret of all success, for it is "to come into the possession of unknown riches, and into the realization of undreamed of powers." (*Spirits* 166)

Trine derived this metaphysical mechanism from Swedenborgian understandings of God and influx and their ample prominence in American Romanticism, but eventually many later writers, such as Zig Ziglar, would entirely leave behind the religious moorings of New Thought in order to advocate simple right-thinking as a wholly sufficient (and wholly secular) means of tapping into, and utilizing the power inherent in, the fabric of the universe. In these secular expositions, God or divine principle, if they were invoked at all, had little to do. All one had to do was to "get in tune with" the eternal laws of reality that were just always there, making use of their power to effect the fulfillment of personal desires. With such gradual and subtle shifts, the "infinite" as God or divinity slowly but surely slid entirely out of the picture.

While not at all a significant figure in intellectual histories of American culture or, for that matter, even in New Thought histories, for Trine was not an innovator, Ralph Waldo Trine's contribution to American culture looms large. *In Tune with the Infinite: Fullness of Peace, Power, and Plenty* served as an efficient and powerful conduit, probably far more than any other single book, at least until Norman Vincent Peale's *The Power of Positive Thinking* (1952), for New Thought ideas into the main currents of American culture. Trine was perhaps an unlikely figure for this task, for his youth and schooling in rural Illinois lay a long way from Boston, the movement's birthplace and hotbed and, for that matter, from Chicago, one of New Thought's livelier outposts. What is perhaps most striking and indicative of the extent to which New Thought ideas had already begun to pervade the culture is that the movement's biggest popular success was written by someone not from the environs of Boston but from rural Illinois. That perhaps offers a telling emblem of the extent to which the founding ideas and leaders of metaphysical cure had made inroads into the main currents, and sometimes the obscure reaches of turn-of-the-century American culture.

Emma Curtis Hopkins

Perhaps the most influential person in the budding New Thought movement in the late nineteenth century was Emma Curtis Hopkins, an exile from Mary Baker Eddy's Christian Science. Henry Warner Bowden places Hopkins "at the headwaters of New Thought in modern America" (252). A charismatic personality and a "teacher's teacher," Charles Braden counts no less than fourteen major New Thought leaders as her students and friends at one time or another (*Spirits* 143). Moreover, Hopkins took significant strides in highlighting the significance of the feminine in religion, both theologically and professionally. While not the first woman to inspire a new religious movement in the United States, she was the "first such founder who celebrated her womanhood and called upon the name of a decidedly female God" (Prothero 299). Further, she declared herself a bishop and forthwith ordained many of her female students as ministers in mental healing.

Emma Curtis was born to well-to-do parents in Killingly, Connecticut, in September 1853. While not much is known of Hopkins's private life, the public outlines of her career are well known. She graduated from Woodstock Academy and then taught there for a while. She married in 1874, but the marriage soon ended in divorce. By 1883 she had moved to Boston and enrolled in a class on Christian Science taught by Mary Baker Eddy. Three months later she emerged as a practitioner and a trusted assistant. Eddy first made the young Hopkins assistant editor of Eddy's prime mouthpiece, the *Christian Science Journal*, and then, for a period of thirteen months, editor. For reasons that, to some extent, remain mysterious, the teacher and the student had a falling out, and Hopkins was fired as editor in October 1885. The cause usually cited blames Hopkins's eclecticism in her far-ranging search for religious wisdom, a search that took her from Mrs. Eddy and Christianity but, in the near and long term, to other world religions and their founders. Others suggest that Hopkins seemed to pose a threat to Mrs. Eddy with her considerable intelligence and independence. Over the years Eddy mentored and then discarded a number of promising assistants if they seemed to look like potential rivals.

If fear of rivalry did, indeed, lead to the dismissal of Hopkins, Eddy's action confirmed her fear, for in 1886 Mrs. Hopkins went off to Chicago, which soon became something of a hotbed of Christian Science dissidence, to begin her own Christian Science healing practice and to open her own school, the Emma Hopkins College of Christian Science, which was later renamed the Christian Science Theological Seminary. In 1887 she began her own journal, the *Christian Metaphysician*, which ran for ten years. Despite denunciations from Mrs. Eddy, Hopkins drew a large following in Chicago and throughout the Midwest. Within a year of her arrival in Chicago she had organized followers in seventeen other cities (Braden, *Spirits* 300). Hopkins's greatest success came with her effectiveness as a healer, teacher, and mentor to other leaders in the mental healing movement. Henry Warner Bowden counts fourteen Hopkins students who went on to become leaders in the New Thought movement. Almost all those who would become prominent in the twentieth century and contribute to the lasting institutional representations of New Thought had studied with Hopkins. The most notable of those were Charles and Myrtle Fillmore, who started the Unity School in Kansas City; Ernest Holmes, who established the Church of Religious Science; and Malinda Cramer, who taught Divine Science. Through her many students, Mrs. Hopkins also exerted considerable influence in the formation in 1914 of the International New Thought Alliance, a loose amalgam of different New Thought groups and teachers.

A "teacher's teacher," Hopkins transfixed her students. Hopkins's most famous disciple, Charles Fillmore, who had heard many of the great orators of the Gilded Age, contended that Hopkins was the most affecting speaker of all by virtue, to borrow Charles Braden's phrase, of the "sweet spirit of charity" that pervaded her public discourse (*Spirits* 144). Hopkins spread her influence by traveling coast to coast to offer courses in her thought, sometimes teaching as many as 1,000 students at a time. In addition to influencing many through teaching, Mrs. Hopkins did add significant elements to Eddy's Christian Science teaching and in the process made distinctive contributions to what would become New Thought. Foremost among these was her emphasis on a broad, inclusive theology that derived from her appreciation of the religious and metaphysical insights provided by different world religions. The culmination of her vision of a kind of universal spiritual harmony was the publication, beginning in 1920 and continuing for two years, of her life work, *Higher Mysticism: A Series of Twelve Studies in the Wisdom of the Sages of the Ages*. Originally offered as a series of bound pamphlets, they were later collected into a single volume. The volume also highlighted Hopkins's other major contribution, namely, her emphasis on mysticism, a theme that becomes clearly evident in the work of disciples like Ernest Holmes. According to Charles Braden, Hopkins's mystical bent did much to humanize the abstract, intellectualist approaches of some early mental healing thinkers.

In her last years Hopkins faded from view, essentially retiring to New York City, where she died in 1925 at age seventy-six. Unlike many of her disciples, she never formed her own church and organization to propagate her ideas or practices. A few of her followers devoted themselves to preserving her legacy, purchasing a farm in Connecticut for a retreat center and publishing and distributing her writings. Over the years Joy Farm became High Watch Fellowship, which has since faded from existence.

Charles and Myrtle Fillmore and the Unity School of Christianity

One oddity of the New Thought movement has been that for all of its enormous influence in American culture, it has not fostered either prominent or lasting religious organizations and institutions. To some extent, this seems to be the product of design, for unlike its powerful, exclusive, and tightly managed cousin, Christian Science, and perhaps in reaction to Christian Science, New Thought has historically not insisted on close fidelity to doctrinal statements, except for rather broadly tolerant and inclusive ones, or the creation of significant organizational identity or embodiment. The exception to this has been one relatively large and influential New Thought institution, which often goes by the simple names of Unity or the Unity movement. Founded in Kansas City, Missouri, in 1887 by married couple Myrtle and Charles Fillmore, today Unity consists of two distinct entities: the Association of Unity Churches, a loose confederation of congregations that take their inspiration and identity from the Fillmores and the institution they founded, and Unity's other major entity, the Unity School of Christianity, a multifaceted ministry and school now located on an expansive campus in the Kansas City suburb of Lee's Summit. Despite the fact that Unity's founders never contemplated or desired starting a church or denomination of their own, Unity has grown into a worldwide ministry and has its own Unity "churches," its own seminary, and a trained ministry. In its own right a large and steadily thriving organization, the Unity School of Christianity, more than any other mental healing organization, has served as a conduit for many New Thought currents into the mainstream of American religious culture, preparing the way, in large measure, for the appearance of that melding of New Thought and traditional orthodox Protestantism under the banner of positive thinking.

The founders of Unity were the firstborn of the second generation of mental healing popularizers. Charles Sherlock Fillmore was born in 1854 in St. Cloud, Minnesota, which was then wild frontier, where his father was an Indian trader. Raised by an Episcopalian mother and largely self-educated, Fillmore moved in 1874 at age twenty to Oklahoma and then to Dennison, Texas, where he became a railway clerk and met his future wife, schoolteacher Myrtle Page, whom he would marry seven years later in 1881. Born in 1845, nine years before her future husband, Mary Caroline "Myrtle" Page came originally from Ohio, where she was raised a strict Methodist and educated at Oberlin College. After graduating, she first moved to rural Missouri, where her brother taught school, and then on to Texas, where she taught. After the couple married, they settled in Pueblo, Colorado, where Charles worked in mining and real estate, becoming the partner of the brother-in-law of Nona Brooks, who later founded the Divine Science Church, one of the many "churches" that grew out of the New Thought movement. In 1884, after a slide in the real estate market, the Fillmores moved to Kansas City, where Myrtle fell seriously ill with tuberculosis. Her condition steadily worsened until 1886, when, in desperate straits, Myrtle went to hear lecturer E. B. Weeks, a protégé of Chicago Christian Scientist Emma Curtis Hopkins. Myrtle was greatly impressed and began to practice what she heard, focusing on the hopeful phrase "I am a child of God and therefore do not inherit sickness." Exactly how significant the event really was for Myrtle is a matter of some dispute. New Thought partisan Martin Larson says that after hearing Weeks Myrtle was "totally transformed. . . . a new and different conviction . . . blazed in her mind" (217). Other critics suggest that the change was more gradual, both religiously and physically. What is clear is that over the next year Myrtle improved remarkably, so much so that her initially skeptical husband began to investigate and study New Thought and occult subjects.

By 1889 Charles had become convinced of the truth of Myrtle's healing and the reality of spiritual forces behind her recovery, and he soon began to publish his own magazine on healing and religion, called *Modern Thought*, which Gordon Melton describes as a "magazine for the discussion of all of the new religious impulses which were emerging in America at the time" (*Cults* 137). Before long, however, according to Martin Larson, Fillmore had discarded all forms of the occult—spiritualism, palmistry, astrology, and others—and embraced the singularity of Christian healing (218). In 1890 the Fillmores arranged for the visit to Kansas City of Emma Curtis Hopkins and then journeyed to Chicago to become two of her students. Perhaps under the influence of Hopkins's Christian Science teaching, Fillmore changed the name of his magazine to *Christian Science Thought*, seeking by this strategy to incorporate the many kindred metaphysical healing movements that took some measure of inspiration from Christianity. In any case, Fillmore dropped that name upon protests from the very self-protective Church of Christ, Scientist and took up the name of *Unity*, which thereafter remained its title. Charles's commitment to a healing ministry no doubt became all the stronger when he began his own practice of healing strategies for a badly withered limb, which recovered sufficiently for him to live without pain or the use of a cane.

In 1890 Myrtle Fillmore announced in the pages of the Fillmores's magazine the creation of a new department and, with it, a new program, what she called the Society of Silent Help, whose purpose was to beckon farspread people to pray at the same time each day for the distressed in circumstance, body, and mind. This practice fitted well within Christian tradition but in Mrs. Fillmore's case was revivified by the notion of "absent treatment" first formulated by Quimby and practiced by sundry Christian Science and New Thought practitioners. Letters petitioning for prayers poured into the office of the magazine, most requesting physical healing but many others seeking prayer for material need or "supply," as the metaphysical movement often called this dimension of human need. The Fillmores themselves took to writing letters of counsel and encouragement to petitioners. Later still, Silent Unity, as the program became known in 1891, moved from letters to telegraph and telephone, and the program continues today as one of Unity's most distinctive ministries, one that has been widely imitated by well-known televangelists, often with little integrity and with the primary purpose of raising money. Presently, Silent Unity employs hundreds of paid workers and volunteers in a toll-free, round-the-clock prayer and counseling ministry (Martin Larson 220). By 1903, when the Fillmores incorporated their group as the Unity School of Practical Christianity, 10,000 people belonged to Silent Unity, and by 1906, 15,000. By the early 1960s Unity received 600,000 requests annually, by 1978 more than 1 million, and by the last published count in 1982, 2.5 million (Braden, *Spirits* 236–37; Martin Larson 220). The continuing popularity of Unity's work is indicated by the fact that presently Unity sends out, in letters, books, pamphlets, and tapes, over 34 million pieces of mail annually and has its own postal zip code (Melton, *Religions* 638).

As indicated by the growth in just this one facet of Unity's ministry, Unity grew by leaps and bounds and soon repeatedly outstripped its physical accommodations. The Fillmores held their first meetings in their home, were forced by attendance to move to Charles's real estate office, and soon after that to its own rented offices, building its own building in 1906, and then another next door in 1914, adding to that four times—a total of twelve moves and expansions in less than twenty years. The long-range solution to the ongoing space problems and the possibility of continuing expansion came in 1920, when Unity purchased a fifty-eight-acre parcel of farmland in Lee's Summit, Missouri, about fifteen miles from downtown Kansas City (by acquiring adjoining land over the years, by the late 1980s Unity's campus consisted of over 1,600 acres). Over three decades, as finances for construction allowed, all the functions of Unity were relocated in Lee's Summit (Martin Larson 222). Throughout planning and the thriving life of the suburban campus, what is now called Unity Village, one of the Fillmore sons, Rickert, served as the chief designer, architect, landscaper, and manager. First residences were built, then a swimming pool and golf courses and a hotel for guests attending courses offered at the Unity School. Silent Unity briefly occupied a building there until the depression stopped future construction and forced a return to Kansas City. The 1940s saw the completion of construction and the move of the entire, sizable operation to the new site. Its most notable landmark is a 165-foot tower office building. In many ways Unity Village seems to be the model for California possibility-thinker

Robert Schuller's Crystal Cathedral complex, which started with its own highly visible Tower of Hope. In the mid-1980s, Unity's workforce hovered around 500 paid employees, and they work and play in a location that seems designed to foster workforce contentment (Martin Larson 223). As Charles Braden comments, it "would be difficult to find a more beautiful set of buildings than that which Unity now occupies, or one in lovelier surroundings" (*Spirits* 243). The estimated value for the Lee's Summit campus is now over $50 million. Also notable, located in Kansas City itself, is the impressive Unity Temple, constructed in the 1940s for a cost of more than $1 million (Martin Larson 222). All of this was apparently accomplished without any long-standing indebtedness and without any sort of fundraising campaign or solicitation of clientele.

While the growth of Silent Unity and its own striking physical facilities indicate some of Unity's extraordinary success, bricks and golf courses hardly begin to gauge the fullest effect of the ministry. Probably the fullest measure of Unity appears in its long-running and far-reaching publications program, which is one of the most characteristic dimensions of Unity School's century-long engagement with American culture. Once he became convinced of the truth of an invisible spiritual reality that could heal, just about the first thing Charles Fillmore undertook, as discussed earlier, was the publication of a magazine, *Modern Thought* (which later became *Unity*), in which to share and explore his own and others' religious discoveries. A plethora of other periodicals, books, and pamphlets followed, and these are very likely the means by which the Unity School of Christianity is best known. Only a few years after the birth of Charles's magazine came Myrtle's *Wee Wisdom* (1893), which started as an eight-page paper and became the oldest and probably most popular children's magazine in American history, in 1960 reaching a circulation of .25 million (Braden, *Spirits* 246). It ceased publication in 1991 (Melton, *Cults* 137).

The other mainstay in Unity School's periodical repertoire was *Daily Word*, which began publication in 1924 as a pocket-sized, monthly devotional magazine. It contains a devotional for each day of the month, prayers, poems, and "affirmations" of Unity truths. By 1960, its circulation had reached 800,000, and by the mid-1980s, 2.5 million (Braden, *Spirits* 246; Martin Larson 247). Presently, it is printed in thirteen languages and reaches 153 countries (Melton, *Religions* 638). Perhaps its greatest significance lies in the fact that *Daily Word* seems, in many ways, to have served as an inspiration for the format and substance of positive thinker Norman Vincent Peale's highly successful *Guideposts*, which first appeared in the 1950s. In addition to these perennial favorites, Unity has over the years published a very popular weekly, a combination of inspiration and news, *Weekly Unity*, a *Reader's Digest*-style magazine for adolescents called *Progress* (although it has also gone under other names), and finally a magazine for businessmen in 1922. Probably the most important of the Unity School magazines is

Unity, originally founded by Charles Fillmore in 1897, whose circulation in the mid-1980s was 430,000. While *Unity* shares some of the same inspirational and practical features of other Unity periodicals, at the same time it contains the fullest and most substantive presentations of Unity's theological suppositions and tradition, with hefty excerpts from the founder's writing and theologically oriented essays. Its readership stretches far beyond Unity's membership, which now stands at approximately 115,000 (Melton, *Religions* 638). As with all Unity School publications, *Unity* draws a wide clientele that includes many from mainline denominations who apparently turn to Unity School for practical spiritual sustenance that more conventional churches often fail to provide.

Unity School does more than circulate magazines. It publishes a long list of books and pamphlets, many translated into as many as nine languages, that make their way from Missouri to just about every spot on the globe. Surprisingly, its most popular book, *Lessons in Truth*, was not written by one of the Fillmores but by a young female osteopathic physician, Dr. Harriet Emilie Cady, whom Charles enticed into writing a column in the early years of *Modern Thought*. When followers suggested that it would be helpful to have a series of statements delineating the substance of Unity's beliefs, many suggested Cady as the best author for the task. Compiled into book form in 1894, Cady's *Lessons in Truth* has since become the theological guide of the Unity School, which has, over the years, distributed almost 2 million copies of the book (Martin Larson 226). Charles Fillmore himself began teaching, which he did throughout his life, and in 1905 he started to write and publish his own largely instructional articles on Christian healing, and four years later those also were compiled into book form under the title of *Christian Healing* (1909), and it has become a perennial Unity favorite. Fillmore published three other books, the most notable of those being *The Metaphysical Bible Dictionary* (1931), which is a lengthy exposition of Unity's allegorical, interpretive approach to the Christian Bible. In addition, Unity sends out to all who ask any of their virtually countless pamphlets on its many topics of spiritual-material counsel, although most have to do with their mainstays of the "good life": health, wealth, and happiness. The general tone of these is optimism, hope, and a kindly helpfulness. All these are dispensed without charge, although sometimes nominal costs are mentioned, but payment usually rests on voluntary donation.

Nor has Unity confined itself to print. In its very early days, in another of its innovative gestures, Charles Fillmore in 1922 initiated radio broadcasts on WOQ in Kansas City, the oldest licensed radio station in the Midwest, and two years later Unity purchased the station, making Unity one of the first religious organizations in America to broadcast its message. Charles Fillmore often gave radio talks two or three times a week and advertised Unity's many publications on the air. This method of dissemination came to be rather costly, and in 1934 Unity discontinued its use of the station.

That did not, however, end its broadcast ministry. Unity's radio department continued to produce programming but, instead of broadcast, distributed it to local stations around the country. Unity either paid for the radio spots or simply offered them free to agreeable stations. The format and purpose of the programs have changed greatly over the years, ranging from the evangelistic to the inspirational, as Unity has tried to remain timely, especially with the advent of television (Braden, *Spirits* 250–51). One of the more recent series comprised brief inspirational messages featuring Hollywood celebrities, such as the late Ernest Borgnine, and was often seen on late-night commercial television.

One of the major elements of Unity's publications enterprise has been teaching, which can serve as a general rubric for almost everything Unity has attempted, but education also has more specific application that has found concrete, formal expression in Unity's many training programs, and of all New Thought churches Unity has the most extensive educational enterprise, most conspicuously in its own seminary on the campus of Unity Village. In the early days of their success the Fillmores faced a happy, but unexpected, challenge. Students who had profited from the Fillmores's own teaching wanted to share with others, by teaching and ministry, the good that had come to them. Thus arose the need to create structures and processes whereby new followers in the movement might learn Unity's essentials so they might follow in the footsteps of the founders. Another significant impetus for Unity's educational venture lay in Charles Fillmore's desire to keep Unity closely tied to a distinctive Christian foundation. Even though Unity's theological tradition is by no means conventional and can probably be best described as esoteric, Fillmore was never able to accept the religious eclecticism that abounded among other New Thought groups or in the International New Thought Alliance. To serve their ever-growing number of followers and to guard against a free-ranging theological hodge-podge, Unity very early in its history undertook the task of providing some theological explanation and direction for its students. As early as 1897 Charles Fillmore regularly taught a series of lessons in their Kansas City headquarters. In 1909 came a correspondence course for Unity's far-flung students and would-be teachers and ministers, a number reaching into the thousands. From the correspondence course came a two-week summer intensive course, from which in 1980 developed the Unity School of Religious Studies, which offers a wide variety of programs for ministerial training, the education of teachers and laypeople, and the conducting of national retreats (Melton, *Religions* 638). Over the decades the number of courses at the Unity Village campus has steadily grown, and the length of time in study and quantity of material resemble what is required by most evangelical and mainstream Protestant seminaries.

One of the intentions that the Fillmores did not have when they began their small ministry in Kansas City was starting a church of their own. Like most in the New Thought movement, they were markedly individualistic and strongly antiecclesiastical, especially in regard to what they considered to be the historic doctrinal distortion and rigid institutional control of traditional Catholicism and Protestantism. They certainly did not want to perpetuate more of the same; nor did they think so much of their small enterprise to anticipate that it would be the occasion for a movement or church. The necessity to forge something akin to a church, including congregations, ministers, and ordinations, emerged only slowly. As suggested earlier, many Unity followers wished in their enthusiasm to replicate the Fillmores's work in Kansas City. The most obvious expression of this desire appeared in the necessity to provide Unity-trained ministers, which the Fillmores attended to in establishing correspondence courses and summer training. The trained and ordained ministry in the field was brought together for the first time in 1923 for the first annual Unity convention with the effect of making the members aware of the great variety of teachings and beliefs that were being spread under the banner of Unity. As a result, in 1925, at the third annual conference, an official Unity Annual Conference was formed with the explicit purpose of governing teaching and regulating leaders of local Unity groups. The organization became independent in 1933 but worked closely with Unity's Field Department to establish standards for ministerial education and ordination. After several more changes in name and relationship the ministerial body became in 1966 the Association of Unity Churches, and it is charged with "oversight of all Unity ministers and the servicing of all churches in the United States" (Melton, *Religions* 638). The control of Unity as a church or denomination has shifted from the enterprise and leadership of Unity Village, still controlled by descendants of the Fillmores, to the ministers and leaders throughout the organization.

The precise doctrinal or theological content of any New Thought thinker or movement, the Unity School included, is always difficult to pinpoint with a reasonable measure of exactitude. Temperamentally, New Thought thinkers seem averse to dogmatic formulations or the possibility of exclusion and intellectual intolerance, particularly so since many of the founders reacted against the authoritarianism of Mary Baker Eddy and the Church of Christ, Scientist. There are also a considerable antitraditionalism and a strong streak of rationalistic, commonsense antiecclesiasticism. Further, many of the founders of New Thought regularly changed their minds. From the first, many enjoyed, indeed relished, perhaps as a part of their philosophical optimism, eclecticism and a sense of pilgrimage that would lead them to ever greater understandings of truth. As opposed to orthodox Christianity, which has predominantly located its source of revelation in the past, New Thought in particular (and here it departs drastically from the now rigidly codified teachings of Christian Science) has looked to the future for increasing measures of knowledge, truth, and light. Together these traits seem to apply with special fittingness to Charles Fillmore, who was more the seeker-teacher than wife Myrtle, and even within the broader New Thought movement, Charles very much went his own way intellectually and organizationally, the latter in his notable refusal to align Unity with the International New Thought Alliance. While Unity was liberal heterodox in relation to traditional Protestantism, amid other New Thought groups, Charles Fillmore found himself decidedly conservative, especially in his allegiance to some sort of special status or uniqueness for the person of Jesus.

Indeed, one distinctive feature of Unity that has characterized it from the beginning is the extent to which it has historically retained the theological emphases and language of traditional Protestantism, although it has, like all New Thought groups, poured its own very distinctive meanings into traditional terminology. This practice has often drawn the critical fire of evangelical Christian groups that see Unity as a wolf parading in sheep's clothing. Staunchly theistic, Unity nonetheless sees God as impersonal principle, a transcendent Mind or Spirit, although this often mixes with a more personalistic set of images, like Father, especially in relation to understandings of Jesus, who is seen as the son of God and as divine. However, in sharp departure from Protestant orthodoxy, divinity is not confined to Jesus, for all people are made in the image of God, and consequently all are potentially divine. God already dwells within the self, and the task of the self or the self's mind is to recognize that in-dwelling reality. "Jesus is regarded as the great example, the Wayshower, in the regeneration of each person" (Melton, *Religions* 638). People encounter God and find health in the course of conceiving of God properly. Unity affirms the idea of a Trinity, but within that the notion of the atonement, that Jesus had to die for humankind's sin, is put aside to emphasize "at-one-ment," a preexisting union between God and humanity. The death on the cross was not to repair a moral or spiritual fracture but to illustrate the wrongness of mortal ideas about disease, sin, and death; salvation lies in the recognition of sinlessness and immortality (MacMaster 3613). Unity stresses the significance of the Bible but, as is common to New Thought, interprets it in a spiritual or allegorical sense that departs drastically from traditional literal readings. Insofar as it possesses a doctrinal core, the preceding description catches its gist, although late in life Charles Fillmore came to believe in, and emphasize, reincarnation. This new ingredient, while not a core element in Unity, is embraced by many of Unity's ministers. How prominent this was in Fillmore's belief or how large a place it occupies in the thought of contemporary Unity ministers or members differs among commentators. What is clear is that in many ways Unity stands apart from other New Thought groups. Historian Stephen Gottschalk distinguishes Unity's theology from others in its insistence on Christian identity and its "key emphasis . . . on meditation and prayer that allow one to attain unity with God, outwardly manifested in greater peace, health, and abundance in daily life" ("Harmonialism" 913).

Unity is one of the few New Thought organizations that seem to have hard figures on its size, and, according to these, Unity continues to prosper. According to J. Gordon Melton's *Encyclopedia of American Religions*, in 1995 the Association of Unity Churches reported 628 ministries and 172 study groups in North America and 75 ministries and 100 study groups abroad. Total membership stands at approximately 115,000 (638). Its influence in American culture through its vast publishing enterprise and Silent Unity greatly exceeds what membership statistics alone might suggest. While these figures and a sketch of its institutional history tell something of its influence, the genealogy and spread of its ideas remain a story that waits a full, careful, and dispassionate telling.

TWENTIETH-CENTURY HEIRS TO NEW THOUGHT

Emmet Fox (1886–1951)

Probably the most prominent of all those preachers and writers who claimed New Thought as their theological heritage (Peale and Schuller have located themselves within the contours of mainstream American Christianity) was Emmet Fox, who was born Roman Catholic in Ireland in 1886 and educated at Stamford Hill Jesuit College near London. Fox soon became a successful electrical engineer while devoting all his spare time to the study of Higher Thought, which is what New Thought was called in England. He studied for many years before venturing to speak on his own distinct version of New Thought ideas, but then his success was rapid, regularly lecturing and drawing ever bigger crowds. From his start in England in 1928 he then moved to New York City in 1930, where he became a popular, independent lecturer attracting large crowds to the meetings he held in the ballrooms of large New York hotels. In the midst of this success he was ordained in the Church of Divine Science, a New Thought group that was started in Denver by Nona Brooks. When A. C. Grier resigned from the pastorate of New York's Church of the Healing Christ, Fox was chosen to follow him, and there he remained until his death in 1951. "Thus began," says Charles Braden, "one of the most remarkable ministries of any church in America in that or any other period" (*Spirits* 352). Fox's crowds grew larger and larger until his church was forced to rent the enormous old Hippodrome until it faced the wrecking ball. From there the congregation moved to the Manhattan Opera House and then eventually to Carnegie Hall, where Fox spoke to crowds that packed the auditorium and its overflow rooms. Soon the Englishman was ministering to "the largest congregation in New York City, and probably the greatest in all America" (353). Soon after becoming a noted New Thought speaker, Fox began to write books that spread his message still further, many of which became bestsellers and all of which are still in print, published by mainstream Harper imprint. *The Lord's Prayer* came in 1932, to be followed in 1934 by *The Sermon on the Mount*, which by the 1960s had sold 600,000 copies and remains Fox's most famous book, having become something of a Christian classic even among those with no sympathy for New Thought (354). In 1940 Fox published his best-selling *Power through Constructive Thinking*, a title that would later clearly influence another soon-to-be-famous New York City preacher, Norman Vincent Peale, who lifted the title for the most popular New Thought book of all time, *The Power of Positive Thinking* (1952). More books followed, whose titles amply suggest the general contours of Fox's thought: *Sparks of Truth* (1941), *Make Your Life Worth While* (1946), *Alter Your Life* (1950), *Stake Your Claim* (1952), and *The Ten Commandments: The Master-Key to Life* (1953). Two other Fox books remain in print, *Diagrams for Living* and *Find and Use Your Inner Power*, as well as a fat devotional book, *Around the Year with Emmet Fox: A Book of Daily Readings.*

In Sydney Ahlstrom's judgment Fox was the twentieth century's purest representative of the New Thought tradition, the one who most fully relied on New Thought concepts and vocabulary (1031). In their 1958 study of inspirational books in America, *Popular Religion*, sociologists Louis Schneider and Sanford Dornbusch concluded that Fox relied heavily on technique and was the most "mentalistic" of popular twentieth-century religious writers (8, 9). In their effort to understand the functional appeal of mid-twentieth-century best-sellers, especially what those books "do" for their readers, Schneider and Dornbusch focus less on the complete theology of their subjects than on the extent to which writers' ideas present an instrumentalist view of religion. Consequently, their reading of Fox's thought as expressed in his books, particularly *Power through Positive Thinking*, stresses those elements in his thought that speak most directly to the needs and desires of readers. Markedly different readings of Fox's appeal and ideas come from Henry Warner Bowden in his *Dictionary of American Religious Biography* and from Charles Braden, who attended one of Fox's services in Carnegie Hall.

Schneider and Dornbusch argue that Fox's foundational beliefs held that the external world is a projection of human thought, evil is false belief, the body is spiritual, and people are divine spirit, which comprises the "good news." Life and experience emanate from one's own mental concepts and imaginings (9). Along with Peale, Fox continued the New Thought theme that "religion brings wealth," and the riches indicate personal goodness (30). Again, along with Peale, Fox emphasized that religious belief has marked psychological results in imparting greater calm and peace to the believer, putting "God and prayer in the service of man's purposes and in making him 'feel better' " (34). In this regard, Fox is in the forefront of the practice of instrumentalizing God for personal benefit. Fox emphasizes prayer and Bible reading, both falling under the heading of what he calls "treatments," as a means to results of all kinds, both spiritual and material, equaling any help that can be offered by modern psychiatry (59, 112). More than any other writer examined by Schneider and Dornbusch, Fox is "committed to the magicalization of the spiritual" (63). In this regard, physical healing formed a major part of Fox's appeal, and he conducted weekly healing services that emphasized not only health but its attainment as a by-product of greater spiritual consciousness (Bowden 186). For Schneider and Dornbusch, Fox offers the best example of a "*mentalized* version of the Protestant ethic" insofar as he assumes that prosperity is an indication of positive religious thought (105).

Little of this emphasis is found in the brief, twenty-minute sermon Charles Braden heard Fox deliver in May 1947. The service itself seemed conventionally Protestant, except for a meditation on healing. A confident speaker, Fox's message seemed focused on reassurance, reminding his audience of God's "love, his power, his healing, his desire for men's good, not in some distant future, but now." In the sermon, Fox "spoke to and of God in the most personal and intimate terms, though occasionally referring to him impersonally," and urged his listeners not to let guilt overcome them, for everyone errs, and forgiveness is readily available in repentance (*Spirits* 352). Braden wonders, to some extent, at Fox's enormous success because he "was in no way sensational either in his language, in his ideas, or in his illustrations"; rather, his services were models of "quiet, thoughtful, prayerful worship" and were very "down-to-earth." Braden locates Fox's success in his humility, warmth, directness, sincerity, and hopefulness. Mostly, though, it seems to lie in his "quiet confidence" in the truth of his message and its applicability to the lives of his listeners. His influence persisted in several of his best-selling books on the Lord's Prayer and the Sermon on the Mount, in which the New Thought influence is undetected by the many mainstream ministers who read and borrow from them for their sermons. Braden does not examine the substance of Fox's conspicuously New Thought books, such as *Power through Constructive Thinking*.

Quite a different summary of the contours of Fox's thought comes from Henry Warner Bowden in his brief essay on Fox in his encyclopedia of the lives of religious figures in American history. Bowden's reading stresses Fox's embrace of metaphysical harmony as the central notion in his theology. "God is the Law of Being; man's understanding and obedience to that basic principle was the key to harmonizing body, soul, and mind" (186). All of the apparently different domains of the self—physical, emotional, intellectual, and spiritual—really possessed an essential harmony. As people progress spiritually, discovering "their oneness with the Divine Being," the aspects of the self merge into an "eternal self" that is aware of its status as a focal point of "God's self-expression." The full realization of one's soul results in a "peace and harmony that comes through unity with every other living creature." In this context, physical healing was a manifestation of a spiritual consciousness of the "glory of God in themselves." In his conclusion, Bowden shies away from the instrumentalist reading offered by Schneider and Dornbusch: "Instead of miracles or instantaneous wealth, he offered them strength based on faith, a format primarily for living *right* now and living right *now*." The prominence and exact role of instrumentalist factors in Fox's thought and appeal pose a question for fresh analysis.

Ernest Shurtleff Holmes and the Church of Religious Science

Still another variety of New Thought that enjoyed considerable success was Religious Science, which started out as a two-man show and ended up with a large church structure, a long-running magazine, a venerated leader, and one of the more lasting groups in the New Thought movement. Its founder, Ernest Shurtleff Holmes, was born in January 1887, into a large, but poor, family in rural Maine, the youngest of nine children. He left school at age fifteen, making his way to Boston, where he worked and went to school, for a time studying speech at the Leland Powers School of Expression, where he met Christian Scientists and read Mary Baker Eddy's *Science and Health*. In 1912, at age twenty-five, he moved to California to meet up with his older brother Fenwicke, who had become a Congregational minister and was pastoring a church in Venice, California, and who, like his brother, showed an interest in New Thought ideas and literature. There the younger brother ran across the writings of Judge Thomas Troward, a British judge who served in Punjab, India. Ernest enthusiastically responded, for Troward articulated much of what the young man had come to conclude on his own (Braden, *Spirits* 289). Ernest took a correspondence course and soon began to lecture locally on Troward and New Thought. By 1917 Ernest and brother Fenwicke had become sufficiently convinced of the superiority of New Thought that they together founded the Metaphysical Institute and the magazine *Uplift*, which merged two years later with *Truth Magazine* published by A. C. Grier of Los Angeles's Church of Truth. The pair then began to lecture regionally. Before long they were lecturing and teaching nationally; the lectures were free and served to entice audiences into classes for which there was a charge, from which the Holmes boys earned a healthy income. In 1919 they published their first books, Ernest's *Creative Mind* and Fenwicke's *The Law of Mind in Action*, each going through twenty printings in the next forty years (Braden, *Spirits* 290). In 1925 the brothers ceased their working relationship, Ernest choosing to settle in Los Angeles and Fenwicke continuing to travel.

In 1927 Ernest founded the Institute of Religious Science and School of Philosophy and began *Science of Mind* magazine, which Holmes intended to instruct morally and religiously from a scientific point of view and to increase consciousness of the divine (Braden, *Spirits* 295). After more than seventy years, the magazine is presently a monthly, is widely available on newsstands, and is subtitled *A Philosophy, a Faith, a Way of Life*. Attractively designed, *Science of Mind* offers a compendium of articles of New Thought inspiration, ads for books distributed by the magazine, and a directory of Religious Science churches and study groups. From the start, the movement grew, requiring several moves to larger quarters, and in 1935 the movement reorganized and moved into headquarters on Wilshire Boulevard in Los Angeles. In 1949 Holmes began a weekly radio broadcast called *This Thing Called Life* on the Mutual network, and in 1956 he began a twenty-six part series on television (Melton, *Biographical* 115). This notoriety translated into marked growth of interest in the movement. By 1954, with numerous branch centers, Holmes's movement had grown so large that the leader dropped his lasting aversion to turning the institute into a church, and the Church of Religious Science came into being. Holmes designated affiliate centers as churches, a move that was met with opposition, and the creation of Religious Science International and various independent Science of Mind churches. The larger movement has since had complex and changing relations with the founding center and Board of Trustees as all have struggled with notions of control, ordination, and education. Wealthy and respected, Holmes died in 1960 at age seventy-three, leaving behind a church that in the 1980s numbered over 100,000 members, not including the various churches that splintered from official linkage to Holmes's church (Ward, "Holmes" 209). In 1967 the Church of Religious Science added the title United to the front of its name.

Always a voracious reader, Holmes continued to devour all sorts of matter, including both mystic Meister Echardt and Christian Science exile Emma Curtis Hopkins, who in some ways was the mother of New Thought and with whom he established a deep friendship. In 1926 Ernest published his major work, *The Science of Mind*, which shows Holmes's penchant, perhaps more than any other New Thought writer, for abstract, impersonal language in his conception of God, perhaps resulting from his desire to "scientize" explanations and proofs of divine reality. By Mind, Holmes meant the study of Spirit, Cause, or "the ultimate Intelligence underlying the cosmos" (Melton, *Biographical* 115). Charles Braden catalogs other terms for divine Being employed by Holmes: "invisible Essence, the ultimate Stuff and Intelligence from which everything comes, the Power back of creation, the Thing Itself" (*Spirits* 293). This apprehension of the divine is shared by all world religions, "One Reality, an Unseen upon which men of all faiths have an instinctive reliance." While ultimately mysterious but nonetheless residing in each person, Mind manifested itself in each person through Law, the essence of which was Love (Melton, *Biographical* 115). Each individual is an expression of the divine. While it works through us, it can work for people when they consciously tap into its power to accomplish their ends. As Braden summarizes, "By conscious thinking we make use of the Universal Law of Mind, and cause It to do things for us through us.

. . . It is ever ready and willing to operate in obedience to our creative belief" (*Spirits* 293–94). The best means of access to this power is through meditation and the inner life, and these can greatly enrich health, happiness, and the good life, which Holmes intended to transpire here and now and not in a distant heavenly kingdom. Braden points out that along with what might sound like a justification for hedonism, Homes advocated "a vigorous gospel, ethically based and deeply Christian in spirit, for both the individual and social life of man" (*Spirits* 294). While Holmes published several books during his career, what he felt to be his great accomplishment appeared shortly before his death, *The Voice Celestial* (1960), an epic poem that expresses Holmes's profound awareness of a mystical "cosmic consciousness," as his brother called it, of which all the world's religions partake.

Bibliography

"Accord Reached on Christian Science Book." *Christian Century* 110 (1993): 1233.

Adams, James Truslow. *The Founding of New England*. Boston: Atlantic, 1921.

Ahlstrom, Sydney E. *A Religious History of the American People*. New Haven, CT: Yale University Press, 1972.

Albanese, Catherine L. *America, Religions and Religion*. Belmont, CA: Wadsworth, 1981.

———. *Corresponding Motion: Transcendental Religion and the New America*. Philadelphia: Temple University Press, 1977.

———. *Nature Religion in America: From the Algonkian Indians to the New Age*. Chicago: University of Chicago Press, 1990.

———. "Transcendentalism." In Lippy and Williams, 1117–28.

Aldridge, A. Owen. "The Alleged Puritanism of Benjamin Franklin." In Lemay, *Reappraising Benjamin Franklin*, 362–71.

———. *Benjamin Franklin and Nature's God*. Durham, NC: Duke University Press, 1967.

———. "Enlightenment and Awakening in Edwards and Franklin." In Oberg and Stout, 27–41.

Allen, David Grayson. " 'Both Englands.' " In Hall and Allen, 55–82.

———. *In English Ways: The Movement of Societies and the Transferal of English Local Law and Custom to Massachusetts Bay in the Seventeenth Century*. Chapel Hill: University of North Carolina Press, 1981.

Anderson, Virginia DeJohn. "Migrants and Motives: Religion and the Settlement of New England, 1630–1640." *New England Quarterly* 58 (1985): 339–83.

———. *New England's Generation: The Great Migration and the Formation of Society and Culture in the Seventeenth Century*. New York: Cambridge University Press, 1991.

Anker, Roy M. "Doubt and Faith in Late Nineteenth-Century American Fiction." Diss., Michigan State University, 1973.

———. "Self-Help Tradition and Popular Religion." In *Handbook of American Popular Culture*, 2nd ed., ed. M. Thomas Inge. Westport, CT: Greenwood, 1989, 1229–76.

Appleby, Joyce. "The Radical *Double-Entendre* in the Right to Self-Government." In *The Origins of Anglo-American Radicalism*, ed. Margaret C. Jacob and James R. Jacob. Atlantic Highlands, NJ: Allen, 1991, 304–12.

———. "Value and Society." In Greene and Pole, 290–316.

Atkins, Gaius Glenn. *Modern Religious Cults and Movements*. New York: Revell, 1923.

Baida, Peter. *Poor Richard's Legacy: American Business Values from Benjamin Franklin to Donald Trump*. New York: Morrow, 1990.

Bailyn, Bernard. *The New England Merchants of the Seventeenth Century*. Cambridge, MA: Harvard University Press, 1955.

———. *The Peopling of British North America: An Introduction*. New York: Knopf, 1986.

Baltzell, E. Digby. *Puritan Boston and Quaker Philadelphia: Two Protestant Ethics and the Spirit of Class Authority and Leadership*. Boston: Beacon, 1979.

Banner, Lois W. "Religious Benevolence as Social Control: A Critique of an Interpretation." In Mulder and Wilson, 218–35.

Banta, Martha. *Failure and Success in America: A Literary Debate*. Princeton, NJ: Princeton University Press, 1978.

Barbour, Brian M., ed. *Benjamin Franklin: A Collection of Critical Essays*. Englewood Cliffs, NJ: Prentice-Hall, 1979.

Barbour, Ian G., ed. *Science and Religion: New Perspectives in the Dialogue*. New York: Harper, 1968.

Barck, Oscar Theodore, and Hugh Talmage Lefler. *Colonial America*, 2nd ed. New York: Macmillan, 1968.

Barkun, Michael. *Crucible of the Millennium: The Burned-Over District of New York in the 1840s*. Syracuse, NY: Syracuse University Press, 1986.

Baym, Nina. *Novels, Readers, and Reviewers: Responses to Fiction in Antebellum America*. Ithaca, NY: Cornell University Press, 1984.

———. *Woman's Fiction: A Guide to Novels by and about Women in America 1820–1870*. Ithaca, NY: Cornell University Press, 1976.

Bednarowski, Mary Farrell. *American Religion: A Cultural Perspective*. Englewood Cliffs, NJ: Prentice-Hall, 1980.

———. *New Religions and the Theological Imagination in America*. Bloomington: Indiana University Press, 1969.

———. "Outside the Mainstream: Women's Religion and Women Religious Leaders in Nineteenth-Century America." *Journal of the American Academy of Religion* 48 (1980): 207–31.

Benedict, Philip. "The Historiography of Continental Calvinism." In Lehmann and Roth, 305–25.

Bercovitch, Sacvan. *The American Jeremiad*. Madison: University of Wisconsin Press, 1973.

Bercovitch, Sacvan, ed. *The American Puritan Imagination: Essays in Revaluation*. New York: Cambridge University Press, 1974.

———. "The Puritan Vision of the New World." In *Columbia Literary History of the United States*, ed. Memory Elliott et al. New York: Columbia University Press, 1988, 33–44.

Bernhard, Virginia. "Cotton Mather and the Doing of Good: A Puritan Gospel of Wealth." *New England Quarterly* 49 (1976): 225–41.

Berthoff, Warner. "Culture and Consciousness." In *Columbia Literary History of the United States*, ed. Memory Elliott et al. New York: Columbia University Press, 1988, 482–98.

Bier, Jesse. "Weberism, Franklin, and Transcendental Style." *New England Quarterly* 43 (1970): 179–92.

Bonomi, Patricia U. *Under the Cope of Heaven: Religion, Society and Politics in Colonial America*. New York: Oxford University Press, 1986.

Bowden, Henry Warner. *Dictionary of American Religious Biography*, 2nd ed. Westport, CT: Greenwood, 1993.

Braden, Charles S. *Spirits in Rebellion: The Rise and Development of New Thought*. Dallas: Southern Methodist University Press, 1963.

———. *These Also Believe: A Study of Modern American Religious Cults and Minority Religious Movements*. New York: Macmillan, 1949.

Breen, T[imothy] H[all]. "Creative Adaptations: Peoples and Cultures." In Greene and Pole, 195–232.

———. "The Non-Existent Controversy: Puritan and Anglican Attitudes on Work and Wealth." *Church History* 35 (1966): 273–87.

———. *Puritans and Adventurers: Change and Persistence in Early America*. New York: Oxford University Press, 1980.

———. *Tobacco Culture: The Mentality of the Great Tidewater Planters on the Eve of the Revolution*. Princeton, NJ: Princeton University Press, 1985.

Breen, T. H., and Stephen Foster. "Moving to the New World: The Character of Early Massachusetts Migration." *William and Mary Quarterly* 3rd ser. 30 (1973): 189–222. Rpt. in Breen, *Puritans* 46–67.

———. "The Puritans' Greatest Achievement: Social Cohesion in Seventeenth-Century Massachusetts." *Journal of American History* 60 (1973): 5–22.

Breitenbach, William. "Religious Affections and Religious Affectations: Antinomianism and Hypocrisy in the Writings of Edwards and Franklin." In Oberg and Stout, 13–26.

Breitweiser, Mitchell Robert. *Cotton Mather and Benjamin Franklin: The Price of Representative Personality*. Cambridge: Cambridge University Press, 1984.

Bridenbaugh, Carl. *Early Americans*. New York: Oxford University Press, 1981.

Bromberg, Walter. *From Shaman to Psychotherapist: A History of the Treatment of Mental Illness*. Chicago: Regnery, 1975.

Buell, Lawrence. *Literary Transcendentalism: Style and Vision in the American Renaissance*. Ithaca, NY: Cornell University Press, 1973.

Burns, Rex. *Success in America: The Yeoman Dream and the Industrial Revolution*. Amherst: University of Massachusetts Press, 1976.

Bushman, Richard. *From Puritan to Yankee: Character and the Social Order in Connecticut, 1690–1765*. Cambridge, MA: Harvard University Press, 1967.

Butler, Jon. *Awash in a Sea of Faith: Christianizing the American People*. Cambridge, MA: Harvard University Press, 1990.

Butts, Francis T. "The Myth of Perry Miller." *American Historical Review* 87 (1982): 665–94.

Buxbaum, Melvin H. *Benjamin Franklin and the Zealous Presbyterians.* University Park: Pennsylvania State University Press, 1975.

———. *Benjamin Franklin, 1721–1906: A Reference Guide.* Boston: Hall, 1983.

———. *Benjamin Franklin, 1907–1983: A Reference Guide.* Boston: Hall, 1988.

———. "Introduction." In Buxbaum, *Essays,* 1–18.

———, ed. *Critical Essays on Benjamin Franklin.* Boston: Hall, 1987.

Caldwell, Patricia. *The Puritan Conversion Narrative: The Beginnings of American Expression.* Cambridge: Cambridge University Press, 1983.

Carden, Allen. *Puritan Christianity in America: Religion and Life in Seventeenth-Century Massachusetts.* Grand Rapids, MI: Baker, 1990.

Carter, Paul A. *The Spiritual Crisis of the Gilded Age.* DeKalb: Northern Illinois University Press, 1971.

Cawelti, John G. *Apostles of the Self-Made Man: Changing Concepts of Success in America.* Chicago: University of Chicago Press, 1965.

Cayleff, Susan E. "Gender, Ideology, and the Water-Cure Movement." In Gevitz, *Other,* 82–98.

Chase, Elise. *Healing Faith: An Annotated Bibliography of Christian Self-Help Books.* Westport, CT: Greenwood, 1985.

Clebsch, William A. *From Sacred to Profane America: The Role of Religion in American History.* New York: Harper, 1968.

Cohen, Charles. *God's Caress: The Psychology of Puritan Religious Experience.* New York: Oxford University Press, 1986.

Cohen, I. Bernard. "The Empirical Temper of Benjamin Franklin." In E. Wright, *Benjamin Franklin,* 60–75.

Conner, Paul W. *Poor Richard's Politicks: Benjamin Franklin and His New American Order.* New York: Oxford University Press, 1965.

Cott, Nancy F. *The Bonds of Womanhood: "Woman's Sphere" in New England, 1780–1835.* New Haven, CT: Yale University Press, 1977.

Cross, Whitney R. *The Burned-Over District: The Social and Intellectual History of Enthusiastic Religion in Western New York, 1800–1850.* New York: Harper, 1965.

Cunningham, Raymond J. "From Holiness to Healing: The Faith Cure in America, 1872–92." *Church History* 43 (1979): 499–513.

D'Andrade, Hugh. *Charles Fillmore: Herald of the New Age.* New York: Harper, 1974.

Dawson, Hugh J. "Fathers and Sons: Franklin's 'Memoirs' as Myth and Metaphor." *Early American Literature* 14 (1979–1980): 269–92. Rpt. in Buxbaum, *Essays,* 19–40.

Deamer, Robert Glen. "The American Dream and the Roman Tradition in American Fiction: A Literary Study of Society and Success in America." *Journal of American Culture* 2 (1979): 5–16.

Degler, Carl. *Out of Our Past: The Forces That Shaped Modern America.* New York: Harper, 1959.

Delp, Robert W. "Andrew Jackson Davis: Prophet of American Spiritualism." *Journal of American History* 54 (1967): 43–56.

Demos, John. *A Little Commonwealth: Family Life in Plymouth Colony.* New York: Oxford University Press, 1970.

de Tocqueville, Alexis. *Democracy in America.* Ed. J. P. Mayer and Max Lerner. New York: Harper, 1966.

Douglas, Ann. *The Feminization of American Culture.* New York: Knopf, 1977.

Dresser, Horatio W. *A History of the New Thought Movement.* New York: Crowell, 1919.

———, ed. *The Quimby Manuscripts.* New York: Crowell, 1921.

Dunn, Elizabeth E. " 'A Wall between Them Up to Heaven': Jonathan Edwards and Benjamin Franklin." In Oberg and Stout, 58–74.

Eliade, Mircea, ed. *The Encyclopedia of Religion.* 16 vols. New York: Macmillan, 1987.

Ellwood, Robert S. *Alternative Altars: Unconventional and Eastern Spirituality in America.* Chicago: University of Chicago Press, 1979.

———. "Occult Movements in America." In Lippy and Williams, 711–22.

Elson, Ruth Miller. *Myths and Mores in American Best Sellers, 1865–1965.* New York: Garland, 1985.

Elzey, Wayne. "Liminality and Symbiosis in Popular American Protestantism." *Journal of the American Academy of Religion* 43 (1975): 746–56.

———. "Popular Culture." In Lippy and Williams, 1727–41.

Fellman, Anita Clair, and Michael Fellman. *Making Sense of Self: Medical Advice Literature in Late Nineteenth-Century America.* Philadelphia: University of Pennsylvania Press, 1981.

Fichter, Joseph Henry, Jeffrey K. Hadden, and Theodore E. Long, eds. *Religion and Religiosity in America: Studies in Honor of Joseph H. Fichter.* New York: Crossroad, 1983.

Fiering, Norman S. "Benjamin Franklin and the Way to Virtue." *American Quarterly* 30 (1978): 199–223.

Finke, Roger, and Rodney Stark. *The Churching of America, 1776–1990: Winners and Losers in Our Religious Economy.* New Brunswick, NJ: Rutgers University Press, 1992.

Foster, Stephen. "The Godly in Transit: English Popular Protestantism and the Creation of a Puritan Establishment in America." In Hall and Allen, 185–238.

———. *Their Solitary Way: The Puritan Social Ethic in the First Century of Settlement in New England.* New Haven, CT: Yale University Press, 1971.

Frankiel, Sandra Sizer. *California's Spiritual Frontiers: Religious Alternatives in Anglo-Protestantism, 1850–1910.* Berkeley: University of California Press, 1988.

Franklin, Phyllis. *Show Thyself a Man: A Comparison of Benjamin Franklin and Cotton Mather.* The Hague: Mouton, 1969.

Freeman, James Dillet. *The Story of Unity.* Unity Village, MO: Unity, 1978.

Fuller, Robert C. *Alternative Medicine and American Religious Life.* New York: Oxford University Press, 1989.

———. *Americans and the Unconscious.* New York: Oxford University Press, 1986.

———. *Mesmerism and the American Cure of Souls.* Philadelphia: University of Pennsylvania Press, 1982.

Galbreath, Robert. "Explaining Modern Occultism." In *The Occult in America: New Historical Perspectives*, ed. Howard Kerr and Charles L. Crow. Urbana: University of Illinois Press, 1983, 11–37.

Gans, Herbert J. *Popular Culture and High Culture: An Analysis and Evaluation of Taste*. New York: Basic Books, 1974.

Gaustad, Edwin S. "The Nature of True—and Useful—Virtue: From Edwards to Franklin." In Oberg and Stout, 42–57.

Gevitz, Norman, ed. *Other Healers: Unorthodox Medicine in America*. Baltimore: Johns Hopkins University Press, 1988.

———. "Three Perspectives on Unorthodox Medicine." In Gevitz, *Other* 1–28.

Giddens, Anthony. "Introduction." In *The Protestant Ethic and the Spirit of Capitalism* by Max Weber, trans. Talcott Parsons. New York: Scribner's, 1976, 1–12(b).

Gilbert, James B. "Popular Culture." *American Quarterly* 35 (1983): 141–54.

Gilmore, Michael T. "Franklin and the Shaping of American Ideology." In B. Barbour, 105–24.

Gottschalk, Stephen. "Christian Science and Harmonialism." In Lippy and Williams, 901–16.

Granger, Bruce. "The Almanac." In B. Barbour, 129–45.

Green, Robert W., ed. *Protestantism and Capitalism: The Weber Thesis and Its Critics*. Boston: Heath, 1959.

Greene, Jack P. *Imperatives, Behaviors, and Identities: Essays in Early American Cultural History*. Charlottesville: University Press of Virginia, 1992.

———. *Pursuits of Happiness: The Social Development of Early Modern British Colonies and the Formation of American Culture*. Chapel Hill: University of North Carolina Press, 1988.

———. "Reconstructing British-American Colonial History: An Introduction." In Greene and Pole, 1–17.

Greene, Jack P., and J. R. Pole, eds. *Colonial British America: Essays in the New History of the Early Modern Era*. Baltimore: Johns Hopkins University Press, 1984.

Greenfield, Tohomas Allen. *Work and the Work Ethic in American Drama 1920–1970*. Columbia: University of Missouri Press, 1982.

Greven, Philip J., Jr. *Four Generations: Population, Land, and Family in Colonial Andover, Massachusetts*. Ithaca, NY: Cornell University Press, 1970.

Griswold, A. Whitney. "The American Gospel of Success." Diss., Yale University, 1934.

———. "Three Puritans on Prosperity." *New England Quarterly* 7 (1934): 475–93.

Gutman, Herbert G. *Work, Culture, and Society in Industrializing America: Essays in American Working-Class and Social History*. New York: Vintage-Random, 1976.

Hall, David D. "On Common Ground: The Coherence of American Puritan Studies." *William and Mary Quarterly* 3rd ser. 44 (1987): 193–229.

———. "Religion and Society: Problems and Reconsiderations." In Greene and Pole, 317–44.

———. "Toward a History of Popular Religion in New England." *William and Mary Quarterly* 3rd ser. 41 (1984): 49–55.

————. "A World of Wonders: The Mentality of the Supernatural in Seventeenth-Century New England." In Hall and Allen, 239–74.

Hall, David D., and David Grayson Allen, eds. *Seventeenth-Century New England.* Boston: Colonial Society of Massachusetts, 1984.

Halttunen, Karen. *Confidence Men and Painted Women: A Study of Middle-Class Culture in America, 1830–1870.* New Haven, CT: Yale University Press, 1982.

Hambrick-Stowe, Charles E. *The Practice of Piety: Puritan Devotional Disciplines in Seventeenth-Century New England.* Chapel Hill: University of North Carolina Press for the Institute of Early American History and Culture, 1982.

Harrell, David Edwin, Jr. "Divine Healing in Modern American Protestantism." In Gevitz, *Other*, 215–27.

Hart, James D. *The Popular Book: A History of America's Literary Taste.* New York: Oxford University Press, 1950.

Hatch, Nathan O. *The Democratization of American Christianity.* New Haven, CT: Yale University Press, 1989.

Hawkins, Ann Ballew. *Phineas Parkhurst Quimby, Revealer of Spiritual Healing to This Age: His Life and What He Taught.* Los Angeles: DeVorss, 1951.

Henretta, James A. "The Protestant Ethic and the Reality of Capitalism in Colonial America." In Lehmann and Roth, 327–46.

————. "Wealth and Social Structure." In *Colonial British America: Essays in the New History of the Early Modern Era*, ed. Jack P. Greene and J. R. Pole. Baltimore: Johns Hopkins University Press, 1984, 262–89.

Henry, Stuart C. "Revivalism." In Lippy and Williams, 799–812.

Hofstadter, Richard. *The Progressive Historians: Turner, Beard, Parrington.* New York: Knopf, 1968.

Holifield, Brooks E. *A History of Pastoral Care in America: From Salvation to Self-Realization.* Nashville: Abingdon, 1983.

Hollinger, David A. "Perry Miller and Philosophical History." *History and Theory* 7 (1968): 189–202. Rpt. in Hollinger, *In the American Province: Studies in the History and Historiography of Ideas.* Bloomington: Indiana University Press, 1985.

Hoopes, James. "Art as History: Perry Miller's New England Mind." *American Quarterly* 34 (1982): 3–25.

Howe, Daniel Walker. "The Decline of Calvinism: An Approach to Its Study." *Comparative Studies in Society and History* 14 (1972): 306–27.

————. "Franklin, Edwards, and the Problem of Human Nature." In Oberg and Stout, 75–97.

————. "The Impact of Puritanism on American Culture." In Lippy and Williams, 1057–74.

Huang, Nian-Sheng. *Benjamin Franklin in American Thought and Culture, 1790–1990.* Philadelphia: American Philosophical, 1994.

Huber, Richard M. *The American Idea of Success.* New York: McGraw, 1971.

Innes, Stephen. *Labor in a New Land: Economy and Society in Seventeenth-Century Springfield.* Princeton, NJ: Princeton University Press, 1983.

————. *Work and Labor in Early America.* Chapel Hill: University of North Carolina Press for the Institute of Early American History and Culture, 1988.

Jackson, Carl T. *The Oriental Religions and American Thought: Nineteenth-Century Explorations.* Westport, CT: Greenwood, 1981.

Johnson, Curtis D. *Islands of Holiness: Rural Religion in Upstate New York, 1790–1860.* Ithaca, NY: Cornell University Press, 1989.

Johnson, Paul E. *A Shopkeeper's Millennium: Society and Revivals in Rochester, New York, 1815–37.* New York: Hill, 1978.

Judah, J. Stillson. *The History and Philosophy of the Metaphysical Movements in America.* Philadelphia: Westminster, 1967.

Kelsey, Morton T. *Healing and Christianity: In Ancient Thought and Modern Times.* New York: Harper, 1973.

Kishlansky, Mark A. "Community and Continuity: A Review of Selected Works on English Local History." *William and Mary Quarterly* 3rd ser. 37 (1980): 139–46.

Klaw, Spencer. *Without Sin: The Life and Death of the Oneida Community.* New York: Penguin, 1993.

Kleinberg, S. J. "Success and the Working Class." *Journal of American Culture* 2 (1979): 123–38.

Knight, Janice. *Orthodoxies in Massachusetts: Rereading America Puritanism.* Cambridge, MA: Harvard University Press, 1994.

Kyle, Richard G. *The Religious Fringe: A History of Alternative Religions in America.* Downers Grove, IL: InterVarsity, 1993.

Labaree, Benjamin W. *Colonial Massachusetts: A History.* Millwood, NY: KTO, 1979.

Larkin, Jack. "The View from New England: Notes on Everyday Life in Rural America to 1850." *American Quarterly* 34 (1982): 244–61.

Larson, David. "Franklin on the Nature of Man and the Possibility of Virtue." *Early American Literature* 10 (1975): 111–20.

Larson, Martin A. *New Thought Religion: A Philosophy for Health, Happiness, and Prosperity.* New York: Philosophical, 1987.

Lazerow, Jama. "Religion and Labor Reform in Antebellum America: The World of William Field Young." *American Quarterly* 38 (1986): 265–86.

Leach, William. *True Love and Perfect Union: The Feminist Reform of Sex and Society.* New York: Basic Books, 1980.

Leavitt, Judith Walzer, ed. *Women and Health in America: Historical Readings.* Madison: University of Wisconsin Press, 1984.

Lehmann, Hartmut, and Guenther Roth, eds. *Weber's Protestant Ethic: Origins, Evidence, Contexts.* Washington, DC: German Historical Institute and Cambridge University Press, 1993.

Lemay, J. A. Leo. "Benjamin Franklin." In *Major Writers of Early American Literature*, ed. Everett Emerson. Madison: University of Wisconsin Press, 1972, 205–43.

———. "Franklin and the Autobiography: An Essay on Recent Scholarship." *Eighteenth Century Studies* 1 (1967): 185–211.

———, ed. *Reappraising Benjamin Franklin: A Bicentennial Perspective.* Newark: University of Delaware Press, 1993.

Levin, David. "The Autobiography of Benjamin Franklin: The Puritan Experimenter in Life and Art." In E. Wright, *Benjamin Franklin*, 41–59.

———. "Edwards, Franklin, and Cotton Mather: A Meditation on Character and Reputation." In *Jonathan Edwards and the American Experience*, ed. Nathan

O. Hatch and Harry S. Stout. New York: Oxford University Press, 1988, 34–49.

———. *Forms of Uncertainty: Essays in Historical Criticism.* Charlottesville: University Press of Virginia, 1992.

———. "Introduction." In *Bonifacius: An Essay on the Good* by Cotton Mather. Boston: Harvard University Press, 1966, vii–xxviii. Rpt. in *The American Puritan Imagination: Essays in Revaluation*, ed. Sacvan Bercovitch. Cambridge: Cambridge University Press, 1974, 139–55.

Levy, Babette M. *Cotton Mather.* Boston: Twayne, 1979.

Lindberg, Stanley W. "Institutionalizing a Myth: The McGuffey Readers and the Self-Made Man." *Journal of American Culture* 2 (1979): 71–82.

Lippy, Charles H. *Modern American Popular Religion: A Critical Assessment and Annotated Bibliography.* Westport, CT: Greenwood, 1996.

Lippy, Charles H., and Peter W. Williams, eds. *Encyclopedia of the American Religious Experience: Studies of Traditions and Movements.* 3 vols. New York: Scribner's, 1988.

Lockridge, Kenneth A. *A New England Town: The First Hundred Years, Dedham, Massachusetts, 1636–1736.* New York: Norton, 1970.

———. *Settlement and Unsettlement in Early America: The Crisis of Political Legitimacy before the Revolution.* Cambridge: Cambridge University Press, 1981.

Long, Elizabeth. *The American Dream and the Popular Novel.* Boston: Routledge, 1985.

Lovelace, Richard F. *Dynamics of Spiritual Life: An Evangelical Theology of Renewal.* Downers Grove, IL: Inter-Varsity, 1979.

Lucas, Paul R. *Valley of Discord: Church and Society along the Connecticut River, 1636–1725.* Hanover, NH: University Press of New England, 1976.

Lynen, John F. "Benjamin Franklin and the Choice of a Single Point of View." In Bercovitch, *The American Puritan Imagination,* 173–95.

Lytton, Kam. *Unity for the Millions.* Los Angeles: Sherbourne, 1969.

MacKinnon, Malcolm H. "The Longevity of the Thesis: A Critique of the Critics." In Lehmann and Roth, 211–43.

MacMaster, R. K. "Unity School of Christianity." In *Encyclopedic Dictionary of Religion*, vol. 3, ed. Paul Kevin Meagher, Thomas C. O'Brien, and Consuelo Maria Aherne. Washington, DC: Corpus, 1979, 3613.

Marsden, George M. *Religion and American Culture.* San Diego: Harcourt, 1990.

Marshall, Gordon. *In Search of the Spirit of Capitalism: An Essay on Max Weber's Protestant Ethic Thesis.* New York: Columbia University Press, 1982.

Marty, Martin E. *Modern American Religion.* Vol. 1: *The Irony of It All: 1893–1919.* Chicago: University of Chicago Press, 1987.

———. *Pilgrims in Their Own Land.* Boston: Little, 1984.

———. *Righteous Empire: The Protestant Experience in America.* New York: Dial, 1961.

Mather, Cotton. *Bonifacius: An Essay upon the Good.* Ed. David Levin. Cambridge, MA: Harvard University Press, 1966.

Mathews, Donald G. "The Second Great Awakening as an Organizing Process, 1780–1830." In Mulder and Wilson, 199–217.

Matthews, Glenna. *"Just a Housewife": The Rise and Fall of Domesticity in America.* New York: Oxford University Press, 1987.

May, Henry F. *The Enlightenment in America*. New York: Oxford University Press, 1976.

———. *Ideas, Faiths, and Feelings: Essays on American Intellectual and Religious History 1952–82*. New York: Oxford University Press, 1983.

McConnell, Donald. *Economic Virtues in the United States: A History and Interpretation*. New York: Arno, 1973.

McCoy, Drew R. "Benjamin Franklin's Vision of a Republican Political Economy for America." *William and Mary Quarterly* 3rd ser. 35 (1978): 605–28.

McDannell, Colleen. *The Christian Home in Victorian America, 1840–1900*. Bloomington: Indiana University Press, 1986.

McLoughlin, William G. "Faith." *American Quarterly* 35 (1983): 101–15.

———. *Modern Revivalism: From Charles Grandison Finney to Billy Graham*. New York: Ronald, 1959.

———. *Revivals, Awakenings, and Reform: An Essay on Religion and Social Change in America, 1607–1977*. Chicago: University of Chicago Press, 1978.

McNeill, John T. *The History and Character of Calvinism*. New York: Oxford University Press, 1954.

Meade, Sydney E. *The Lively Experiment: The Shaping of Christianity in America*. New York: Harper, 1963.

Melton, J. Gordon. *The Encyclopedia of American Religions*, 5th ed. Detroit: Gale, 1996.

———. *Encyclopedic Handbook of Cults in America*, rev. ed. New York: Garland, 1992.

———, ed. *Religious Leaders of America: A Biographical Guide to Founders and Leaders of Religious Bodies, Churches, and Spiritual Groups in North America*. Detroit: Gale, 1991.

Meyer, Donald B. *The Positive Thinkers: Religion as Pop Psychology from Mary Baker Eddy to Oral Roberts*. Reissue, with New Preface and Conclusion. New York: Pantheon, 1980.

———. *The Positive Thinkers: A Study of the American Quest for Health, Wealth, and Personal Power from Mary Baker Eddy to Norman Vincent Peale*, 2nd ed. Garden City, NY: Doubleday, 1965.

Meyer, D[onald]. H. "Franklin's Religion." In Buxbaum, *Essays*, 147–67.

Middleton, Richard. *Colonial America: A History, 1607–1760*. Cambridge, MA: Blackwell, 1992.

Miles, Richard D. "The American Image of Benjamin Franklin." *American Quarterly* 9 (1957): 117–43.

Miller, Perry. *Nature's Nation*. Cambridge, MA Harvard University Press, 1967.

———. *The New England Mind: From Colony to Province*. Boston: Harvard University Press, 1953.

———. *The New England Mind: The Seventeenth Century* (orig. pub. 1939). Boston: Beacon, 1961.

Mitchell, Robert M. *Calvin's and the Puritan's View of the Protestant Ethic*. Washington, DC: University Press of America, 1979.

Moore, Laurence R. *In Search of White Crows: Spiritualism, Parapsychology, and American Culture*. New York: Oxford University Press, 1977.

————. "The Occult Connection? Mormonism, Christian Science, and Spiritualism." In *The Occult in America: New Historical Perspectives*, ed. Howard Kerr and Charles L. Crow. Urbana: University of Illinois Press, 1986, 135–61.

————. *Religious Outsiders and the Making of Americans*. New York: Oxford University Press, 1986.

Morantz, Regina Marrell. "Making Women Modern: Middle-Class Women and Health Reform in 19th-Century America." In Leavitt, 346–58.

Morgan, Edmund S. "The Historians of Early New England." In *The Reinterpretation of Early American History*, ed. Ray Allen Billington. San Marino, CA: Huntington, 1966, 41–63.

————. "Perry Miller and the Historians." *Harvard Review* 2 (1964): 52–59.

Morison, Samuel Eliot. *Builders of the Bay Colony*. Boston: Houghton, 1930.

Morton, Marian J. *The Terrors of Ideological Politics: Liberal Historians in a Conservative Mood*. Cleveland: Press of Case Western Reserve University, 1972.

Moseley, James G. *A Cultural History of Religion in America*. Westport, CT: Greenwood, 1981.

Mott, Frank Luther. *Golden Multitudes: The Story of Best Sellers in the United States*. New York: Macmillan, 1947.

Mott, Tracy, and George W. Zinke. "Benjamin Franklin's Economic Thought: A Twentieth Century Appraisal." In Buxbaum, *Essays*, 111–27.

Mulder, John M., and John F. Wilson, eds. *Religion in American History: Interpretive Essays* (orig. pub. 1973). Englewood Cliffs, NJ: Prentice-Hall, 1978.

Murrin, John M. "Review Essay." *History and Theory* 11 (1972): 226–75.

Nash, Gary. *Class and Society in Early America*. Englewood Cliffs, NJ: Prentice-Hall, 1970.

————. "Social Development." In Greene and Pole, 233–61.

Niebuhr, H. Richard. *Christ and Culture*. New York: Harper, 1951.

————. *The Kingdom of God in America*. New York: Harper, 1937.

————. *The Social Sources of Denominationalism* (orig. pub. 1927). Cleveland: World, 1957.

Noll, Mark A., et al. *Eerdmans' Handbook to Christianity in America*. Grand Rapids, MI: Eerdmans, 1983.

Noll, Mark A., Nathan O. Hatch, and George M. Marsden. *The Search for Christian America*. Grand Rapids, MI: Eerdmans, 1983.

Numbers, Ronald L., and Rennie B. Schoepflin. "Ministries of Healing: Mary Baker Eddy, Ellen G. White, and the Religion of Health." In Leavitt, 376–89.

Oakes, Guy. "The Thing That Would Not Die: Notes on Refutation." In Lehmann and Roth, 285–94.

Obelkevich, James, ed. "Introduction." *Religion and the People, 800–1700*. Chapel Hill: University of Carolina Press, 1979, 3–7.

Oberg, Barbara B., and Harry S. Stout, eds. *Benjamin Franklin, Jonathan Edwards, and the Representation of American Culture*. New York: Oxford University Press, 1993.

O'Connell, Laura. "Anti-Entrepreneurial Attitudes in Elizabethan Sermons and Popular Literature." *Journal of British History* 15.2 (1976): 2–20.

Parker, Gail Thain. *Mind Cure in New England: From the Civil War to World War I*. Hanover, NH: University Press of New England, 1973.

Parrington, Vernon Louis. *Main Currents in American Thought: The Colonial Mind, 1620–1800.* New York: Harcourt, 1927.

Peterson, Mark A. "From Founding Fathers to Old-Boy Networks: The Declension of Perry Miller's Puritans." *Reviews in American History* 23 (1995): 13–19.

Pope, Robert G. "New England versus the New England Mind: The Myth of Declension." *Journal of Social History* 3 (1969–1970): 95–108. Rpt. in Mulder and Wilson, 45–56.

Powell, Sumner Chilton. *Puritan Village: The Formation of a New England Town.* Middletown, CT: Wesleyan University Press, 1963.

Prothero, Stephen R. "Emma Curtis Hopkins." In Queen, Prothero, and Shattuck, 299–300.

Queen, Edward L., II, Stephen R. Prothero, and Gardiner H. Shattuck, Jr., eds. *Encyclopedia of American Religious History.* New York: Facts on File, 1996.

Reay, Barry. "Popular Religion." In *Popular Culture in Seventeenth-Century England,* ed. Barry Reay. London: Croom, 1985, 91–128.

Rischin, Moses, ed. *The American Gospel of Success: Individualism and Beyond.* Chicago: Quadrangle, 1965.

Rodgers, Daniel T. *The Work Ethic in Industrial America 1850–1920.* Chicago: University of Chicago Press, 1978.

Ross, John. "The Character of Poor Richard: The Source and Alteration." *PMLA* 55 (1940): 785–94. Rpt. in E. Wright, *Benjamin Franklin,* 27–40.

Rothstein, William G. *American Physicians in the Nineteenth Century: From Sects to Science.* Baltimore: Johns Hopkins University Press, 1992.

Runkle, Gerald. "Does Spiritual Faith Insure Physical Benefits?" *Theology Today* 11 (1955): 483–94.

Rutman, Darrett B. *Winthrop's Boston: Portrait of a Puritan Town, 1630–1649.* Chapel Hill: Institute of Early American History and Culture and University of North Carolina Press, 1965.

Rutman, Darrett B., and Anita H. Rutman. *A Place in Time: Middlesex County, Virginia 1650–1750.* New York: Norton, 1984.

Ryken, Leland. *Worldly Saints: The Puritans as They Really Were.* Grand Rapids, MI: Zondervan, 1986.

Sanford, Charles, ed. *Benjamin Franklin and the American Character.* Boston: Heath, 1955.

Sayre, Robert F. *The Examined Self: Benjamin Franklin, Henry Adams, Henry James.* Madison: University of Wisconsin Press, 1988.

Schneider, Louis, and Sanford M. Dornbusch. *Popular Religion: Inspirational Books in America.* Chicago: University of Chicago Press, 1958.

Seaver, Paul. "The Puritan Work Ethic Revisited." *Journal of British Studies* 19.2 (1980): 35–53.

Selement, George. *Keepers of the Vineyard: The Puritan Ministry and Collective Culture in Colonial New England.* New York: University Press of America, 1984.

———. "The Meeting of Elite and Popular Minds at Cambridge, New England, 1638–45." *William and Mary Quarterly* 3rd ser. 41 (1984): 32–48.

Shea, Daniel B., Jr. "Franklin and Spiritual Autobiography." In B. Barbour, 93–104.

Shi, David E. *The Simple Life: Plain Living and High Thinking in American Culture.* New York: Oxford University Press, 1985.

Shriver, George H. "Romantic Religion." In Lippy and Williams, 1103–15.

Sicherman, Barbara et al., eds. *Notable American Women: The Modern Period: A Biographical Dictionary.* Cambridge, MA: Harvard University Press, 1980.

Silverman, Kenneth. "From Cotton Mather to Benjamin Franklin." In *Columbia Literary History of the United States,* ed. Memory Elliott. New York: Columbia University Press, 1988, 101–12.

———. "Introduction." In *The Autobiography and Other Writings* by Benjamin Franklin. New York: Penguin, 1986, vii–xxii.

———. *The Life and Times of Cotton Mather.* New York: Harper, 1984.

Sizer, Sandra S. "New Spirit, New Flesh: The Poetics of Nineteenth-Century Mind-Cures." *Soundings* 63 (1980): 407–22.

Skotheim, Robert Allen. *American Intellectual Histories and Historians.* Princeton, NJ: Princeton University Press, 1966.

Smith, James Ward, and A. Leland Jamison, eds. *The Shaping of American Religion.* Princeton, NJ: Princeton University Press, 1961.

Sommerville, C. John. "The Anti-Puritan Work Ethic." *Journal of British Studies* 20.2 (1981): 70–81.

———. *Popular Religion in Restoration England.* Gainesville: University of Florida Press, 1977.

Stout, Harry S. "Moral Philosophy in Colonial New England: From Early Puritan Piety to Perry Miller's Mistakes." *Fides et Historia* 15.2 (1983): 97–102.

———. *The New England Soul: Preaching and Religious Culture in Colonial New England.* New York: Oxford University Press, 1986.

Sweet, Leonard I. "Nineteenth-Century Evangelicalism." In Lippy and Williams, 875–99.

Swihart, Altman K. "Stetson, Augusta Emma Simmons." In Sicherman, 364–66.

Tatham, Campbell. "Benjamin Franklin, Cotton Mather and the Outward State." *Early American Literature* 6 (1971): 223–33.

Teahan, John F. "Warren Felt Evans and Mental Healing: Romantic Idealism and Practical Mysticism in Nineteenth-Century America." *Church History* 48 (1979): 63–80.

Tenner, John W. "Unity School of Christianity." Diss., University of Chicago, 1942.

Thomas, George M. *Revivalism and Cultural Change: Christianity, Nation Building, and the Market in the Nineteenth-Century United States.* Chicago: University of Chicago Press, 1989.

Trilling, Lionel. *The Liberal Imagination: Essays on Literature and Society.* New York: Doubleday, 1953.

"Unity School of Christianity." In *Encyclopedic Handbook of Cults.* New York: Garland, 1992, 136–44.

Van Doren, Carl. *Benjamin Franklin.* New York: Viking, 1938.

Vaughan, Alden T., and Francis J. Bremer, eds. *Puritan New England: Essays on Religion, Society, and Culture.* New York: St. Martin's, 1977.

Vogel, Morris J., and Charles E. Rosenberg, eds. *The Therapeutic Revolution: Essays in the Social History of American Medicine.* Philadelphia: University of Pennsylvania Press, 1979.

Walters, Ronald G. *American Reformers 1815–1860.* New York: Hill, 1978.

Walzer, Michael. *The Revolution of the Saints: A Study in the Origins of Radical Politics.* Cambridge, MA: Harvard University Press, 1965.

Ward, Gary L. "Ernest Shurtleff Holmes." In Melton, *Religious Leaders of America,* 419.

Warren, Robert Penn, Cleanth Brooks, and R.W.B. Lewis. "A National Literature and Romantic Individualism 1826–1861." In *Romanticism: Critical Essays in American Literature,* ed. James Barbour and Thomas Quirk. New York: Garland, 1986, 3–24.

Weber, Max. *The Protestant Ethic and the Spirit of Capitalism.* Trans. Talcott Parsons. New York: Scribner's, 1958.

Wecter, Dixon. *The Hero in America: A Chronicle of Hero-Worship.* 1941. Ann Arbor: University of Michigan Press, 1963.

Weil, Andrew. *Health and Healing: Understanding Conventional and Alternative Medicine in America.* Boston: Houghton, 1983.

Weintraub, Karl J. "The Puritan Ethic and Benjamin Franklin." *Journal of Religion* 56 (1976): 223–37.

Weiss, Richard. *The American Myth of Success: From Horatio Alger to Norman Vincent Peale.* New York: Basic Books, 1969.

Welter, Barbara. *Dimity Convictions: The American Woman in the Nineteenth Century.* Athens: Ohio University Press, 1976.

Wentz, Richard E. *Religion in the New World: The Shaping of Religious Traditions in the United States.* Minneapolis: Fortress, 1990.

Whalen, William J. *Faiths for the Few: A Study of Minority Religions.* Milwaukee: Bruce, 1963.

White, Charles W. *Benjamin Franklin: A Study in Self-Mythology.* New York: Garland, 1987.

Whorton, James C. "Patient, Heal Thyself: Popular Health Reform Movements as Unorthodox Medicine." In Gevitz, *Other,* 52–81.

Williams, Peter. *America's Religions: Traditions and Cultures.* New York: Macmillan, 1990.

———. *Popular Religion in America: Symbolic Change and the Modernization Process in Historical Perspective.* Englewood Cliffs, NJ: Prentice-Hall, 1980.

Wilson, R. Jackson. *Figures of Speech: American Writers and the Literary Marketplace, from Benjamin Franklin to Emily Dickinson.* Baltimore: Johns Hopkins University Press, 1989.

Wise, Gene. *American Historical Explanations: A Strategy for Grounded Inquiry,* 2nd ed. Minneapolis: University of Minnesota Press, 1980.

Witherspoon, Thomas E. *Myrtle Fillmore, Mother of Unity.* Unity Village, MO: Unity, 1977.

Wright, Esmond. *The American Dream: From Reconstruction to Reagan.* Cambridge, MA: Blackwell, 1996.

———. *Franklin of Philadelphia.* Cambridge, MA: Harvard University Press, 1986.

———, ed. *Benjamin Franklin: A Profile* (orig. pub. 1963). New York: Hill, 1970.

Wright, Louis B. *The Cultural Life of the American Colonies, 1607–1793.* New York: Harper, 1957.

———. "Franklin's Legacy to the Gilded Age." *Virginia Quarterly Review* 22 (1946): 268–79.

Wrobel, Arthur, ed. *Pseudo-Science and Society in Nineteenth Century America*. Lexington: University of Kentucky Press, 1987.

Wyllie, Irvin G. *The Self-Made Man in America: The Myth of Rags to Riches*. New York: Free, 1954.

Young, Arthur P., E. Jens Holley, and Annette Blum. *Religion and the American Experience, 1620–1900: A Bibliography of Doctoral Dissertations*. Westport, CT: Greenwood, 1992.

Zaret, David. "The Use and Abuse of Textual Data." In Lehmann and Roth, 245–72.

Ziff, Larzer. *Puritanism in America: New Culture in a New World*. New York: Viking, 1973.

Zuckerman, Michael. *Almost Chosen People: Oblique Biographies in the American Grain*. Berkeley: University of California Press, 1993.

———. "Doing Good While Doing Well: Benevolence and Self-Interest in Franklin's Autobiography." In Lemay, *Reappraising*, 441–51.

———. "The Fabrication of Identity." *William & Mary Quarterly* 3rd ser. 34 (1977): 183–214.

———. *Peaceable Kingdoms: New England Towns in the Eighteenth Century*. New York: Knopf, 1970.

———. "The Social Context of Democracy in Massachusetts." *William and Mary Quarterly* 3rd ser. 25 (1968): 523–44.

Zweig, Paul. *The Heresy of Self-Love: A Study of Subversive Individualism*. Princeton, NJ: Princeton University Press, 1980.

Zweig, Stefan. *Mental Healers: Franz Anton Mesmer, Mary Baker Eddy, Sigmund Freud*. New York: Ungar, 1962.

Index

About the Author

ROY M. ANKER teaches English and Film at Calvin College in Grand Rapids, Michigan. In addition to many scholarly and popular essays, he edited and co-wrote *Dancing in the Dark: Youth, Popular Culture, and Electronic Media* (1991).

ISBN 0-313-31136-6

HARDCOVER BAR CODE